optimal *stress*

living in
your best
stress
zone

carol j. scott, m.d.

WILEY

John Wiley & Sons, Inc.

To my husband, Alex.
Thank you for your unlimited unconditional love.

Published by John Wiley & Sons, Inc., Hoboken, New Jersey
Published simultaneously in Canada

Design by Forty-five Degree Design LLC

The illustration on page 75 copyright © by Richard Karasek.

For general information about our other products and services, please contact our Customer Care Department within the United States at (800) 762-2974, outside the United States at (317) 572-3993 or fax (317) 572-4002.

Wiley also publishes its books in a variety of electronic formats. Some content that appears in print may not be available in electronic books. For more information about Wiley products, visit our Web site at www.wiley.com.

Library of Congress Cataloging-in-Publication Data:

Scott, Carol, date.
    Optimal stress : living in your best stress zone / Carol Scott.
      p. cm.
    Includes bibliographical references and index.
    ISBN 978-0-470-06851-9
      1. Stress management—Popular works. 2. Self-care, Health—Popular works. I. Title.
  RA785.S39 2008
  155.9'042—dc22
                                       2009033991

Printed in the United States of America

10 9 8 7 6 5 4 3 2 1

contents

part two
optimal stress: living in your beststress zone

preface

Stress is inevitable and generally unavoidable. Our response to stress—the automatic unconscious changes in our bodies and minds when we confront a crisis—often is the key to our survival. Most people don't think about it this way, but a life without stress is very likely not much of a life at all. We are most alive when we are challenged, and we respond by becoming sharper, stronger, and faster in both body and mind. That's the right and healthy way that people cope with the world around them.

The human body, however, as marvelous and miraculous as it is, hasn't had a chance to evolve with the lightning speed of the world around it. A few thousand years ago we were fighting off predators with sticks and stones. A few hundred years ago we got our food directly from the earth or the sea. A few generations ago we still communicated by pen and paper. The body hasn't changed much in that time, yet today we cope with everything from cell phones, text messages, and virtual meetings to traffic jams, viruses transported across oceans by airlines, instant 'round-the-world communication, and what feels like a complete loss of privacy, control, and the illusive "balance" we seek on a day-to-day basis.

You might think that you're still better off. None of that craziness represents any real danger or physical threat. In fact, nothing could be further from the truth. Research has proved that the tiny little stress triggers represented by each buzzing cell phone or obnoxious driver in front of you produce exactly the same physiological reactions in your body that a face-to-face encounter with a grizzly bear would. The chemical and neurological changes might be smaller on an individual basis, but the buildup caused by prolonged and relentless triggers can be fatal. I see it every day in the emergency room.

The truth is, having a "balanced" life is about having a "balanced" body-mind chemistry. Realizing this is at the core of understanding how to think about optimal stress. Stress is a condition that results from the interaction of the mind and the body. It is the mind that interprets situations and communicates with the whole body—the heart, the immune system, the gastrointestinal tract, the skin, and other bodily systems. In this book, I'll give you a doctor's-eye view of exactly how stress affects the body.

There is no denying that the stress response is absolutely necessary for peak experiences and performances, for joy and creativity, and for maximum productivity. It can literally protect us in critical situations. But when your stress response is activated too often or for too long, it can become counterproductive and even fatal. The goal of my program is to ensure that your "good" stress never tips over into bad or dangerous stress, or at least not too often. When you examine your life using the assessment tools I've provided here, I want you to be able to focus and channel your activities so that you can optimize your stress response and truly harness it for greater productivity and satisfaction. This is what I call living with optimal stress in the BestStress Zone. It may not be easy, but nothing could be more important. This is the work of discovering what really makes you tick.

Let's begin the journey together.

acknowledgments

. . . .

This book has been a labor of love. As an emergency physician, I've learned to expect the unexpected. Still, I never expected quite so many unexpected hurdles in the writing process. The greatest was the passing of my mother two years ago. She was thrilled when my book contract arrived, and I so wish that she could have seen the project come to completion. My mother and father (who both passed away several years ago) were hardworking teachers on Chicago's South Side. I was fortunate to grow up in a household where hard work, integrity, simple pleasures, and achievement were treasured. They ideals continue to inspire me on a daily basis. Writing this book was a clarifying and therapeutic process for me. It would be quite an understatement to say that the writing process required me to take more than the occasional dose of my own medicine. "Physician, heal thyself," they say, but there are many people who helped me get this task done.

To be sure, this book would not have been possible without my book agent, Jill Kneerim of Kneerim & Williams. Jill believed in me and the value of this project from the day we first met almost five years ago. Thank you for your generosity, kindness, perseverance, and patience.

There would be no book without my writing partner, David Sobel. David was with me every step of the way, from the concept to the actual writing and editing. He helped give shape and clarity to a great overabundance of material and never gave up hope. I thank him for his skill and his insight, his patience, and his persistence.

I am indebted to the well-orchestrated team at John Wiley & Sons. Tom Miller, executive editor, was unusually accessible and understanding and made the publishing process effortless. Christel Winkler, editor, and Kimberly Monroe-Hill, senior production editor, combined their talent and expertise to finalize the manuscript with meticulous attention to detail.

Gratitude also to supportive colleagues and friends: Elizabeth Weed, Shirley Hanley and the late Edgar Hanley, Vanessa Stovall, Dr. Gloria Williams and Victor Williams, Dr. Cynthia Morgan, Dr. John Payne and Judy Payne, Linda Kesselring, Karen Harrop, Tony Williams, Alice Cherbonnier and Marc Cherbonnier, Dr. Thomas LaViest and Bridgette LaViest, Coach Frank Keefe, Laura and Glenn Miller, Mrs. Ethel Reed, Dr. Roger Blumenthal, Jacinta Gauda, Barbara Johnson, Dr. Patrice Boddie, Lily May Johnson, Dr. Charles Terrell, Dr. Carin Basgal, Dr. Marshall Goldsmith, Carol Evans of Working Mother Media, Juanelle Teague of People Plus, James Huggins, Peggy Henderson at IBM, Al Martella, Rosanna Innis and Catherine Kapferer at Merrill Lynch, Terry McClure and Adrienne Holland at UPS, Verna Felton and Robyn Hendrickson at Microsoft, Wendy Brieterman at Johnson & Johnson, and my sisters, Patrice and Karen, who have given me special motivation during this venture.

My work in emergency medicine has privileged me to work with and get to know many patients and families, including those in the military. This book focuses on the stress of nonmilitary individuals in their day-to-day lives. I am obliged to give special thanks to active duty and retired military soldiers and their families. I know that it is their mission and focus that enable them to harness and channel the stress in their lives so that it becomes a means to gratification. I salute them, and I thank them.

Finally, the men in my life, my husband, Alex, and my sons, Alec and Douglas, have been, like any family members, occasional sources of stress, as I have been to them, but on a deeper level, they have represented the cure. As you'll discover later in my book, the secret of optimal stress is aligning the activities of your life with your purpose, your passions, and your priorities—exactly what these three magnificent men represent to me.

introduction

Always expect the unexpected. I'm an emergency room (ER) doctor, so you'd think I would have known that. I'm sure my boys knew it as they sat waiting for me to pick them up from school one afternoon a few years back. I'm sure they expected me to be late, and I didn't disappoint them.

They wouldn't have been surprised if they had seen me behind the wheel in full multitask mode: banking smoothly into the carpool lane with one hand, while talking on my cell phone with the other and somehow managing to scarf down a candy bar despite nagging indigestion.

When the boys, eight and ten at the time, jumped into the car, they bounced around with the wild energy of kids just released from school, yelping about which fast-food restaurant we would eat at that night. They knew the routine: my husband worked every day until six, and I had pulled the eleven p.m. to seven a.m. shift at the Johns Hopkins Emergency Room, my fourth in a row. I really needed some rest.

1

Thankfully, it was a light afternoon. No piano lessons or play rehearsals, only gymnastics. With luck, I thought, I'd be able to catch a nap before I had to be back at the hospital.

But something felt off that day. My indigestion just wouldn't go away. All of a sudden, my thoughts were bouncing around, first to all of the patients who had shown up in my ER complaining of indigestion, only to be diagnosed with a heart attack, and then to my precious sons in the backseat and how much they depended on me. I changed direction and drove straight to our local ER. The boys barely even registered the change of plan, having spent so much time in and around hospitals. They were probably as excited about hospital food for dinner as they had been about a quickie burger and fries.

Two hours later, after a "normal" EKG, I was still under observation. My risk factors dictated that they keep me overnight in the chest-pain-observation area and give me a serial blood test and a stress test the next day. I called my own chief, who arranged to have someone cover my shift. I convinced myself that I was most likely in the clear health-wise and took the opportunity to get a good night's sleep.

Things changed pretty quickly the next morning. Only six minutes into my stress test, the cardiologist (someone I had only met that morning) came into the room with surprise and concern written all over his face.

"Carol, I really didn't expect this. We need to get you to the cath lab immediately. I think you have major heart damage. You'll probably need a balloon and a stent, and we have to move fast."

I was stunned. After years of moving patients in and out of emergency rooms, I finally saw what it was like from the patient's point of view, and it really opened my eyes. I had understood intellectually about the fear and uncertainty that patients wrestle with, but I had never experienced these feelings myself until that moment. Before long I was lying on a gurney, staring up at the white hospital ceiling tiles, while a nurse laid a sterile drape over me. I couldn't count the times I had told a patient not to worry or that some procedure would be "a little uncomfortable," as I covered him or her with a drape, without having any real sense of how much it might hurt or what the ultimate outcome might be. I tried to calm myself with a silent prayer as the sedation took effect.

The next voice I heard was the doctor cheerfully telling me, "Good news! Are you listening? Your cath was normal—entirely normal—and your cardiac stress test was a false positive. We think the burning was just esophageal reflux. I do have a question for you, though: have you been under any stress lately?"

Enormous relief washed over me, but that serenity didn't last long. It seemed at the time like my ordeal was over, but in truth the battle was just beginning. All of those years I had spent examining patients and I'd never really examined my own life. At that moment my goals were very simple and clear: to be the perfect homemaker, mom, wife, daughter, congregant, neighbor, friend, coworker, medical doctor, and scholar. As I remember that day now, I realize that we never feel quite as fully and acutely alive as we do in times of crisis. This idea became a key part of my new journey and understanding of the role of stress in our lives. The process of self-discovery that was triggered on this very frightening day enabled me to realign my life and outlook in wonderful and exciting ways. I continue on this journey though I depart from it at times. But I'm eager to share what I've learned with you in the hope that it will help you, too, live your life in the fullest and most rewarding way you choose.

Note: This book contains comprehensive exercises that will guide you to your BestStress Zone; however, you should only feel obligated to answer the ones that are most meaningful to you. I recommend that you keep a notebook handy as you read through the exercises, or, if you prefer, you can photocopy the relevant pages to record your progress.

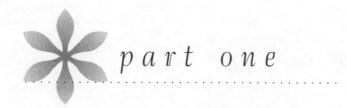

part one

stop stressing about stress

understanding stress and how it can work for you

Most of my stress is work related. This job has proved not to be full of "balance," as it was described to me before I accepted it, and instead is more out of balance and full of stress than any other job I've ever had in this industry. The volume of work is unmanageable with the resources allocated, so it's a hole we will never get out of, a shore we will never reach (which is inherently stressful if you are a person who cares about accomplishment and doing a good job). As it has been at every other company where I have worked, mine is a thankless job, but in many ways it feels worse here. We never have a sense that we can celebrate our accomplishments because there is never a lull in the work after you finish a difficult project. My hours "suck" . . . my work is primarily West Coast based, and as a result I come in a bit later and am often in the office three or more hours later than my coworkers, which leaves me little time to have much of a social life during the week. In addition, Fridays are usually my worst day of the week, with some crisis that needs immediate attention, so I can never make plans on a Friday night, leaving me with only the weekends (sort of . . . in the first year and half here, I worked the weekends, too). I am single. I feel isolated and alone. I uprooted myself and moved across the country for this job, leaving my friends and family behind. I knew only a few people (from school) living in the area, but they are all married with kids and living in the suburbs, so I never see them. And, unlike my previous work environments, the company feels more assembly line in its structure and location . . . everyone does the work and goes home, with little interaction (I think being located in the suburbs exacerbates this). My floor is so noisy that we all work with our doors closed . . . so we sit alone in our dark, windowless offices, connecting only via phone or e-mail—sometimes the only times you see anyone in the flesh is in the bathroom.

—Joann, 32, business analyst

Stress for me is feeling like there is not enough time to take care of all my responsibilities and my personal well-being. Feeling rushed all the time. Feeling like there is always something left undone or done in haste. And feeling like I am always behind. In Asia, family and parents have a lot of influence on one's life. I feel a lot of stress is felt due to these family and social pressures. I think different races define and deal with stress differently. Here in the U.S.A., people are more aware of stress, whereas in India people barely use the term stress. *It is just accepted as a part of daily life, and very few people give it a second thought.*

—Rohiti, 28, certified public accountant

My second husband and I have been married for sixteen years, and we have one elderly Labrador retriever (she is thirteen and a half years old). We currently live in Atlanta. We moved here four years ago from NYC. My husband is originally from Wisconsin. I have other sisters in Texas and Tennessee. We moved to Atlanta since my largest client was located here and I was traveling all the time. My husband has moved for me twice. This last move has resulted in an extended period of unemployment for my husband, and although he is currently working, he is significantly underemployed. At a point where finances shouldn't be a problem in our lives, we are not where we want to be. This causes me a great deal of stress.

—Debbie, 60, lawyer

I'm an upper-level executive for a growing company in a rapidly changing market. I've worked hard to get where I am, and I continue to put in long hours and to make myself available at all times of the day, whenever the market demands snap decisions and quick action. I work for the kind of boss who thinks nothing of sending e-mails to his staff at eleven o'clock at night, and I regularly get to work in the morning to discover that many of my colleagues have already responded because they logged on from home while I was busy trying to put my children to bed. My workload makes me feel like I'm giving my family short shrift, but when I focus on being a good wife and mother, I feel like I'm ignoring my job. By the time I figured out that my husband was finding the love and attention he needed elsewhere, it was too late.

—Melissa, 39, logistics manager

I run a national nonprofit organization that I've successfully piloted through a period of enormous growth. I am the sole breadwinner in my household, supporting my stay-at-home partner and our adopted son. I also bear most of the responsibility for caring for my aging father, who not only has begun to show early signs of Alzheimer's disease but has also recently been diagnosed with colon cancer. I constantly feel the weight of the many people who depend on me, but I am somehow always there when I am needed. There is only one person for whom I never seem to find time: myself.

—Gina, 45, executive director of a nonprofit organization

I don't have a paying job. I am the mother of three school-age children, one of whom suffers from a seizure disorder. My husband, a home contractor, has been on disability since being injured on a job site. The time I spend arguing and negotiating with insurance companies, lawyers, doctors, and the insane bureaucracies of Workers' Compensation and Social Security is almost like a full-time job. There are thousands of details for me to keep straight, and the slightest mistake can mean the loss of some income. The precarious health of my one child requires constant monitoring, and a day doesn't go by when I don't worry about which of my other children will start acting out in a desperate plea for emotional attention.

—Marie, 29, stay-at-home mother

Each of these women has a unique story to tell, but the one word that comes up in all of their stories is *stress*. Discussing stress has become so common in our culture. Many books have been written about it, and "experts" appear every day on television selling their stress-reduction secrets. We say we're stressed as often and as easily as we say we're tired or we're hungry. With so much overuse, the word itself has lost its meaning and power. It's time for us to take a fresh look at this phenomenon we call stress and to get a clear picture of what stress really is. And maybe if we can truly understand stress—its symptoms, its triggers, its effects, and, yes, even its benefits—we can start to put it in perspective. Ultimately, I intend to show you how to accept stress as an unavoidable part of life, to make it work in your favor, and thus help you free yourself from the worries and complaints and poor health that stress causes.

What Is Stress?

How many times have you complained about stress in your life? What do you mean by the word? Is it the people in your life who drive you crazy—your tyrannical boss, your misbehaving children, your aging parents, your demanding spouse, your gossipy coworkers, or your noisy neighbors? Is it the situations and chaos that you can't seem to get a hold of—maxed-out credit cards, unrelenting housework, long commutes to and from work, or conflicting demands on your time? Or have you gotten to the point where you expect these to be constant factors in your life, and the only things that you label stressful are unexpected disasters: an exploding water heater, the sudden collapse of your employer, a debilitating illness, or some other bolt from the blue? Perhaps the external factors themselves are not stressful, but instead stress is a response that erupts inside you as you interact with your chaotic world: the insomnia, the high blood pressure, the headaches, the irritability, the weight gain—in short, any or all of the things that will eventually land you in my emergency room. Is stress the trigger or the response? The cause or the effect?

In my view, it is neither, and it is both. Stress is the pressure that life exerts on us, and it is also the way this pressure makes us feel. Stress refers to situations and experiences that cause you to feel anxious, frustrated, and angry because you're pushed beyond your ability to successfully cope. You feel out of balance. It is essentially a state of arousal, involving both the body and the mind. Stress is a process that incorporates both cause and effect, and it has emotional, psychological, behavioral, biological, and physical aspects. No two people are alike. Our unique physical and personality traits and the individual circumstances of our lives ensure that our stressors and the ways that we experience them will be ours and ours alone. No off-the-shelf stress-reduction scheme can possibly work for every woman. The packaged wisdom of pop-psych gurus can be very seductive, and the appeal of exotic relaxation techniques is undeniable, but too often these approaches provide only short-term relief. They ease our symptoms without ever resolving the fundamental internal conflicts at the root of the problem.

My approach for discovering optimal stress rests on developing an understanding of what stress is and what it is not and, most important, of the stress-health connection. Because no two people experience stress in exactly the same way, it won't surprise you that doctors and scientists can't agree on a single clear definition of stress. Yet even though there is no scientific consensus on the subject, you and I can still have a shared understanding about what I mean when I use the term *stress*.

We all know stress when we experience it. Whether it's due to the challenges of a fast-paced, competitive business environment, uncertainty and change, team dynamics, client expectations, family and interpersonal relationships, caretaking responsibilities, or expectations that we have of ourselves, stress is inevitable—but one of my core beliefs is that despite being inevitable, stress doesn't "just happen."

A little historical background may be useful here. At the beginning of the twentieth century, Dr. Walter B. Cannon was a medical student at Harvard when he first posed questions about the stress phenomenon that eventually led to his lifelong research pursuits in physiology. In 1900, he received his medical degree and later became the chairman of the department of physiology at Harvard Medical School. It was at Harvard where he developed the concept of *homeostasis*, which is the notion that there are ideal steady-state conditions, such as temperature and body chemistry, that the body tends to maintain. Cannon coined the term *fight or flight* in 1915 to describe an animal's response to a threat. This discovery was published in 1915 in *Bodily Changes in Pain, Hunger, Fear and Rage: An Account of Recent Researches into the Function of Emotional Excitement.* His research revealed valuable information about the role of adrenaline in the body and it provided new insight into the workings of the nervous system. But it was Dr. Hans Selye, an Austrian scientist working at the University of Montreal in Canada, who is most widely regarded as the father of stress research.

Selye's writings on stress date back to the 1930s, and he is credited with authoring more than seventeen hundred papers and thirty-nine books on the subject. He studied the neuroendocrine effects of the fight or flight response, and as the undisputed expert on stress, he observed that common symptoms were present in many diseases. In a landmark study published in 1950, he applied engineering principles to his observations about humans. In engineering, *stress* refers to the pressures exerted on a system: too many appliances in a single electrical outlet, too much snow on the roof, too much speed for a car's tires on a slick road. Selye had trained as a neuroendocrinologist (a physician specializing in hormones and other chemicals in the brain and the nervous system), and he proposed that these pressures are a normal part of human life, just as they are in any physical system. He believed that humans have a well-designed natural mechanism to respond and adapt to stress. What's important to understand is that this mechanism is designed to protect us and preserve homeostasis for short-term challenges. His understanding and description of stress form the foundation for most of today's work in the field. Selye was the first researcher to describe the link between stress and disease. He suggested that long-term exposure to demands and challenges, such as the ones that many of us face daily, can cause increasing levels of adaptation to stress and eventually result in physical exhaustion and perhaps even death.

Seyle described stress as a "disease of adaptation" or, more formally, "general adaptation syndrome," and he theorized that poor stress adaptation is the basis of many disease states. He explained this as the syndrome of "just being sick." When he exposed rats to various types of stress and then dissected them, he discovered that three physical changes are always present: (1) enlargement of the adrenal cortex (the site where adrenaline is produced); (2) atrophy of the thymus, the spleen, the lymph nodes, and all other lymphatic structures (which are fundamental components of the immune system); and (3) deep bleeding ulcers in the stomach and the duodenum. Selye described three strategies in the general adaptation syndrome: alarm, resistance, and exhaustion.

The alarm reaction is characterized by surprise and anxiety and is considered to be a general call to arms (the fight-or-flight response). The adrenal glands secrete hormones, including epinephrine, norepinephrine, and hydrocortisone. This phase occurs quickly and accounts for a phenomenon such as a young and petite mother lifting a car to free her trapped child. Resistance represents the second phase of stress, when the body continues to adapt to and fight the stressor. The fight or flight response has ceased at this point. The adrenal glands are pushed to the edge of capacity, and possibly beyond, in this stage. An individual can respond to and meet the demands of the stress as long as this stage continues. If the adaptive stress is resolved, a rapid return to the resting state can be achieved. The third phase, exhaustion, occurs when an individual can no longer meet the demands placed on him or her due to the prolonged stress. According to Seyle, it is in the third phase where illness can occur.

As I discuss in chapter 2, Selye's observations from more than fifty years ago were correct. The Centers for Disease Control states that approximately 70 percent of medical disorders are related to stress. More simply, stress (and the emotional or physical reaction to it) can make people sick or make people with disease even sicker. Selye further divided stress into positive or negative conditions. He called good stress (for example, getting a job promotion) *eustress*. He called negative stress (such as anxiety produced by an abusive working situation) *distress*.

Our world has changed radically in only a few generations. Walter B. Cannon and Hans Seyle might not even recognize the harshness of some modern environments. You don't have to live in a war zone or a bitter arctic climate, and you don't have to suffer food shortages or work long days shoveling coal, to be affected by your surroundings. We hail so many modern technological advances as greatly improving our quality of life, but in reality, these very advances can represent new sources of stress. Cell phones, e-mail, text messaging, and other forms of instant communication have accelerated life and work to an often unmanageable pace. You may be blessed with a full life and professional success and might be fortunate enough to live in a modern society filled with technological wizardry, but you need to understand that all of this can result in a frenetic existence, with pressures and stressors never imagined even thirty years ago.

Around the time that Hans Selye was conducting his research, two other scientists were developing a model to document the effects of stress on the body. In 1967, psychiatrists T. H. Holmes and R. H. Rahe published their work and described a system to measure the relative stressfulness of various life events and circumstances. Their research was based on the principle that major stressors cause a break in the habits and patterns of our daily activities and in our social relationships (the higher the number on the scale, the greater is the need for readjustment and thus the greater effect on our daily lives). In Holmes and Rahe's study, 394 people (215 women and 179 men) were asked to rate a series of life events (which included marriage, divorce, the death of a spouse, retirement, and even vacations) on a scale of 1 to 100 as to the intensity and length of time necessary to readjust regardless of the desirability of the event. The scores were compiled and an average score was determined for each event that indicated the severity and amount of time needed to adjust to it. We can gauge the stressfulness of these life events by comparing the amount of time needed for, and the difficulty of, readjustment and adaptation after the event.

The results of the research are commonly referred to as the Rahe and Holmes Stress Scale (see below).

Rahe and Holmes Stress Scale

Life Event	Life Event Unit
Death of spouse	100
Divorce	73
Marital separation from mate	65
Detention in jail, other institution	63
Death of a close family member	63
Major personal injury or illness	53

Marriage	50
Fired from work	47
Marital reconciliation	45
Retirement	45
Major change in the health or behavior of a family member	44
Pregnancy	40
Sexual difficulties	39
Gaining a new family member (e.g., through birth, adoption, oldster moving, etc.)	39
Major business readjustment (e.g., merger, reorganization, bankruptcy)	39
Major change in financial status	38
Death of close friend	37
Change to different line of work	36
Major change in the number of arguments with spouse	35
Taking out a mortgage or loan for a major purchase	31
Foreclosure on a mortgage or loan	30
Major change in responsibilities at work	29
Son or daughter leaving home (e.g., marriage, attending college)	29
Trouble with in-laws	29
Outstanding personal achievement	28
Spouse beginning or ceasing to work outside the home	26
Beginning or ceasing formal schooling	26
Major change in living conditions	25
Revision of personal habits (dress, manners, associations, etc.)	24
Trouble with boss	23
Major change in working hours or conditions	20
Change in residence	20
Change to a new school	20
Major change in usual type and/or amount of recreation	19
Major change in church activities (a lot more or less than usual)	19
Major change in social activities (clubs, dancing, movies, visiting)	18
Taking out a mortgage or loan for a lesser purchase (e.g., for a car, TV, freezer, etc.)	17
Major change in sleeping habits	16
Major change in the number of family get-togethers	15

(continued)

Life Event	Life Event Unit
Major change in eating habits	15
Vacation	13
Christmas season	12
Minor violations of the law (e.g., traffic tickets, etc.)	11

Data from T. H. Holmes and R. H. Rahe, "The Social Readjustment Rating Scale," Journal of Psychosomatic Research 11 (1967): 213–218, esp. 216.

Although their initial goal was to improve the ability to predict the onset of disease or illness, Holmes and Rahe devised what became an often used measurement of the affect of certain events on our lives. They began with the assumption that the more significant the life change, the greater the biological changes, causing the body to use more energy to readjust and thus increasing the likelihood of illness.

Remember that although smaller chronic stressors may rank lower on the list, as they increase in both number and duration, their cumulative effect can be devastating.

So far, we have looked at the meaning of stress through a historical perspective. What about a more current definition? We know that scientists do not agree on any single definition of stress, but here are some concepts I want to share as we build a definition for the purposes of this book.

- Stress is the pressure that life exerts on us and the way this pressure makes us feel.
- Stress is a state of arousal that involves the body and the mind.
- The reflex response to stress evolved from our need as humans to protect ourselves from real physical dangers—the "lions and tigers and bears" of early human history.
- In modern society, our stressors are more likely connected to common events, daily hassles, technology, time constraints, deadlines, and interpersonal communication.
- Stress involves cause and effect. Demands, challenges, or changes *cause* a series of events that require adjustment. Our thoughts, actions, and behaviors can be considered the *effects* of these triggers.

- Triggers or causes can be external (the boss, the job, the bad news) or internal (your thoughts and unresolved conflicts).
- Triggers may produce different emotional, behavioral, and psychological responses in each of us.
- Being exposed to a stressor is not the same as being vulnerable to it.
- The stress process involves the mind and the body.
- Stress is in the eye of the beholder.

I have come to think of stress as a process showing the relationship between a cause/trigger and a subsequent effect/response.

The stress process incorporates aspects of biology, psychology, coping, and behavior and has three main elements:

1. A stimulus or a stressor that serves as the trigger.
2. A reflex perception, which is unique to each of us and includes coping skills, personality traits, genetics, and so on.
3. A response, of which there are four types: biological, cognitive, behavioral, and emotional. The accumulation of responses determines our general experience of stress. In broad terms, that experience can reflect either healthy adaptation and adjustment or nonadaptive unhealthy responses and conditions.

Understanding how this process works forms the very heart of your ability to adjust or control various factors in your life and to learn when and how to seek creative solutions to challenges. Think of the stress process as your personal automatic "emergency response system." Your unique appraisal of a situation, a demand, or a challenge determines the type and intensity of the response that is triggered. Four levels, or types, of responses can occur, and each generates one part of the total stress experience: biological, behavioral, psychological, and emotional.

At this point, I hope you can see that the only reasonable approach to finding relief from stress is to look inside yourself and assess how the stress process works for you. You can identify the many aspects of your daily life that relate to your personal passions and goals. Once you've determined the areas of balance and imbalance, you can set up an action plan to bring everything into alignment. This is how you regain control and how you become proactive, thus dictating the shape and direction of your life, instead of remaining passive and waiting nervously for the next calamity.

My goal is to give you tools to help you identify symptoms of stress in your own life, so that you can recognize the triggers, sort through your stressors, and distinguish those that serve your goals from the ones that get in your way. I can't promise to eliminate stress from your life. It may surprise you, but I wouldn't even *want* to eliminate all stress. As you will learn, not all stress is inherently bad. I hope to show you how to minimize the damaging stress in your life and turn the rest to your advantage. In this way, you will find your BestStress Zone.

Stress Isn't Always the Enemy

The human body has evolved in remarkable ways. Our physiological response to stress and danger, whether from a confrontation with a prehistoric beast or a dinosaur-brained boss, has been an essential weapon in our long fight to survive in a hostile environment. In today's world, the stress process might be triggered by something as common as having to give a speech, or it might result from an unexpected and cataclysmic event, such as a hurricane or a terrorist attack. In either case, the body responds in consistent ways. First, the brain activates the autonomic nervous system, which controls involuntary processes—in this case, stimulating the output of key hormones that in turn regulate other functions. Our heart rate and blood pressure increase, boosting our energy, strength, and reflexes. Even our immune system is put on heightened alert. With its defenses up, so to speak, the body is ready to meet a challenge.

Everyone is familiar with the feelings of heightened alertness and intensity that occur during this stress response. For many of us, our most vivid and important memories are of such moments—not necessarily times of danger but simply of our increased engagement and awareness, which were made necessary by the events around us. We often hear people say that they "felt so alive" in these unusual circumstances. We might lump all of these experiences together as "stress," but that would be a misleading term. Sometimes it's more accurate to say that our lives are very full, complex, or overly busy, but these demanding situations don't always represent danger. Instead, the experiences are inevitable, and we're extraordinarily lucky that we're equipped to handle them. So stress, or the stress response or stress process, is at times beneficial and even vital to our continued health.

What happens, though, when the stress response is stimulated all the time? As much as the body needs to be able to enter a higher gear when necessary, it isn't designed to operate at that level on a constant basis. Imagine if you ran your car in the highest gear all the time; the engine would wear out in a hurry and would be in constant danger of breaking down entirely. The same is true for your body. The cumulative effect of being in a perpetual state of arousal—a state of chronic stress—can have an extremely damaging effect on your health. Just as an overtaxed stress system means too much of a good thing, however, you can also have too little stress. If your system doesn't respond quickly enough, strongly enough, or often enough to stress, your body won't be able to defend itself when it needs to.

Clearly, you can have too much stress in your life, and you can have too little. Trying to eliminate stress from your life completely is like going on a radical diet. It may seem logical to banish potentially unhealthy substances like carbohydrates, fats, or salt, but your body actually needs each of these nutrients, to some degree. Likewise, your body requires occasional periods of heightened stimulation or arousal to stay in peak performing condition.

What's true for your body is true for your mind as well. You tell yourself that you need more peace and quiet, more serenity, yet you can't stop yourself from pushing forward. You complain about the pressure of your job, but you like being in the middle of the action. You can't stand the long hours at the office and being away from your family, but then you think that buying a bigger house might be nice. You don't really have time for the church sisterhood group, but you swore to yourself that community service would be a part of your family's values. You think that if you have to sit through one more Little League game you'll go insane, but you always wanted a big family, and you still catch yourself looking enviously at mothers pushing newborns in strollers down the street.

You want what you want, and generally there's nothing wrong with that. It's okay to have professional ambitions, to want to build a safe home life for your children, to want to be a big wheel in your community, or even simply to get fit and lose twenty pounds. It makes no sense to feel guilty about the choices you make in life or to resent the effort you must expend to realize your dreams. If you feel torn between your commitments to your family, your job, your parents, and your community, take a step back and reflect. Remembering that your life is the result of your choices makes it easier to embrace all of the challenges that those choices entail. It also reminds you that you are free to reconsider. Naturally, life is full of random events, and wisdom comes from expecting the unexpected. No amount of planning can ensure that you avoid such calamities, but you can put yourself in a position to minimize the damage by having support systems and contingency plans in place and by knowing how to quickly bring your emotional and psychological selves back into alignment. The problem arises when all of the busy activity of your daily life directs you away from the things you really hold dear or prevents you from focusing on the things that give your life meaning and satisfaction. Again, it's this lack of alignment, this imbalance, that triggers stress.

It's Time to Get Beyond Stress

I hope to give you a new way to think about the stress process in your life, so that you can restore balance and control. We will be exploring concepts that are in the domain of mind-body medicine. One of the central tenets of mind-body medicine is the recognition that the mind plays a key role in health and that the historical medical concept of Cartesian dualism—that is, separation of mind and body—is false. Please keep one additional incentive in mind: learning how to think about stress in a new way puts you on the path to more successful aging. Optimal stress and the BestStress Zone approach is unique because it incorporates a better understanding of the stress-health connection. The evidence is clear that the biological by-products of constant stress accumulate in the body and, over time, reduce your mental and physical capacities. Although currently there is no single way to measure this deterioration, certain medical tests help us assemble a picture of the overall physical effects of stress on the body.

I want to give you practical tools to help you assess your stressors and their symptoms and to determine which stress is good and which is bad. I'll take you through the physical and medical signs and dangers of stress and will show you how to recognize the symptoms—which differ for every individual—and how to minimize their effects. We'll go through the exercise of determining your three Ps—purpose, passions, and priorities. You will learn which of your daily challenges are worth the effort and the stress, because they bring you closer to your goals, and which are merely obstacles and distractions. This process of self-evaluation and self-discovery will enable you to envision and establish a life that works for you, in which you've minimized dangerous stress and embraced productive challenges. You'll then be living in your BestStress Zone. I'll give you strategies for maintaining, nurturing, and defending that zone, and I'll show you how to prepare for those inevitable moments when life deals you a bad hand and even the most careful planning falls apart.

The best thing about this approach is that there are no right and wrong answers. There is no one-size-fits-all system. You don't need to change anything about yourself or your attitudes that you don't want to change. Each person's BestStress Zone will be unique. My aim is to help you clarify your own values and goals, reorder your commitments, and refocus your energies so you can live the life that you want to live.

measuring the risk
stress, health, and wellness

Don't think that stress is a mysterious monster hiding in the closet. Problems loom larger in our lives when they remain abstract or intangible. It's much easier to tackle life's challenges when you break them down into concrete, manageable parts. In this chapter, I'll help you understand the stress process by focusing on how your responses to stress create the stress-health connection. Finally, and most important, you will have the opportunity to assess yourself. Is your health at risk because of stress?

I want to clarify that when I talk about stress, I'm referring to a very specific set of processes in your mind and body. Our lives are complex and cluttered, and this often causes *anxiety* or *burnout*. We need to understand the difference between these conditions and *stress*. The American Psychological Association defines anxiety as a syndrome characterized by "apprehension, tension or uneasiness from the anticipation of danger, usually from a source which is largely unknown or unrecognized." Experts consider anxiety a natural underlying part of an individual's psychological makeup, whereas stress is usually tempo-rary, arising in response to a specific set of circumstances. The natural overlap between stress and anxiety often causes people to confuse the two, but they exist independently, although anxiety can certainly be a subset or a component of stress. Doctors can help you manage anxiety with therapy and with newly developed medications, but often you can attack anxiety more effectively by better understanding the stressful circumstances in your life.

Burnout sets in when stress is left unaddressed for too long. It is the end result of your failure to cope successfully with stress, so it requires a lot effort and attention to undo before you can get back on track. Psychologists have identified three fundamental components of burn-out: depersonalization, disengagement, and exhaustion or irritability. My goal is to help you resolve the stress in your life long before you have to think about the serious problem of burnout.

There's no getting around the fact that much of the stress and sub-sequent burnout in contemporary society has been work related. The economic crisis and subsequent recession has added a new layer of com-plexity for interpreting work-related stress. The demands placed on people in today's streamlined and downsized workforce are often unreasonable, yet most of us need to recognize that we contribute in important ways to our own work stress, through our ambition and our desire for success. In 1971, Wayne Coates defined a new phenomenon in his book *Confessions of a Workaholic.* Most experts agree that what we call workaholism is best understood as a form of addiction or compulsive behavior. I'll address this more fully later in a separate chapter on the crucial relationship between work, stress, and health, but for now, simply understand that our obses-sion with our jobs, whether we perceive them as a source of pleasure or of pain, contributes greatly to stress and can later lead to burnout.

Let's get back to the stress response. The stress response might be physical (an increased heart rate, fatigue, sweaty palms), emotional (elation, anger, moodiness), psychological (problematic thoughts, rumination, depression), or behavioral (eating or sexual problems, overexercising, substance abuse).

Although you may think of stress in vague terms such as uneasiness, nervousness, irritation, or exhaustion, the stress response has many clear and specific signs that you can learn to recognize. Many of these signals are physical, but even the less obvious emotional and psycho-logical responses cause physical or behavioral symptoms that you can learn to track and manage. The first step in bringing the stress process under control is to identify these signs, which will differ in some ways for each individual, and to connect them to the events and situations in your life that trigger the stress response.

The range of potential triggers is extremely broad, from a sud-den, unexpected crisis to the incessant barking of the dog next door. Random disruptions to your life, such as the loss of a spouse or a loved one, a natural disaster, getting laid off, or a serious illness or injury, fall into the category of *acute stressors*. These events are sharply delineated, meaning they have a recognizable beginning and end, and they require you to make a rapid adjustment of some kind, whether physical, practi-cal, or psychological. Consider this real-life example of how the loss of a loved one can affect an entire family.

The sudden death of my father four years ago was very stressful. He had been a consistent source of support to me. Since his passing, our family dynamic has changed. My middle sister has taken on much of the burden for handling my mother's finances and making major decisions. My oldest sister has sort of checked out of any responsibil-ity for my mom. During the time that I lost my dad, I was single and had just purchased my first house.
—Angela, 49, middle school teacher

Research has shown that you can experience acute stress either directly or indirectly. You could have been living in New Orleans's Ninth Ward when Hurricane Katrina struck in August 2005, or perhaps you were traveling in Asia when the earthquake that shook China's Sichuan province in May 2008 occurred that left seventy thousand dead, eighteen thousand missing, and almost five million homeless, and you would have experienced a sudden and direct feeling of stress. Or you may have been at home watching either event on television and still have experienced very real stress. The stress response—the pro-cesses triggered in your body and your brain by these occurrences—would have been the same.

As often as not, your stress isn't tied to a single, unexpected event. *Chronic stressors* are the ongoing annoyances that gradually become part of your personal landscape—a difficult relationship with a coworker or a family member, money problems, or simply having too much to do. Here's how chronic stressors affect one woman's life.

> *Traffic, traffic, traffic! I sometimes spend up to four hours every day in traffic. A two-hour commute in the morning gets my day off to a bad start, and after a long, exhausting day, a two-hour commute home almost kills me. I telecommute one day a week, but it just isn't enough.*
> —Susan, 47, IT account executive

Chronic stressors usually represent an imbalance, a state of basic conflict, between what you want and what you've got. The daily hassles and frustrations of your life—a job you dislike, the climate, the squabbling with your spouse or children—all represent chronic stressors.

Interestingly, the human body doesn't distinguish between acute and chronic stressors. The stress response is triggered either way, and the physical processes are essentially constant, with minor variations depending on the individual and the situation. Your health and well-being are no more or no less at risk from one kind of stress than they are from another. Perhaps you've heard the old adage about how if you drop a frog into a pot of boiling water, the frog reflexively recognizes the danger and jumps right out, but if you put it in a pot of cold water and then turn up the heat gradually, it will boil to death. Chronic stress is like being immersed in a slowly simmering pot of water, and it is a big part of most people's lives. Bad situations develop slowly over time, usually with your own inadvertent participation, so that you may not even be conscious of them. Awareness is the first step.

The Stress Response in the Body

As I've mentioned, stressful situations spark certain processes within the body. As an emergency-room doctor, I see the outcome of these processes all the time.

It may be helpful to describe the biologic response to stress. The purpose of the response to stress is the mobilization of energy from the body's storage sources (such as liver and fat cells) to fuel the fight-or-flight response. This energy is delivered to the systems that are critical for fight or flight: namely, to the muscles in your legs in case you need to run away and to the brain for improved thinking and memory. When you are stressed, the body halts processes such as digestion, growth, reproduction, recalcification of the bones, and the immune system's surveillance of your body. This so-called shutdown happens regularly. For instance, when you are nervous before giving a public presentation, your body senses this as stress and shuts down the digestive process; you experience this as dry mouth. This is how the stress response works.

The autonomic nervous system and stress hormones form the core of the stress response of the body. When faced with a challenge or a threat, the brain kick-starts the autonomic nervous system, which shifts the body's systems into a higher gear. First, the brain sends a message to the adrenal glands to release the powerful hormone *adrenaline* into the body. The adrenal glands are powerful, triangular-shaped organs about half an inch in height and three inches in length that sit atop the kidneys. Adrenaline speeds up your heart rate. Remember, a fast heart rate is necessary to get oxygen-rich blood to your muscles and brain. In response to the increase in heart rate, your blood vessels constrict and your blood pressure increases, giving you that tingly, hair-standing-on-end feeling. Your breathing rate increases, too, as you bring greater amounts of oxygen into your lungs. From there, the oxygen moves through the bloodstream into your muscles and your brain, increasing your strength, reflexes, endurance, and alertness. Adrenaline also stimulates your body to release glucose and fatty acids from storage, boosting your energy. The additional release of fibrinogens, which assist blood clotting, endorphins, which blunt the sensation of pain, and antibodies to defend against infection shows once again how the stress response evolved to protect us from real physical danger. In this heightened state of readiness, the body also temporarily shuts down the digestive process.

If adrenaline represents the first line of defense in your emergency-response system, the secondary component is *cortisol*. Cortisol's main function is to replenish the various bodily systems and stores in the body. Cortisol stimulates the release of glucose (sugar) and fatty acids from the liver, which are then converted into energy. Cortisol also makes you hungry, causing you to replenish the body's fuel. In times of crisis or trauma, the body needs cortisol. But cortisol becomes a problem when produced in high quantities. It blocks the normal insulin process, which make you prone to developing diabetes. It also promotes the loss of protein from the muscles as it converts protein into burnable fat. Adrenaline, cortisol, and other chemical messengers involved in the stress response are called stress *mediators*.

When, and if, the brain senses that a threat in an acute situation has subsided, these mediators turn off and hormone levels return to normal, or what doctors call *baseline*, which can differ among individuals. The body begins to restore and rebalance itself. You relax, each of your systems—heart, circulation, nervous system, breathing, and so on—recover, and you return to neutral. Later, we'll explore some techniques for consciously initiating this recovery process—the *relaxation response*—that have been popularized in recent years.

Although these processes occur in all of us when we are stressed or challenged, they aren't exactly the same in any two people. Some of us may have more sensitive triggers or may release greater or lesser amounts of the different hormones. These differences are largely tied to your genetic makeup. Some people may actually be predisposed to have a severe biological response to stress, just as some people are predisposed to developing a certain illness. Let's say you have a family history of high blood pressure (hypertension). Your body, already at risk, is likely to recover more slowly from an episode of acute stress, meaning that it might take longer for your heart rate to return to baseline or for your blood vessels to return to normal than it would for other people. These are exactly the kinds of conditions that cause heart attacks. If your family has a history of diabetes, you'll probably be more likely to feel the long-term effects of increased blood sugars that are released via cortisol with chronic stress.

Believe it or not, research has shown that behavioral patterns, which can be genetic in nature, are linked to stress. Some people simply have a natural tendency to put themselves into situations that have a higher probability of producing stressful events. Likewise, hardwired aspects of your personality can put you at greater risk for feeling stress or can make you more vulnerable to the physical effects of the stress response. Having a high-strung or neurotic temperament will more readily expose a person to stressful events or episodes of depression. Hostility (a lethal component of type A behavior) can increase the frequency of stressful events and heighten the intensity of the experience. If you experience trauma in early life, whether psychological or physical, this can also aggravate the stress response, because it is tied to traits such as a negative mood, depression, anxiety, defensiveness, and hostility.

The good news is that personality traits and behavior patterns—the ones we might consider positive—also influence the stress response regardless of your genes. Among the most important ones are the following:

- A clear and coherent sense of meaning in life
- Optimism
- Tolerance for ambiguity
- Flexibility
- Relience
- Hardiness
- High self-esteem

Hardiness has been researched extensively, most notably by Dr. Salvatore Maddi of the University of California, Irvine. Currently the director of the Hardiness Institute, which he founded, Maddi began his work by studying the traits of employees of Illinois Bell Telephone when it was acquired by AT&T in the 1980s. His goal was to determine who survived in good mental and physical health and why. Maddi's work revealed similar tendencies as those noted by clinical psychologist Dr. Susan Kobasa, from the City University of New York, who studied the lives of concentration camp survivors as an integral part of her research. Being hardy or resistant to stress is a typical characteristic of people who can remain healthy and balanced despite adverse circumstances or a heavy workload. Essentially, a hardy or resilient person lives in alignment with his or her inner values. Individuals with hardy personalities thrive and remain healthy in the midst of enormously stressful situations.

Hardiness, which we might also call resiliency, has at its foundation a set of common characteristics, including these "3 Cs":

1. *Commitment.* You engage fully in your life's activities, with no restrictions on imagination or effort. This engagement adds meaning to your life.
2. *Control.* You believe that your efforts can influence the outcomes of events, and you can distinguish between the aspects of a situation that you can control and those you can't. This clearheadedness helps you accept that which is beyond your control and focus your energy where it will have the biggest impact.
3. *Challenge.* You accept change as a constant, a normal and expected part of life. When faced with new demands, you are able to seek understanding and move forward to solve problems. This willingness to face and engage with new developments fosters confidence, openness, and optimism.

In contrast, individuals who do not thrive physically in stressful environments hold very different attitudes. In general, they

- are bored with life;
- find life to be meaningless;
- consider change to be threatening;
- believe themselves to be at the mercy of their circumstances;
- prepare for the worst; and
- consider the status quo to be normal and view change as unusual.

Understanding that you can have a healthy response to stress with simple, learned personality and behavioral adjustments can help you to respond effectively to both acute and chronic stressors and to dampen their dangerous effects on your mood, your health, and your life.

Identifying the Symptoms

All forms of the stress response—physical, behavioral, emotional, and psychological—have recognizable symptoms that provide simple and measurable evidence of the existence of stress. Take some time now to identify the most common signs and symptoms of stress in your life. Ask a friend or a loved one to help you because sometimes others can notice these signs better than you can. Here are some of the most common symptoms.

Physical Symptoms
- Sleep disorders
- Headaches
- Neck and back pain
- Cardiovascular problems (chest pain, palpitations, shortness of breath)
- Gastrointestinal problems (constipation, diarrhea, heartburn)
- Dizziness
- Chronic fatigue
- Memory problems

Emotional/Psychological Symptoms
- Anxiety
- Irritability
- Impulsiveness
- Anger or hostility
- Loss of control
- Periods of confusion
- Inability to concentrate
- Impatience
- Frustration
- Inability to feel appropriate extremes of joy or sadness
- Fatigue

Behavioral Symptoms
- Increased smoking
- Increased use of prescription drugs
- Increased intake of alcohol or nonprescription drugs
- Binge eating
- Compulsive dieting
- Chronic procrastination

Following is a checklist I devised, "Understanding My Personal Stress Responses." Try to be as objective as possible when completing it. Don't downplay symptoms that might embarrass you, and don't exaggerate anything. Be honest, and trust the checklist to provide a clear picture of your physical self as it relates to stress.

Understanding My Personal Stress Responses

Read each symptom and choose the response that best describes you.

0 = Never
1 = Rarely (no more than once per month)
2 = Sometimes (once a week)
3 = Often (at least three times per week)
4 = Very often (more than four times per week)
5 = Constant

Body (Physical Symptoms)

Tension headaches __
Migraine (vascular) headaches __
Twitching eyelid __
Twitching nose __
Facial or jaw pains __
Dry mouth or throat __
Difficulty in swallowing __
Ulcers on tongue _
Neck pains __
Dizziness __
Speech difficulties, slurring, stuttering __
Blackaches __
Muscle aches __
Weakness __
Constipation __
Indigestion __
Nausea and/or vomiting __
Diarrhea __
Gain or loss of weight __

Swollen joints __
Sexual problems __
Increased allergies __
Frequent colds and flu __
Trembling and/or nervous tics __
Accident proneness
Excessive/distressed menstruation __
Rapid or difficult breathing __
Acidic stomach __
Shaking hands __
Burping __
Gassiness __
Oily skin __
Panting __
Dry mouth __
Hand tremor __
Neck stiffness __
Gum chewing __
Grinding teeth __

(continued)

Understanding My Personal Stress Responses (continued)

Loss of appetite or constant
  appetite __

Rashes, hives, or other skin
  problems __

Chest pains __

Heartburn __

Heart palpitations __

Frequent urination __

Excessive sweating __

Excessive sleeping __

High blood pressure __

Chronic fatigue __

Tightness in the chest or
  the heart __

Skin blemishes __

Colitis __

Asthma __

Hyperventilation __

Arthritis __

Allergy __

Cold hands and/or feet __

Insomnia __

Please count the number of items for which you chose 3, 4, or 5.

  Number of items that you rated as 3 (often): __

  Number of items that you rated as 4 (very often): __

  Number of items that you rated as 5 (constant): __

Please complete the following two sentences.

  The body symptom(s) that I am most aware/conscious of is (are): __

  The body symptom(s) that interfere(s) with my day-to-day functioning most
  is (are): __

Mind (Emotional/Psychological Symptoms)

Irritability __

Depression __

Loss of memory or concentration __

Nervousness about little things __

Nervousness about little things __

Impulsive behavior __

Withdrawal from other people __

Racing thoughts or disorientation __

Inability to make decisions __

Feelings of panic __

Frequent episodes of crying __

Thoughts of suicide __

Lack of sexual interest __

Moodiness __

Unusual aggressiveness __

Restlessness or
  overexcitability __

Nightmares __

Feelings of helplessness or
  frustration __

Neurotic behavior __

Anger __

Anxiety __

Feelings of losing control __

General anxiety (regardless of the
  situation or the people involved) __

(continued)

Understanding My Personal Stress Responses (continued)

Periods of confusion __   Powerlessness __
Depression __   Hostility __
Poor self-esteem __   Phobias __
Resentment __   Obsessions, unwanted thoughts __
Fears __

Please count the number of items for which you chose 3, 4, or 5.
    Number of items that you rated 3 (often): __
    Number of items that you rated 4 (very often): __
    Number of items that you rated 5 (constant): __

Please complete the following two sentences.
    The mind symptom(s) that I am most aware/conscious of is (are): __
    The mind symptom(s) that interfere(s) with my day-to-day functioning most
    is (are): __

Behavioral Symptoms

Gnashing or grinding of teeth __   Wrinkling forehead __
High-pitched, nervous laughter __   Foot or finger tapping __
Nail biting __   Hair pulling or twirling __
Increased smoking __   Increased use of prescribed
Increased alcohol consumption __   medication __
Binge eating __   Compulsive dieting __
Chronic procrastination __   Pacing the floor __
Sudden change in social habits __   Loss of interest in physical
Chronic tardiness __   appearance __

Please count the number of items for which you chose 3, 4, or 5.

    Number of items that you rated 3 (often): __
    Number of items that you rated 4 (very often): __
    Number of items that you rated 5 (constant): __

Please complete the following two sentences.
    The behavioral symptom(s) that I am most aware/conscious of is (are): __
    The behavioral symptom(s) that interfere(s) with my day-to-day functioning
    most is (are): __

You may have struggled to choose a dominant symptom from each category, but it's worth the effort. This work is necessary to establish your personal BestStress Zone. You may discover that you have different symptoms in various settings (i.e., workplace, family gatherings, social situations, or place of worship). Most of my clients have a dominant tendency that will reveal itself in some form in most settings. I want you to focus on the dominant symptoms. Each of us is different. If you must distinguish separate symptoms for various dimensions of your life, please do so.

Based on this exercise, you should now have a self-portrait of your current tendencies in response to the demands and challenges in your life. The next step is to link the symptoms to a stress source. This can be done easily with a daily record of what you experience. You can call it a "Stress Diary." Either jot things down on paper or create a diary on your favorite electronic device. The idea is to write down each symptom immediately—as soon as you notice it. Make note of the situation, the time, and the activity that you engaged in just prior to experiencing the symptom. Following is a sample of what your diary might look like.

Sample Stress Diary

Time	Symptom	Trigger	Preceding Activity
6 a.m.	Headache	Stood on the scale	Getting the kids up for school
8 a.m.	Chest pain	Traffic	Thinking about the car payment
10 a.m.	Anxiety	Sixty-five new e-mails	Received a call that my son forgot his trumpet
Noon	Smoking	Thinking about the car payment	My supervisor "dropped in" to see me in my cubicle
10 p.m.	Diarrhea	Argument with my son	Thinking about the car payment
1 a.m.	Insomnia	Anger about an argument	Remembered the deadline for a report

After making entries in your diary for a week, you should be able to spot some trends and patterns. Do symptoms occur at a certain time of day? Does a specific symptom accompany a certain situation or thought? Once you recognize the symptoms and link them to their sources, the next step is to determine why the sources are causing the symptoms. Ask yourself the following questions:

- Does the trigger generate the symptom because of the time of day?
- Does the trigger generate the symptom because of the nature of the situation itself or how you are managing it?
- Does the activity just prior to the trigger generate the symptom?
- Is there a solution?

Answering these questions may provide some relief. For example, a careful examination may reveal that your headache is due to your frenzied morning routine or ongoing concern about your finances. You might see that each day starts with a mad rush to get the kids off to school, resulting in a headache, an upset stomach, a rash, or some other physical ailment. If you know that your children constantly forget things and are anxious themselves, it may be that getting up earlier or enlisting the kids in an effort to get organized the night before would decrease the frenzy and alleviate your symptoms. Other simple steps, from taking time to get the traffic report before you leave in the morning or blocking out time to regularly review your finances, will decrease your overall symptoms. A little effort to keep track of your life in a stress diary for a short period of time can show you where many of these simple stress triggers and solutions lurk.

The physical symptoms I'm talking about may seem minor, but they are a cause for concern. Remember, it's not just about what you can "handle." We women think we can handle a huge amount of work and responsibility, and often we can. But too much stress is bad for your health, and that's my particular area of expertise. So let's talk about the stress-health connection.

The Medical Risks of Stress

When you are chronically stressed, the hormones that regulate your body's responses—adrenaline and cortisol, or the mediators—build up in your body, with no chance to return to their baseline levels. This creates a real burden on your system. Although you can deal with the "symptoms" noted earlier, your body is really taking a "hit" in terms of short- and long-term biological consequences.

The scientific name for this "hit" or biological burden is *allostatic load*, a term derived from the word *allostasis*. Allostasis refers to the combination of automatic adaptive responses that enables the body to maintain stability, or homeostasis, through change. The term was introduced by Dr. Peter Sterling of the University of Pennsylvania.

There are many components of the allostatic load, but here is an important general yardstick: the lower it is, the more successfully you age, meaning the better you are able to maintain a high level of mental capacity and physical well-being. The "load" is a measure of the mediators and biological by-products of ongoing stress in your body. It reflects your genetics, lifestyle choices, and exposure to chronic stress. It is important to know that factors such as exercise, smoking, and drinking also influence the reactivity of the stress response system and the release of mediators. The fact is that the acute response to demands and challenges in your life is protective and necessary. Only when stress is constant are the natural mechanisms for homeostasis altered and "toxic" by-products become a "load" on your body.

Dr. Bruce McEwen of the Rockefeller Institute and Dr. Teresa Seeman of UCLA developed a research battery of tests that measure this biological effect of ongoing stress—allostatic load—that can predict the amount of wear and tear your body has already been exposed to. It is not surprising that these tests also predict successful aging. Specifically, the results help anticipate any decline in cognitive and physical functioning. McEwen and Seeman's tests include the following:

- Urine (collected after twelve overnight hours) is tested for:
  1. Ur. norepinephrine (adrenaline)
  2. Ur. epinephrine (adrenaline)
  3. Ur. free cortisol
- Salivary cortisol: six saliva samples measured over one day
- Blood is tested for:
  1. Total and high-density lipoprotein cholesterol

   2. Glycosylated hemoglobin
   3. Interleukin-6
   4. C-reactive protein
   5. Fibrinogen
- Other:
   1. Waist-hip ratio
   2. Systolic and diastolic blood pressure
   3. Heart rate variability

This battery of tests also measures cardiovascular functioning and heart rate variability, which is correlated with cardiovascular activity and resistance to sudden death. Also included in the tests are indicators of metabolism (how efficiently your body processes what you put into it), such as the lipid profiles, your fasting insulin and glucose, and a gauge of your abdominal obesity based on your waist circumference. Finally, the tests measure inflammation; determine sympathetic nervous system activity based on the levels of neurotransmitters, such as epinephrine and norepinephrine; measure excess hypothalamic pituitary activity, based on cortisol levels; and survey the cortisol rhythm over the course of the day. In the context of my stress-relief coaching programs, I look at the allostatic load to judge how overworked an individual's stress response might be or how much time the body spends in overdrive because of stress. I call this the NetStress Load, and later we'll examine how it endangers the various systems in your body.

We can use these tests measuring the effects of stress as one component of a detailed picture of what I call the stress-health connection. When you live a life consumed by ongoing, long-term stress, you create a situation in which the cumulative effect is unhealthy, generating high NetStress Load. The same processes that protect you in the face of acute stress become harmful over the long term.

In the next section, we will look more closely at this stress-health connection, with the goal of gaining insights to prevent the development of NetStress Load and reduce the symptoms listed earlier. Let's start with an important area of the body that we all need to prioritize—the cardiovascular system.

Women, Cardiovascular Disease, and Stress

Today's women, juggling family, work, self, and other activities, are under pressures unlike those of previous generations. In the following account, one woman gives her opinion on stress and heart problems.

Stress is trying to be everything to everyone. When work is demanding longer hours and the family is "asking" for you to attend basketball games, take the kids somewhere, or just engage and join them for dinner without making phone calls, it is hard to be fully attentive. A few years back, I thought I was having a stroke, and now I'm on medication for hypertension and cholesterol. Given my family history and the pace I work at, I am predisposed to cardiac problems.
—Dorianne, 55, midlevel manager

It is no coincidence that we are noticing a clear increase in daily stress at the same time that our society is experiencing an epidemic of cardiovascular disease, especially in women. Let me give you some background before I go into details about the connection between stress and cardiovascular disease.

According to the American Heart Association's 2007 update, cardiovascular disease (CVD) includes:

- *High blood pressure, or hypertension*: an elevation in the force of blood pumping through your arteries, making the heart have to work harder than it should.
- *Coronary heart disease*: the hardening or clogging of coronary arteries.
- *Myocardial infarction* (or heart attack): the temporary interruption of blood flow to the heart muscle itself.
- *Angina pectoris*: chest pain caused by coronary heart disease.
- *Heart failure*: any structural or functional problem with the heart that prevents it from pumping blood properly.

Since 1900, in every year except 1918, CVD accounted for more deaths than any other single cause or group of causes of death in the United States. Data show that CVD is the underlying cause in 36.3 percent of all 2,398,000 deaths in 2004, or 1 of every 2.8 deaths in the United States.

Nearly 2,400 Americans die of CVD each day, an average of 1 death every thirty-six seconds. CVD claims more lives each year than cancer, chronic lower respiratory diseases, accidents, and diabetes combined. According to the American Heart Association, CVD is the largest single cause of death among women worldwide, accounting for more than one-third of all deaths. This statistic underscores the enormity of cardiovascular disease in women as a global health issue and the need for prevention.

Today, most Americans are aware of the causes of heart disease and the concept of prevention, but this was not always the case. In 1948, the Framingham Heart Study—under the direction of the National Heart Institute (now known as the National Heart, Lung, and Blood Institute)—embarked on an ambitious project in health research. At the time, little was known about the general causes of heart disease and stroke, but the death rates for CVD had been increasing steadily since the beginning of the century, and it had become an American epidemic. The objective of the Framingham Heart Study was to identify the common factors or characteristics that contribute to CVD by following its development over a long period of time in a large group of participants who had not yet developed overt symptoms of CVD or suffered a heart attack or a stroke.

In the original study, in 1948, the researchers recruited 5,209 men and women between the ages of thirty and sixty-two from the town of Framingham, Massachusetts, and began the first round of extensive physical examinations and lifestyle interviews that they would later analyze for common patterns related to CVD development. After 1948, the subjects returned to the study every two years to undergo detailed medical histories, physical examinations, and laboratory tests. In 1971, the study enrolled a second-generation group—5,124 of the original participants' adult children and their spouses—to participate in similar examinations. In the twenty-first century, a third generation, also related to the original participants, was recruited to continue this research.

Over the years, careful monitoring of the Framingham Study population has led to the identification of the main CVD risk factors—high blood pressure, high blood cholesterol, smoking, obesity, diabetes, and physical inactivity. The study has also provided a great deal of valuable information on the effects of related factors, such as blood triglyceride and LDL cholesterol levels, age, gender, and psychosocial issues, including stress.

Here is what we know today about the connections among stress, health, and the heart. The heart and the blood vessels are particularly sensitive to acute and chronic stress. With every beat, the heart not only pumps blood, but it also transmits complex patterns of neurological, hormonal, pressure, and electromagnetic information to the brain and throughout the body The heart is uniquely positioned as a powerful communication hub that connects the body, the mind, the emotions, and the spirit. Research suggests that an elaborate feedback network of hormones, chemicals, and nerves exists connecting the heart and the brain's centers of thoughts and emotions. Dr. Candace Pert describes this phenomenon and process in her book *The Body Is the Subconscious Mind*. It was in her laboratory at the National Institutes of Health that the naturally produced, powerful "informational substances" known as endorphins were discovered and biochemically defined. Her pioneering research laid the groundwork for our understanding of how the heart sends the brain messages that affect our perceptions, our mental processing, and our feelings. It's no surprise, then, that there is a strong connection between stress and cardiovascular disease.

In a 2008 *Journal of the American College of Cardiology* article, Dr. Joel Dinsdale, a cardiologist and researcher at the University of California in San Diego, published the first meta-analysis of the literature on psychological stress and cardiovascular disease. His review documented overwhelming evidence that stressors contribute to sudden death, myocardial infarction, angina, and heart wall motion abnormalities, as well as alterations in the regulation of the heart by the sympathetic nervous system. Dinsdale differentiated studies investigating the effects of acute stress (lasting one week or less, such as earthquakes and other natural disasters) from studies of chronic stressors (severe continuing adverse stressors, such as wartime), as well as chronic low-level aggravations (hassles). He noted that the distinctions were at times somewhat arbitrary. According to Dinsdale, "The stressor may last an instant (public criticism by a boss), but the patient may continue brooding about the humiliation for weeks or longer."

What we learned is that stress—whether acute or chronic—can lead to CVD via a number of different pathways:

- Type A behavior pattern (hostility and anger are lethal elements).
- Too much adrenaline and cortisol lead to high blood pressure and cause the blood vessels supplying the heart to spasm.

- Adrenaline has a direct effect on the heart in times of acute emotional stress, potentially causing sudden heart failure (Takotsubo cardiomyopathy).
- An acceleration of atherosclerosis (hardening of the arteries) leads to coronary heart disease and heart attacks.
- An increase of fibrinogen, a blood protein that causes thickening or clotting of the blood, adds to the likelihood of suffering a heart attack.
- An abnormal metabolism (the ongoing chemical reactions in the body that are necessary for life) is created, which includes elevation of cholesterol, insulin resistance (diabetes), and obesity.
- Irritation of the heart muscle leads to irregular heart rhythms (ventricular fibrillation), which cause sudden death in the setting of acute emotional stress.

Let's examine some of these specific pathways more closely, first the ones related to chronic stress and then those related to acute stress.

Chronic Stress and Cardiovascular Disease

We all experience some form of chronic stress, whether it is the daily hassle associated with navigating traffic to get to the workplace, the daily worry about how to adequately fund your retirement plan, the misery that may be associated with caring for a loved one with a terminal illness, or the ongoing tension between you and your teenage children. Biological changes can also put you at risk for heart disease. For most women, the risk for heart disease is greater than the risk of acquiring breast cancer. Here are some facts and explanations of the pathways that can lead to cardiovascular disease.

Type A Behavior

In 1959, cardiologists Meyer Friedman and Ray Rosenman published a breakthrough article in the *Journal of the American Medical Association* describing a clear link between stress and health, behavior and specific disease. The two cardiologists had called in an upholsterer to refinish the seats in the waiting room of their medical office. The upholsterer noticed that only the front edges of their seats were worn out and asked the doctors what types of patients they had been seeing. With their curiosity sparked, the doctors launched a study in an effort to determine why so many of their patients seemed to be literally "on the edges of their seats." Were they frightened? Agitated? Excited? Impatient? After close to five years, Friedman and Rosenman's research eventually enabled them to identify a unique condition that they named type A behavior pattern (TABP).

Here is the original description from Friedman and Rosenman's 1959 article:

> Type A behavior pattern "is a particular complex of personality traits, including excessive competitive drive, aggressiveness, in patients, any sense of time urgency as well as a free-floating, but well rationalized form of hostility and almost always a deep-seated sense of insecurity." They also described a Type B behavior pattern characterized by "no free-floating hostility or sense of time urgency. These people are equally as successful, but are not excessively competitive.... The most common measure of hostility measures the constructs of: suspiciousness, resentment, frequent anger, and cynical distrust."

They noted that type A people tended to smoke more cigarettes, have a higher level of serum cholesterol, and develop more coronary heart disease. In addition, they found that type A people who have a heart attack are more likely to have a second one.

More recently, research in the 1980s clarified the specific relationship between TABP and coronary disease. There are two lethal components. The first is the combination of impatience (time urgency) and irritability in striving for achievement. It appears that the second component, a combination of hostility and anger, is even more toxic. In the 1980s two researchers tested 255 medical students for hostility and then examined them annually for twenty-five years. Independent of coronary risk factors such as age, smoking status, and family history of hypertension, the researchers determined that high levels of hostility predicted an increased incidence of potentially lethal coronary disease. Subsequent studies have verified these findings and allow us now to feel comfortable describing hostility and anger as the key factors in people with type A behavior pattern, making them vulnerable to heart attacks or death due to coronary heart disease.

Hardening of the Arteries

Atherosclerosis, what is commonly called "hardening of the arteries," is a direct result of NetStress Load. Remember those jars of white paste you used in grade school? Now imagine this hard pastelike material sticking to the inside walls of your blood vessels. How is this related to stress? Recall that when the body requires increased fuel for the acute stress response described earlier, adrenaline and cortisol generate that fuel by ordering the release of glucose from your liver and fatty acids from your fat reserves. So, if your levels of cortisol are chronically elevated due to continual stress, fat is being generated and not expended. The two places where this extra fat is most likely to accumulate are in blood vessel walls and around the abdomen. Fat inside inflamed arteries is called atherosclerotic plaque. The pattern of fat deposits around the abdomen gives the body an apple shape, as opposed to a healthier pear shape, where fat accumulates lower, around the hips. This is called central obesity. In fact, waist-to-hip ratio is a better indicator of risk for heart disease than BMI (basal metabolic index), which is a common standard used to assess obesity.

Accumulated fat deposits inside the walls of the heart's major blood vessels lead to heart attacks through a sequence of interactions with the immune system's cells. The atherosclerotic plaque must be "activated" to cause a heart attack. Also, coronary spasm, which is more common in women, can trigger a heart attack. Coronary spasm is a reason that women come to emergency rooms with atypical chest pain. Ultimately, the blockage of blood flow in those vessels deprives the heart of oxygen, without which it cannot survive. And just as a blockage in the coronary arteries can cause a heart attack, a blockage in the arteries of the brain can cause a stroke.

Women have been conditioned to fear breast cancer, but they generally fail to realize that cardiovascular disease is currently the number one cause of death for both women and men in the United States. In a recent study, only 9 percent of women identified heart disease as the condition they fear most, even though heart disease kills twice as many women ages forty-five to sixty-four than breast cancer does. Improved heart health is a key benefit of living in the BestStress Zone.

Heart Attacks

The Interheart study was a landmark research project that examined the connection between stress and heart attacks. The study, published in 2004 in *Lancet* by lead researcher Salim Yusuf, M.B., B.S., D.Phil, of McMaster University in Canada, screened all patients admitted to the coronary-care unit or an equivalent cardiology ward for a first myocardial infarction, or heart attack. Thirteen thousand patients at 262 participating centers in fifty-two countries from all corners of the world were studied, along with an equivalent number of control patients who were matched by age and sex but had no history of heart disease.

This is the first study of heart disease to ask specific questions about stress, which was defined as "feeling irritable, filled with anxiety, or as having sleeping difficulties as a result of conditions at work or at home." Questions about psychosocial risk factors in the Interheart questionnaire covered stress at work or home, financial stress, stressful life events, depression, and locus of control (the perceived ability to control life circumstances). The results indicated that those who reported "permanent stress" at work or home had *more than double* the risk of developing a heart attack. Although the global effect was less than that for smoking, it was comparable with hypertension and abdominal obesity! Furthermore, the effects of stress on heart attacks were similar in men and women, in people of all ages, and in all geographic regions of the world that were studied.

Acute Stress and Cardiovascular Disease

Having to give a presentation in front of your peers, answering the phone and learning that there's been an accident involving your child, getting an e-mail from your boss moving up the deadline for a project—these are all situations that present demands and challenges that can be labeled as acute stress. Below, I've outlined some specific cardiovascular problems that can occur in the setting of acute stress.

Takotsubo Cardiomyopathy

In 2005, Dr. Iian Wittstein and his colleagues at Johns Hopkins reported a cardiovascular disorder thought to be due to a direct effect of adrenaline on the heart as a result of stress. The elevated adrenaline can literally stun the heart muscle, causing heart failure. This condition, now called Takotsubo cardiomyopathy, is related to acute emotional stress and mimics acute heart attacks. It is characterized by reversible ballooning of the left heart chamber (the major part of the heart pump) in the absence of blockage of heart (coronary) vessels. Takotsubo cardiomyopathy, which is transient and typically precipitated by acute emotional stress, is also known as "stress cardiomyopathy" or "broken-heart syndrome." It is important for women to be aware of this condition for the following reasons:

- In the cases reported to date, the syndrome is more common in women than in men.
- The condition can be easily overlooked or mislabeled as a lack of disease. Doctors or loved ones might incorrectly interpret it as the overly emotional response of a "drama queen."
- The condition requires a different intervention. Because the coronary arteries are not involved, there is no need for angioplasty or stents. This is a reversible condition that requires that the weakened heart muscle be supported pharmacologically (through medication) and/or mechanically until healing takes place.

Acute Emotional Stress and an Abnormal Heartbeat

The main cause of all sudden cardiac deaths outside the confines of a hospital is the abnormal beating of the heart, or cardiac arrhythmias. The most lethal heart rhythm is *ventricular fibrillation*. The automatic electrical defibrillators that you see displayed in public places are specifically designed to treat ventricular fibrillation. Ventricular fibrillation describes a situation in which the heart's electrical activity becomes disordered. When this happens, the heart's lower (pumping) chambers contract in a rapid, unsynchronized way. The ventricles "flutter," rather than beat, and the heart pumps little or no blood. Lack of blood to the brain and other critical organs will ensure death. Without immediate medical attention, the patient will collapse and can suffer sudden cardiac death. According to Dr. Roy Ziegelstein of Johns Hopkins, at least

20 percent (or one in five episodes) of serious ventricular arrhythmias, including ventricular fibrillation or sudden cardiac death, are precipitated by unusual emotional stress.

Just as styles of thinking are influenced differently by the right and the left sides of the brain, cardiac activity is influenced by each side of the brain in a different manner. This is called *lateralized control* of the heart. Current research suggests that emotional arousal triggers ventricular fibrillation and sudden death through activation of one side of the brain, which in turn causes a net lateralized imbalanced activation of nervous-system input to the heart muscle itself. Early studies suggest that left-sided activation of the heart is more likely to trigger lethal heart rhythms (ventricular fibrillation) than right-sided activation.

What does this mean for you? Quite simply, as you deepen your understanding of stress and your body, never forget that the first step toward living "heart healthy" is reducing the stress in your life.

Stress, Cardiac Deaths, and the Holidays

Did you know that more people die of heart disease on Christmas Day and New Year's Day than any other day of the year? These so-called holiday deaths are called "excess" deaths. There are several mechanisms that are thought to contribute to the increase in cardiac deaths during the winter holiday season:

- Changes in diet and alcohol consumption (alcohol has a direct toxic effect on the heart and can cause atrial fibrillation).
- Increase in respiratory diseases that often weaken patients, making them more vulnerable to cardiac events. Some causes of respiratory illnesses are the environmental toxins created by burning fireplaces and the infections brought on by bronchitis, the common cold, and pneumonia.
- Holiday-induced delays in seeking care due to traveling or not wanting to spoil what is supposed to be a joyous time.
- Increase in emotional stress often related to the responsibilities and tasks surrounding traveling, decorating, shopping, and other holiday-oriented events.

The Immune System

Beginning in the early 1980s, researchers Janice Kiecolt-Glaser, Ph.D., and immunologist Ronald Glaser, Ph.D., of the Ohio State University College of Medicine, were intrigued by animal studies that linked stress and infection. Their pioneering work led to our current understanding of stress, the immune system, and depression

We currently know that the effect of stress on the immune system actually differs depending on whether the stress is acute or chronic. In times of acute stress, the immune system is fortified to defend against pathogens (any biological agent that can cause illness or disease, such as a germ, a virus, a bacterium, or a parasite) by causing the release of immune cells from the bloodstream into the tissues where they are needed. Chronic stress, however, weakens your immune system through the influence of cortisol. Ultimately, the availability of various types of cells that fight infection and the responsiveness of those infection-fighting cells are diminished in the presence of chronic stress. Prolonged exposure to such chronic stress ultimately leaves you more vulnerable to infections, rashes, and certain viral or bacterial disorders.

While there is no evidence at this time that stress is a direct cause of cancer, there is a link between stress and developing certain kinds of cancer, as well as how the disease progresses. Researchers at the National Institutes of Health have reviewed hundreds of studies done over the past thirty years that examined the relationship between psychological factors, including stress, and cancer risk with conflicting results. Evidence from both animal and human studies suggests that chronic stress weakens a person's immune system, which in turn may affect the incidence of virus-associated cancers, such as Kaposi's sarcoma and some lymphomas. Some studies have also suggested an association between certain psychological factors, such as feeling helpless or suppressing negative emotions, and the growth or spread of cancer, although this relationship has not been consistently seen.

Stress and the Brain

Neuroscientists sometimes joke that the more we learn about the brain, the less we know. The processes within the brain are extremely complex and sometimes unpredictable, but we have managed to identify some important patterns for how things work. We know that a particular structure in the brain, the *hippocampus*, stores contextual memory, or the what, where, why, and when of our experiences. We rely on input from the hippocampus to recognize a situation as potentially demanding or challenging. We also need input from the adjacent brain structure, the *amygdala*, which stores emotional memories, particularly fear and anger. The evidence of learning taking place in the brain is called *brain plasticity*, which refers to the stretching and growth of the brain cells in the hippocampus in response to repeated exposure to something. But when we are chronically stressed, those hippocampal cells lose some of their size, and we have problems recalling people, places, or things. Interestingly, the amygdala is less vulnerable to this effect of chronic stress, meaning that a particular cue might trigger bad feelings without your even knowing why!

Things get even more complicated when we examine the relationship between stress and depression. Recently, in a *New England Journal of Medicine* review, Dr. R. H. Belmaker offered some new insights on this topic, yet many questions remain unanswered. According to Belmaker, cortisol elevation is present in patients with both chronic stress and depression. It is possible that chronic mild elevations of cortisol, especially at night, when cortisol levels in normal subjects are very low, may in fact have a role in causing depression. Stress may be a direct cause in some cases but may have a secondary, more undefined relationship to depressed moods in other individuals. Some patients have a single depressive episode in their lifetime, whereas larger numbers of people have recurrent or even chronic cases of depression. It is also possible that certain instances of cortisol elevation only reflect central disturbances in brain signaling, which might fundamentally change the way environmental stresses affect mood. Various types of acute stress, early childhood trauma, or long-term psychosocial problems may be involved and may cause different responses of the stress system.

Stress and the Gastrointestinal System

Here is what we know about the biology of stress and the gut. In the presence of acute stress, we produce less saliva (dry mouth), our intestinal secretions decrease (digestion ceases), and we experience uncontrolla-ble spasms or contractions of the esophagus. For years, most of us have considered ulcers the hallmark of a stressful life, but I see two disorders in the ER with astonishing regularity: gastroesophageal reflux disease (GERD) and irritable bowel disease (IBD).

GERD results from an abnormal amount of acid moving back from the stomach up into the esophagus. The barrier (the sphincter—a spe-cialized muscle in the lower end of the esophagus) between the stom-ach and the esophagus is either too weak to prevent acid from flowing back into the esophagus or is unable to maintain its function as a bar-rier, particularly after meals. This backward flow of acid may result in various symptoms. Heartburn and a sour taste in the mouth are typical symptoms, whereas chest pain, hoarseness, chronic cough, shortness of breath, and others are atypical manifestations of GERD.

In a Gallup poll, 64 percent of individuals with heartburn reported that stress increased their symptoms. But the poll provided even more interesting information: most patients with GERD (up to 80 percent) have typical symptoms of GERD even though they have no evidence of inflammation or damage to their esophagus! This suggests that stress plays an important role in generating symptoms not only in GERD patients but also in people with completely normal esophageal linings. Psychological factors such as anxiety also play a role. Stressed patients have increased esophageal sensitivity to acid, which appears to be the underlying mechanism. Scientists are studying the specific brain mechanisms that help integrate the biochemistry of the gut and the biology of the stress response.

IBD causes bouts of unrelenting diarrhea, alternating with con-stipation. Because up to 40 percent of IBS patients show evidence for increased anxiety and the changes are similar to those reported in a variety of other so-called functional disorders (e.g., fibromyal-gia, chronic fatigue syndrome, and interstitial cystitis), this suggests a model in which alterations in the central stress circuits in predis-posed individuals are triggered by stressors and play a primary role in causing this disease. According to this model, various stressors and specific triggers create changes in the lining of the bowel that regulate the response of the bowel to stress. Stressors also vary in how they produce the symptoms, that is, diarrhea and abdominal cramping, seen in irritable bowel syndrome. Early life stress and trauma, in the form of abuse, neglect, or loss of the primary caregiver, play a major role in individuals' vulnerability to developing functional gastrointestinal disorders later in life. Acute, life-threatening stress episodes in adult life, such as rape, can trigger acute functional bowel disorders or other long-term symptoms if post-traumatic stress disorder develops.

The high incidence of ulcer disease results partly from a chronically suppressed immune system (due to chronic stress) and the increase in the bacteria *Helicobacter pylori*. Symptoms often include nausea, vomiting, and frequent bouts of unexplained abdominal pain. Treatment may include stress reduction and antibiotic therapy.

Stress and Diabetes

Diabetes mellitus occurs when the pancreas doesn't make enough or, in some cases, none of the hormone insulin. It can also occur when the insulin produced doesn't work effectively. In diabetes, the level of glucose in the blood is too high. Like cardiovascular disease, diabetes is at epidemic proportions in the United States. According to the American Diabetes Association, diabetes affects 23.6 million people in the United States.

There are two types of diabetes. In a person with type 1 diabetes, little or no insulin is produced by the body. It is easy for the demands of stress to overwhelm the body's ability to handle the increased glucose produced by chronic stress. In those with type 2 diabetes, the pancreas continues to produce normal amounts of insulin, but the body stops responding to it. For people who are borderline, or have pre-diabetes, stress can add additional demands on their system that lead to full-fledged diabetes symptoms.

Stress contributes to the development or worsening of diabetes through several mechanisms:

- Glucose and fatty acids are present the bloodstream.
- Insulin is unable to be secreted by the pancreas.
- Cortisol makes the body less sensitive to insulin.

The good news is that reducing stress can prevent the development of diabetes in many people. For people living with type 2 diabetes, studies have shown that reducing stress can make the body more sensitive to insulin and thereby reduce blood glucose levels.

Stress and the Musculoskeletal System

When you are acutely stressed, your body shifts the blood to flow into large muscle groups in preparation for running or taking a stand— that is, fight or flight. Stress may also trigger the contraction of small muscles—a tightening in your jaw and back or neck stiffness. The patients with back pain I see in the ER often come seeking care for chronic problems with their lower back or because of overuse injuries to muscles. As you will see in the next chapter, the connection between your work and the physical manifestations of stress is extremely strong.

Finally, I'd like to mention those individuals who have abnormal medical conditions because they lack an adequate response to stressors. Although the mechanism has not been clearly described, people with chronic fatigue syndrome, atypical depression, fibromyalgia, autoimmune disorders, and chronic inflammatory disorders such as rheumatoid arthritis and hypothyroidism often have a poor brain response to stimuli and stressors. They also characteristically have low cortisol levels and are often depressed.

Current Risk for Illness and Disease Due to Stress

Life in the BestStress Zone requires a focus on risk reduction Are you at risk for experiencing illness, disease, premature disability, or premature death because of stress? In the exercise that follows, the statements will help you assess your personal risk for the links between stress and disease.

Stress Health Profile

. . . .

Read each statement carefully and answer true or false honestly and to the best of your knowledge.

1. I am crystal clear about my life's purpose, and I know the greater meaning that shapes all of my life. __

2. A biological parent or sibling has heart disease, high blood pressure, diabetes, clinical depression, or is/was a workaholic. __

3. I have a close friend or a family member with whom I can talk about my true feelings when I need to. __

4. In the last six months, caretaking responsibilities for children in my life and/or parents are a significant source of anxiety or worry due to time conflicts or inability to meet needs of others. __

5. I consider unexpected change to be an opportunity for learning and growth. __

6. In the last month, I have had frequent episodes of at least one of the following; feeling out of control, agitation, anxiety, frustration, irritability, moodiness, resentment, restlessness or overexcitability, inability to concentrate, or forgetfulness. __

7. I currently smoke or drink more than one alcoholic beverage per day __

8. I find it intolerable to watch others perform tasks that I know I can do faster. __

9. In the last six months, I been filled with anxiety, have been irritable, or have had difficulty sleeping as a result of conditions at home—specifically, in managing home responsibilities or elder care; not having enough help with household tasks or children; from abuse or frequent problems with a spouse, a partner, or a teenager; or from a recent change in living conditions or situations. __

10. In the past six months I have lost my job, had a change in my job, or am living with the real possibility of losing my job. __

11. Within the last five years, a doctor has told me that I have at least one of the following health problems or conditions: obesity, high cholesterol, anxiety or depression, or hypertension (high blood pressure). __

12. Within the last six months, I have experienced bias or discrimination because of my primary language, race, ethnicity, or sexual orientation. __

(continued)

Stress Health Profile (continued)

. . . .

13. I am satisfied with my current level of self-care in at least two of the follow-ing five areas of my life: types of foods I eat and when I eat, spiritual life, physical fitness, personal grooming needs, or time for self. __

14. It is hard for me to say no even when I get overloaded and will be person-ally ineffective by saying yes. __

15. In the last twelve months, I have been so angry that one or all of the fol-lowing have occurred: my body tensed, I clenched my fists or teeth, I slammed a door or pounded a table, I threw an object, I felt almost out of control or I lost control, or I physically hurt myself or someone else. __

16. I often engage in leisure or play activities and "lose myself" and time just "stands still." __

17. I struggle to make ends meet and do not have enough money to pay bills and meet other obligations, or I don't have enough money to save or invest for the future for me or my children. __

18. I usually feel emotionally drained and "used up" by the end of the day.

19. Murphy's Law almost always applies to me—if things can go wrong, they will go wrong. __

20. I know what it means to relax and practice some form of true relaxation at least once a day. __

Interpreting Your Responses

At the end of each section are action steps to help you get a jump-start on your quest for better health and less stress.

Statements 1, 3, 5, 13, 16, 29: If you answered true for these statements—congratulations! These statements are generally associated with good or positive health outcomes.

   Action Steps: Continue to nurture supportive and intimate relationships in your life. This is good for your health.

Statements 2, 11: If you answered true for these statements, it likely represents genetic wiring or acquired habits. There is good news, though. Your wiring is not your destiny! According to the Centers for Disease Control, eight of ten vis-its to primary care doctors are due to stress. It is not a coincidence that there is

. . . .

a stress epidemic and, at the same time, epidemics of obesity, heart disease, and diabetes. Take action today to learn more about your specific status. These risks can be reduced and even reversed through simple lifestyle adjustments, a decrease in stress, and, in some cases, medications and nutritional supplements. See your primary care doctor.

Action Steps: Try to tone down your anger and hostility today. Give the gift of forgiveness freely. Go ahead and try it—if only for the rest of the week

Statements 4, 6, 7, 8, 9, 10, 12, 14, 15, 17, 18, 19: If you answered true for these statements, today may be the beginning of the next phase of your life! These emotional, biological, and psychological responses to the demands and challenges of your life put you at a much higher risk of suffering from high blood pressure, a heart attack, obesity, diabetes, and depression. Acknowledging these issues is a great positive first step. Things can and will get better! It's your move.

Action Steps: First, if you are anxious, sad, or depressed to the extent that you feel you may harm yourself or others, contact your primary care doctor or a mental health professional today. Next, back off from your quest for perfection. It is impossible to have a perfect marriage or partnership, kids, career, body, and fitness regimen. Delegation works, if it's done correctly. Learn how to delegate at home and on the job. You can and will be happy without perfection. Next, consider what is really important to you. What are you excited about? Write it down. Learn to "relax." This is not the same as engaging in a leisure activity. True relaxation is a simple learned skill that enables you to trigger at will a biological response that lowers blood pressure and heart rate and counters harmful stress hormones. See chapter 9 for more about relaxation techniques. Finally, self-care is not selfish—it is your duty. In emergency medicine, when faced with a pregnant trauma patient, we say, "Take care of the mom first." Begin today!

Summary

In this chapter, I've outlined the biology of stress. Although I have described four types of responses to stress, all of them are actually integrated. The body is wired with biochemicals, hormones, and nerves that are bundled into what we call organs and systems, but they all work together in a unique manner for each individual. Your own special

DNA, inherited from your parents, not only gave you your eye color and body type (the outer packaging) but, more important, it influences all of your internal processes, from triggering responses in your nervous system to regulating the levels of common stress hormones and to giving you a tendency toward weight gain or heart disease.

Now you should appreciate why and how you can actually *feel* a heartbreak or experience "gut instincts."

Armed with facts about the specific medical risks of stress, you can step back and make a realistic assessment of your physical state. You have to know what's broken before you can fix it. Not all of the physical symptoms you've identified necessarily result from stress, of course, and I want to emphasize the importance of maintaining communication with your regular doctor, who can help distinguish between the manageable, stress-related problems and more serious medical concerns. As you begin to understand your own stressors and responses from reading this book, you'll be able to work with your doctor to recognize serious risks and take all necessary steps to restore and maintain your optimal health.

women and stress

the unique impact of stress on women and how to reduce it

Women are not unique in experiencing stress in the workplace; however, this chapter will focus on what is unique to women when it comes to work-related stress. I'll start with numbers and then will go into what "work" really is—and is not—with the guidance of some well-known and important thinkers in the field. We will then turn our attention to the relationship between work and health, and I will provide you with some self-assessment tools to help you better understand how work affects your overall well-being.

You will recall that stress is a process. Stress occurs because of a disequilibrium and a disharmony in the relationship between the demands and challenges you face and your perception of your ability to cope. So, what is "work"? According to Wikipedia, work in the context of human labor means "one's place of employment . . . the effort applied to produce a deliverable or accomplish a task . . . physical work done by people." Discussions about stress in the lives of women are often distilled to seeking work-life balance. This implies a clear distinction between work and life. Obviously, this is not always the case. In his many books and writings, Dr. Mihály Csíkszentmihályi, of the Quality of Life Research Center at Claremont College in California, makes the argument that work and nonwork are not necessarily opposites. For Csíkszentmihályi, an event or a condition is defined best by the quality of the experience: how you are engaged with the experience and what it feels like to you. Moreover, it is the quality or essence of any experience that makes either stress or enjoyment possible.

Flow is a technical term Csíkszentmihályi coined to describe an experience that is rewarding in and of itself. This quality of intrinsic motivation is also called *autotelic.* When athletes talk about being "in the zone" or "in the groove," they are completely absorbed in the experience, their minds clear except for the immediate task at hand, and they feel as if all of their senses and reflexes are heightened. Flow can also describe a benchmark or a standard for positive psychic functioning. A precondition for the flow or autotelic state is that you have total clarity about the requirements of the task or situation, combined with confidence in your ability to carry it out. To sustain the flow state, you must be increasingly challenged by something that requires more complex and refined skills. I'm sure you know what it's like to experience new levels of accomplishment and discovery. In the same way that athletes constantly seek to "elevate their game," you seek the same satisfactions from work and from life.

Flow typically occurs in clearly structured activities with specific goals in which challenges and skills can be varied, yet controlled. Some amount of familiarity or regularity helps. For example, if you play tennis regularly, you can experience flow when playing an opponent for the first time. The opponent's style may be new and unusual, and no two points in tennis are ever alike, but the general outlines of the game stay the same and offer a setting in which flow can occur. Most important, flow produces harmony within the self. It can distort the experience of time. People talk about being so involved in the moment that they didn't notice hours go by. How many times have you been at work and lost track of time?

Even though work and your life can sometimes feel like an endless string of boring routines, your days are rarely so neatly structured that you can easily slip into a flow state. The truth is that very few of us experience flow in the workplace, and this leads to stress.

An Epidemic

Stress and work have been a problem for men and women in our society for several decades. In 1992, a United Nations report called stress a "twentieth-century disease," and, at the same time, the World Health Organization (WHO) labeled stress a worldwide epidemic. Ten years later, the National Institute for Occupational Safety and Health (NIOSH) published data about the epidemic and declared that "organizational changes in the workplace may have outpaced our understanding of the implication for job health." In 2001, NIOSH suggested that restructuring, downsizing, nontraditional employment practices, and lean production technologies should be listed as the causes of stress. This report was the first attempt in the United States to develop a comprehensive research agenda to investigate and reduce occupational safety and health risks associated with the changing organization of work. Here are some statistics from that report:

- 40 percent of workers reported that their jobs were very or extremely stressful.
- 25 percent viewed their jobs as the number one stressor in their lives.
- 29 percent felt quite a bit or extremely stressed at work.
- 26 percent said they were "often or very often burned out or stressed by their work."
- Job stress was more strongly associated with health complaints than financial or family problems were.

Employers well know the high cost of workplace stress. According to the American Institute of Stress, workplace stress results in more than $300 billion nationally each year in health-care costs. Some common effects of stress in the workplace are reduced employee focus, higher rates of turnover and absenteeism, more accidents, decreased productivity, and higher medical costs and workers' compensation payments. Workers who report that they are stressed account for health-care costs that are 46 percent higher than the costs for employees who do not report being stressed. Roughly 8 percent of all employee medical expenditures are related to stress. Given a 19 to 20 percent prevalence of stress in the workplace, stress has become a great economic burden for employers.

In 2005, Ellen Galinsky and the Families and Work Institute published a study examining work and families. The goal was to better identify contemporary work habits and how the ways we prioritize our lives on and off the job contribute to our being overworked. Here are some highlights:

- One in three American employees is chronically overworked.
- 54 percent of American employees have felt overwhelmed at some time in the past month by how much work they had to complete.
- 29 percent of employees spend a lot of time doing work that they consider a waste of time. These employees are more likely to be overworked.
- More than one-third of employees (36 percent) had not and were not planning to take their full vacations.
- Most employees take short vacations, with 37 percent taking fewer than seven days.
- Among employees who take one to three days off (including weekends), 68 percent return feeling relaxed, compared with 85 percent who take seven or more days off (including weekends).
- Only 8 percent of employees who are not overworked experience symptoms of clinical depression, compared with 21 percent of those who are highly overworked.

Perhaps even more alarming is the Gallup poll "Attitudes in the American Workplace VI," sponsored by the Marlin Company, that found that

- 80 percent of workers feel stress on the job, nearly half say that they need help in learning how to manage stress, and 42 percent say that their coworkers need such help;
- 14 percent of respondents had felt like striking a coworker in the previous year but didn't;

- 25 percent had felt like screaming or shouting because of job stress, and 10 percent are concerned about an individual at work whom they fear could become violent; and
- 9 percent are aware of an assault or a violent act in their workplace, and 18 percent had experienced some sort of threat or verbal intimidation in the previous year.

Today, small businesses, as well as independent laborers, are threatened by large, centralized, multinational organizations. The need for high productivity and profit gains have replaced quality of product and quality of workers' lives as the first priority, driving wave after wave of organizational restructuring, mergers, acquisitions, and downsizing. The economic downturn and recession of 2008–2009 that has been responsible for some of the highest rates of unemployment seen in decades, tanking investments, decreasing home values, and worsening consumer confidence has added several new layers of complexity to the "work stress" phenomenon. Job security has become priority one for most people, and many employees are having to do more with fewer resources. The pace of work and life has become increasingly frantic, contributing to the erosion of leisure time and the unwelcome blending of work and personal time, as shown in this woman's story.

In the last two years, stress has always been present in my life at work, and it leaks over to my personal life. I was promoted back then, and since that time I have felt incredible stress to the point that I have great difficulty finding ways to relax. Then there is the positive stress, which drives me (adrenaline rush). However, there's also stress that has the potential to affect me in an unhealthy manner—not enough sleep, instantly consumed by the job, unable to take time out to live in the moment. Six months ago, my husband lost his job, and now I am doing some home visits to increase my income. There is nothing positive about what I am feeling these days. I feel more like a patient instead of a health-care provider.

—Melissa, 50, home health-care manager

Today, stressors are everywhere in the workplace. Some are small and irritating; others are catastrophic. Stressors can be internal or external; they can be sudden crises or chronic conditions. You may feel intimidated by all of the wonderful new technologies that were supposed to make your life easier. Maybe product shortages due to bad weather in far-off countries caused your own supply lines to dry up. Maybe you have crazy coworkers or customers or bosses. Maybe your industry is shrinking, and you have to hold on for dear life to a job you've hated for years. One thing is certain: not only is the workplace packed with unavoidable stressors, but Americans are also spending more time in that workplace than ever before. The average full-time worker puts in about fifty hours a week in the United States—almost twenty-five hundred hours per year. Workers in the United States have now surpassed the Japanese in the number of hours they work each year.

Policy reforms outside the United States aimed at reducing work time appear to have had an effect. Average work hours in almost every European nation have fallen dramatically since 1979. Even in Japan, known throughout the world for its long work hours, average work hours per person declined by more than three hundred hours a year. By contrast, the United States has not implemented or even seriously debated policies that are designed to reduce work time. Instead, most work-family advocates have focused on the need for child care, paid family leave, and programs that permit flexibility in determining which, rather than how many, hours workers will spend on the job.

We see the magnitude of the effect of workplace stress when we look at the increase in preventable lifestyle disorders: ulcers, migraines, muscle strain, and, of course, cardiovascular disease. Cardiovascular disease is the main cause of death and disability in the industrialized world, and it is the number one cause of death in the United States. It is estimated that 250,000 people die each year from heart disease and another 250,000 die due to chronic cardiac disease. At the core of many heart disorders is hypertension. Evidence suggests that 25 percent of people who have "essential" hypertension—a risk factor for stroke and heart disease—suffer from work-induced hypertension.

Is It Really Tougher for Women?

I put in many extra hours, sacrificing breaks and lunches, coming in early, staying late, and often working on weekends. I have had to let people go, restructure the office, and deal with corporate demands of more and faster production. I came up through the ranks and moved into management. The people that I am laying off or terminating are the same people who were my peers for more than two years.

—Rachel, 42, vice president of a technology company

Let's now focus on women, work, and stress.

Gender influences stress in the lives of all women: executives, managers, support staff, workers on production lines, and the service side of the cafeteria line. The triggers and the experiences may differ, but the effect on health is often the same. Stress affects women across all racial, ethnic, and religious cultures. Understanding this issue will help us better analyze organizational performance—and explore the links between stress and disease. Researchers have identified key differences between women's and men's experiences with stress in the workplace.

The National Study of the Changing Workforce (NSCW) delved even deeper into patterns of work and women and family life. Every five years, the Families and Work Institute conducts the NSCW—the only ongoing study of the U.S. workforce of its kind or scale. By surveying large, nationally representative samples of workers, the NSCW provides a rare glimpse into the work, personal, and family lives of Americans—and how home and work are changing over time. In its most recent report, published in 2003, the NSCW focused on the following five key areas:

1. Women in the workforce
2. Dual-earner couples
3. The role of technology in employees' lives
4. Work-life supports on the job
5. Working for oneself versus someone else

Here are some highlights of the report's results. The proportions of women and men in the wage and salaried workforce are now nearly equal (51 percent men and 49 percent women), and men have become far more accepting of women's participation in the workforce over the last twenty-five years. Two in five men, however, still think that women's place is in the home. Over the last twenty-five years, women have achieved increasingly higher educational levels and have moved steadily into managerial and professional occupations, so that today women employees are significantly better educated and more likely to hold managerial and professional positions than men are. Women's annual earnings, on average, however, are still substantially less than men's earnings ($36,716 versus $52,908). Employees—whether men or women—who have greater responsibility for the care of their children report lower earnings. In dual-earner couples, there is a significant third job that has to be done at home: family work. And women are still much more likely to assume the primary responsibility for family work than men are. The proportion of married wage and salaried employees who are dual-earner spouses has increased substantially over the last twenty-five years, from 66 percent in 1977 to 78 percent today. And together, these couples are working longer and longer hours. Combined work hours for dual-earner couples with children rose ten hours a week, from eighty-one hours a week in 1977 to ninety-one hours a week today. Clearly, today's working couples have less time for their lives off the job. Given this, it comes as a surprise that the combined time that spouses with children spend caring for and doing things with their children on workdays has actually increased—from 5.2 hours in 1977 to 6.2 hours today.

What has been sacrificed? Parents' time for themselves. Today's dads spend 1.3 hours on workdays on themselves, down from 2.1 hours twenty-five years ago. Moms have even less time for themselves—0.9 hours versus 1.6 hours in 1977. Work-life supports on the job—both specific benefit entitlements and less formal policies and practices—have increased somewhat, although not a lot, in the last decade. One work-life program that has increased significantly is elder-care resource and referral services. In 1992, only 11 percent of employees had access to this benefit versus nearly a quarter (24 percent) today. Despite somewhat increased work-life supports on the job, however, employees with families report significantly higher levels of interference between their jobs and their family lives than did employees twenty-five years ago (45 percent versus 34 percent report this as "some" or "a lot").

So what happens when women show up at work? According to David Thomas, a professor at Harvard Business School and a leading authority on diversity in the workplace, variation in team composition has a profound effect on business performance outcomes. Thomas described the manner in which an organization views "differences" as its unique "diversity perspective." There are three perspectives for inclusion of women: equity and fairness, access to markets, and experience and learning. The experience and learning perspective allows women in organizations to feel comfortable, and they don't have to represent or know the feelings of all women. Rather, women in these organizations are valued for their unique contributions to the team, as individuals. They can remain open about their differing perspectives on issues. Dr. Thomas's work also suggests that organizations with the highest level of diversity perspectives provide an environment in which mentoring relationships across gender differences can be as effective as more traditional mentoring relationships.

In 2002, a landmark book edited by Debra Nelson and Ronald Burke, *Gender, Workstress and Health*, offered an analysis of the relationship between gender and stress in the workplace. The evidence they developed revealed that deeply entrenched perceptions of accepted gender roles are the main factor contributing to the extra burden of stress experienced by women in the workplace. They also observed that although men and women may have similar numbers of stressors, the types of stressors and the meaning or importance that each gender attaches to the stressors may differ. Workaholism is another individual variable that has implications for creating work stress. Workaholism has three facets: work involvement, feeling driven to work, and work enjoyment. Nelson and Burke's book suggests that women may have a different experience of workaholism because of greater levels of self-imposed perfectionism.

The effect of these differences comes into focus when we look at some statistics for working women today. According to the U.S. Department of Labor, Bureau of Labor Statistics, as of 2008, of the

121 million working-age women in the United States (defined as age sixteen and older), 68 million were employed—75 percent full-time and 25 percent part-time. Women make up 46.5 percent of the total U.S. labor force. Seventy-one percent of American women with children under age eighteen, 77 percent of women with children ages six to seventeen, 64 percent of women with children under age six, and 56 percent of women with infants (under one year of age) are in the labor force.

These percentages understate how many women raising children are in the paid labor force because they reflect only women raising their own children and do not include the many women who are raising grandchildren, nieces and nephews, or other related children. Note that the labor force includes those who are working and those who are looking for work.

Women are now experiencing the stress associated with leadership positions in the workplace. In 2008, the U.S. Department of Labor reported that women accounted for 51 percent of all workers in upper management and professional occupations. They outnumbered men in such occupations as public relations managers, financial managers, human resource managers, education administrators, medical and health services managers, accountants and auditors, primary and secondary schoolteachers, physical therapists, writers, and registered nurses.

One final demographic change increasingly will have a profound effect on the number and types of stressors to which women are exposed. Although the population as a whole is aging, women continue to outlast men to a significant degree. According to the Alliance for Aging Research, older women in the United States are especially vulnerable to gaps in social services and are more likely than men to experience stressors related to chronic health and financial problems at the end of their lives. Women substantially outnumber men at all ages over sixty-five. In fact, 75 percent of people over age eighty-five are women. Only 40 percent of women over age sixty-five live with a spouse, compared to 74 percent of men. Additionally, women's burden as primary caretakers for children and aging parents creates the potential for us to experience additional stress. A recent study revealed that women who are providing care to their aging parents receive less socio-emotional support from the care recipient than their male counterparts do. One woman describes her stressful role as primary caretaker below.

> *The company's flex-time policies allow me to arrive at work at 5:30 a.m. Managing the demands and deadlines of work, home, and kids is what gets to me. There have been many overlapping deadlines, and managing the priorities and following through leads to some stressful and long days. Stress for me is also having to constantly "play the game" at work without losing my values or who I am. Stress is being there for my kids and my parents when they need me.*
> —Anne, 40, administrative assistant and single mom

Vive la Différence!

Not only do women face challenges and stressors that are unique to their gender, but our very nature also makes our experience of those stressors different from men's experience. In social science, *gender* refers to socially constructed differences between men and women that go beyond the hardwired biological differences. Gender identity and politics are at the heart of the organizing process for the social lives of individuals, families, communities, and societies. We know that gender roles and relationships are often reproduced and reinforced in the workplace. People are often sorted into various working roles based on their sex. In gender-neutral organizations, the psychological demands for women and men tend to be the same within the same profession. Historically, men were paid for work, while women, whose responsibilities involved taking care of their families' needs, went unpaid. Therefore, a woman's paid employment was considered a strain on the family, whereas a man's paid employment was a boon. Recent trends suggest that women have been more successful in retaining or acquiring employment than men when salaries are taken into consideration.

Women are in visible leadership positions as never before. According to the latest Catalyst data (2008), 15.7 percent of corporate officers in Fortune 500 companies are women (2,140 of the 13,673 total). A total of 8 percent of these women hold titles of chairman, vice chairman, chief executive officer, chief operating officer, or senior or executive vice president. Women hold 13.6 percent of the seats on the boards of Fortune 500 companies. I often wonder whether this is good or bad news when I see more professional women coming into the ER as patients. Following is one woman's description of how professional and personal success is defined for her.

> I've been at my current position as chief operating officer for a little more than three years. By all accounts I am very successful professionally. My income has exceeded my expectations, and I am well respected by my colleagues. I have my sister and her family in the area, as well as a huge network of friends. I'm also on the board of a nonprofit organization. But as a woman there are tremendous pressures on me to succeed, to get married, and to be a good daughter—a combination of both my ethnicity and my gender.
>
> —Nina, 34, COO of an engineering company

In the past, researchers suggested that gender differences in coping strategies arose from the fact that women are socialized from an early age to be more emotional, supportive, and dependent, as compared to men, who are portrayed as independent, rational, and instrumental.

Two coping patterns are seen in working women more often than in working men. First is the pattern of *overcommitment*, in which the need for control stimulates the thinking, emotional, and motivational component that triggers an enhanced arousal in demanding situations. Women who use this coping pattern may have an inappropriately high need for approval and may suffer from excessive competitiveness and hostility, impatience, disproportionate irritability, and, most important, an inability to withdraw from work obligations. To these women, commitment means (perhaps unconsciously) making exaggerated efforts, beyond what is usually considered appropriate. This excessive effort may result from an underestimation of the challenges presented or an overestimation of one's coping resources, which in turn may be triggered by an underlying need for approval.

Another gender-specific coping pattern is the strong tendency for women to seek the company and counsel of others—especially other women—when dealing with stress. In general, women maintain more close same-sex relationships than do men. We mobilize more social support during stressful events than men do. *Tend and befriend* is the name given to this response pattern by UCLA psychologist Shelley Taylor. She theorized that the female hormones oxytocin and pitocin, which are present in massive amounts during breast-feeding, are very high when women are stressed. As a result, women are naturally inclined to bond, and they seek to nurture when stressed. It's part of our social understanding that women like to talk and share, but Taylor postulated that this is in fact a unique quality in women, hardwired by biology and refined through ages and ages of evolution.

Other possible gender-based variations in stress coping and health may be related to the unique stressors that women encounter in the workplace and at home. Although men and women share many work-related stressors, some stressors, having to do with organizational politics, work overload, and work-family conflict, are especially prominent for working women. Let's now examine each work-related stressor.

Organizational politics is the general name for the spoken and unspoken rules and informal behaviors within an organization (who sits where and talks to whom at a company event, for instance). Often women may be less familiar with the ways of the workplace than men. Women often lack access to, or awareness of, the "rules," which can lead to stress. Women might find themselves struggling for control of resources and/or information or might feel excluded from the informal networks that keep offices and working groups humming. Furthermore, all of these conditions make women more vulnerable to other stressors in their lives. For instance, problems with organizational politics may create barriers to achievement. The glass ceiling still exists in some male-gendered organizations. Minor inequities and discrimination may be as subtle as stereotypical gender-based discrimination or being denied access to certain developmental opportunities. A simple example is a company activity such as a golf outing, which is more likely to facilitate bonding among male employees and leave many women feeling as if they are still on the outside. Finally, despite federal and organizational guidelines, sexual harassment is still a reality in more work settings than anybody wants to admit. Here is one woman's assessment of how sexual harassment has affected her life since high school.

Dealing with ongoing sexual harassment is probably the single most stressful aspect of my life. I believe that sexual issues have played a major role at my law firm, as I have had former partners who wanted more than just a professional colleague. My looks are fading now, but I used to turn heads every time I walked into a room. It was a curse. Sexual harassment has been a part of my life since I was in high school. I think it is most accurate to say that I didn't deal with it but rather tried to defend myself against too much invasion, while at the same time denying what was happening. I didn't deal with it until about three years ago when my daughter started looking at colleges, and I started freaking out over her safety in college. I have addressed it now. I feel like I am much better, and it is no longer a major issue in my life most days.

—Judy, 52, partner at a law firm

Overload is the second unique stressor for working women. We refer to the sum of all forms of work—paid and unpaid, domestic and vocational—as the *total workload*. Men, particularly in the age groups called Generation X and Generation Y, are taking on more domestic responsibilities among working couples, yet the total workload remains greater for women than for men. Studies of the division of labor within U.S. households have shown that the movement of wives into the paid labor force has not been accompanied by an equivalent shift of husbands to participate more in household work. Married women who are employed do less housework than their unemployed counterparts do, but their husbands do little to take up the slack. In fact, women do more housework than men do, regardless of their family living situation (married, cohabiting, divorced, living with parents, or single). The "double duty" imposed on employed women has real costs in terms of stress and exhaustion. For example, in households with children, child care is the most time-consuming and arguably the most important job at home for both men and women, but women spend more than three times as many hours tending the kids as men do. For many of the women I spoke to in the course of my research, work overload resulted from the multiple roles they have to play in life and, more important, the unclear expectations for each of those roles. Many women stated that they felt they had to work that much harder and longer because they were never fully clear about what was expected of them.

Women tend to perceive their work and family responsibilities as an integrated whole (see my discussion of the work-life conflict in the following paragraphs). Men, on the other hand, generally escape the stress of role overload because they have an independent perception of their various roles. They are also less likely to feel guilty from not taking on tasks that would create overload. Men tend to be clearer about which situations they have control over, and they are better able to let the other situations go. In both men and women, overload stress has been shown to be related to "low schedule control" tasks. These include tasks that are often done under time pressure and with a sense of urgency, such as preparing meals and certain duties that must be performed regardless of other interferences. The number of such tasks in an individual's life helps predict the level of distress: the more there are, the more likely a person is to have an increased NetStress Load. And bear in mind that many of these are gendered tasks that more commonly fall to women. One woman sums up the stress created by trying to balance the responsibilities of work and home.

Am I giving the very best of myself at work and at home? How can I keep up with work demands, with the increased volume, increased urgency, and tighter time lines in the world of instant response? At the same time, I need to be available for a growing child, aging parents, and a husband who I see for maybe twenty hours a week max. Stress is trying to balance being a working woman, wife, and mother. Stress means not taking care of myself—doing things for myself and not feeling selfish in doing so. Stress means being overwhelmed by the many different roles I am required to play in a very limited amount of time on any given day. Not having enough time to

stop and smell the roses, be with my family, spend the time on hob-
bies I'm passionate about, and getting enough sleep.
—Debbie, 43, district manager for a retail sales chain

This conflict between work and home life represents the third unique stressor for working women. The term *work-life conflict* cuts both ways, that is, work can interfere with home or family life, and family or home life can interfere with work. This interference deprives women of the harmony we seek. Studies show that both men and women report conflict, but some studies also have shown that the causes of the conflict and the direction of the relationship differ for men and women. For men, their work involvement spills over in a positive way into their family lives, whereas their family involvement has a negative spillover into their work. The solution for most men is simply to moderate their stress by reducing the amount of time they spend with their families. Furthermore, for many men, three, not two, categories exist: in their minds, they create a separate area of "self," which is independent of both work and family life.

For women, the work-family relationship is more one-dimensional. Family involvement is always present. The amount and quality of family involvement can never be reduced in most women's minds. It is a constant. Women have a fixed level of family involvement that is independent of the influences of work. It is almost impossible to reduce family commitment to relieve anxiety and stress. Most women report only a single mental category—work/family—which is a 24/7 integrated physical and emotional commitment. Most important, there is no discrete "self" factored into the lives of so many working women.

The good news is that, overall, the evidence indicates that work in general actually has positive effects on women's health. We know that employed women can have better health, greater psychological well-being, and more resilience for handling their nonwork stressors than women who do not work outside the home. Here's another woman's take on dealing with her home and work responsibilities.

Stress means juggling diverse projects, while maintaining my pri-
mary responsibilities and roles as mother, wife, and professional.

*But I never give up. I am always trying to please everyone. I just
can't help it.*

—Adrianna, 48, court reporter

I have discussed how gender, stress, and work relate to one another.
But what do women do in response to all of this stress? Interestingly,
the behavioral responses to stress often differ in men and women.
Smoking, alcohol abuse, drug use, and eating disorders are behavioral
symptoms of stress. Women smoke more when under stress, and
the rate of smoking among women is increasing at faster rates than
are those of men. Overuse of alcohol and drugs is also rising among
women, and these behavioral problems often go undetected. Women
are more likely to drink in private but are less likely to engage in binge
drinking. Anorexia and bulimia are also more frequently seen among
women than among men. The rate of suicide among women is double
that of men, and women experience more sleep disorders.

So, what about Csíkszentmihályi's flow, which we discussed earlier, and women in the workplace? Two researchers, Maria T. Allison
and Margaret Carlisle Duncan, have studied women's relationship to
work and flow. They set a goal to identify the context in which working women experience the greatest sense of boredom and frustration,
or what they termed *anti-flow*. They define anti-flow as meaningless,
tedious activities that offer little challenge, are not intrinsically moti-
vating, and create a sense of lack of control.

Interestingly, they compared professional women and blue-
collar women. Blue-collar women found that boredom, often
because of the tediousness of their tasks, made time move quite
slowly. Professional women, on the other hand, had little awareness of the passage of time during an average workday. Initiative
and even creativity are expected and often rewarded in the professional role, but these qualities are rarely encouraged in blue-collar
women. In fact, several reported being chastised by supervisors for
stepping outside of their assigned responsibilities. Professional women
described being judged on their intellectual abilities, and they often
worried about their competency. Both professional and blue-collar
women placed tremendous importance on relationships with their

children. The two groups were equally protective of their family time. This frustration appeared particularly marked among women who had divorced and/or were single heads of households. For both groups of women, a sense of autonomy and freedom was important in making the flow state possible. All women enjoyed activities in which they were able to match their opportunities to act in the environment—the challenges—with their personal skills. Another shared characteristic of flow for both groups was that although the women could experience flow while alone, they often experienced it in interactions with others. Social environments were important, reminding us again of the *tend-and-befriend* response in women.

Despite the similarities, several distinctions emerged between professional women and blue-collar women. Perhaps the largest difference was the degree of control perceived to be important at home. Blue-collar women expressed great satisfaction with the sense of control they felt at home. Such a pattern might reflect the needs of these women to compensate for a lack of control on the job. A second distinction is that the professional women frequently began talking of their home lives and continually reverted to discussions about their jobs or linked their work to their home lives. The blue-collar women, on the other hand, made a clear distinction between the two environments and referred to work only with regard to how work inhibited their enjoyment at home. In general, blue-collar women were forced to compartmentalize work and nonwork more completely than professional women were. It may be that some blue-collar women share characteristics with people who have endured situations of extreme hardship. The most poignant aspect of their lives was their extreme boredom with performing simplistic tasks in their day-to-day routines. The second source of anti-flow was the type and quality of interaction they had with supervisors. Not only were supervisors seen as overbearing and lacking in job competence, but they were also perceived as erratic and unfair in their decision making. These perceptions heightened the feeling of lack of control and lack of flow experienced by blue-collar women. Poor or unskilled supervision was cited as intrusive, and it detracted from work environments where women were otherwise committed to and enjoyed their jobs.

Finally, let's consider the relationship among work, stress, and health—a complex interaction among your thoughts, emotions, behaviors, and environment.

There are no traditional biomedical tests to measure and determine the presence of job stress or even the connection between a particular job and stress. The standard blood, urine, or X-ray tests—such as the measurement of triglycerides, high-density lipoproteins, or low-density lipoproteins, which are known to be potential indicators of heart disease—cannot determine the amount of stress a person has undergone. There is more to it than simple cause and effect. Given the complexity and variability of work-related psychosocial factors, there are a couple of models or theories that can help us. These focus on the components or dimensions that may explain the direct or indirect effects of stress on health. Two complementary models offer valuable insights across the complete spectrum of occupations, gender, and ethnicities: job-strain theory and effort-reward imbalance model.

Job-Strain Theory

Job strain is another term for work-related stress. Dr. Richard Karasek at the University of Massachusetts at Lowell developed the dominant model to describe job strain. His model relies on the relationship between the demands (psychological stress) of work and the lack of control. If we set job demand and control against each other on a grid, we create four distinct categories (or quadrants), each representing a different experience of job strain. (See the illustration on page 75.) On this grid, *control* refers to the worker's ability to control his or her own activities and not to control others. *Decision latitude* is another term for control, and in this model refers to the following:

1. Having authority about decisions on your job
2. Having influence on decisions
3. Having discretion to use or acquire skills in the execution of your job
4. Having the ability to use your skills in unexpected situations

KARASEK'S JOB-STRAIN MODEL

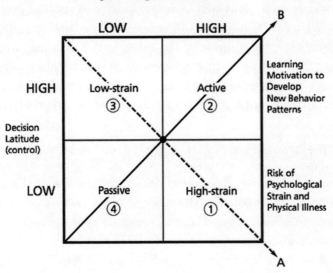

Psychological Demands

A high level of job control means having a nonmonotonous job with possibilities of learning new things to enable you and the organization to grow.

Life in quadrants 3 and 4 is commonly associated with boredom and a lack of flow. What appears to be the most desirable situation is depicted in quadrant 2 (active), in which high-decision latitude (control) is matched with high psychological demands. Most people thrive in such circumstances and become high achievers. Control on the job is high, and psychological demands are also high but not overwhelming. Employees in quadrant 2 are also the most active when it comes to leisure, political, and social activities, despite the heavy demands of their jobs. In this quadrant, most of the energy mobilized by the job's many stressors or challenges is translated into direct action—effective problem solving—leaving little residual strain. The most toxic situation is quadrant 1, where psychological demands are high, but there is little control over how or when to deal with those demands and a lack of adequate support.

Many blue-collar workers are in quadrant 1. But there is a challenge for many high-achieving professional women in quadrant 2. In this quadrant, women often maintain a sense of mastery because of their high levels of control, as well as a strong drive to succeed despite any obstacles. However, this sense of mastery is often false. In reality, these women are likely functioning on the "edge" of this quadrant, aware that they are really outside their BestStress Zone, or the place where they experience flow. This false sense of control and mastery places many high-achieving women at risk for stress-related health problems.

The Effort-Reward Imbalance Model

Developed in the early 1990s, the effort-reward imbalance (ERI) model proposes that an imbalance (psychologists call it a lack of *reciprocity*) between "costs" (effort) and "gains" (reward) activates or triggers the stress response.

When we perceive an imbalance between the effort we are putting in on the job and the rewards we receive, we become stressed, and this leads to negative health outcomes, particularly in people with limited coping abilities.

Research on the ERI model of work stress suggests that the most toxic jobs are those in which high effort (intrinsic or extrinsic) and low reward occur simultaneously. In these settings, workers who have high demands placed on them have high adrenaline levels, while those receiving low rewards have high levels of cortisol. Workers exposed to both high demands and low rewards have high levels of adrenaline and cortisol. Psychological and emotional changes occur in tandem with these biological reactions and may include alterations in motivation, vigilance, memory, and the ability to accurately assess risk.

In summary, key dimensions are shared by the job-strain and ERI models; both control and challenge (demands) are integral parts of each model. Control, however, varies from the micro (task) level in the Karasek model and at a macro level in the effort-reward imbalance model.

Another interesting observation about work and stress is that for many people, the workplace represents an important hub of their social lives, as well as serving as a center of learning. Social psychologists have identified something called the *learning generalization effect*, which describes how, during our leisure time, many of us reproduce the types of activities that we perform in our work environment. For example, there is evidence that workers in passive or repetitive jobs tend to engage in passive leisure-time pursuits, such as watching a lot of television. When our jobs offer higher levels of control over what we do and how we do it, we are more likely to enjoy leisure activities that are intrinsically driven by internal passions and interests. We feel empowered and capable of taking control of and influencing our personal lives. We are also more likely to be involved in volunteer service and giving. So, through this process, the work environment may actually influence your ability to stop smoking, stick with your diet, or engage in healthy leisure activities.

Dr. Peter Schnall, a pioneer in the new field of occupational cardiology, initially began his work at Cornell University. He now leads teams at the University of California, Irvine, and has conducted seminal studies that suggest that approximately 25 percent of Americans who have what doctors call essential hypertension really have high blood pressure that can be related to job stress. Essential hypertension or essential high blood pressure is the catch-all term for unexplainable elevations in blood pressure. Essential hypertension, which afflicts sixty million Americans and six hundred million people worldwide, is a major risk factor for developing coronary artery disease, stroke, renal disease, and many other disease states. Schnall's researchers are leading the way in this new area of medicine called occupational cardiology. It is similar to occupational lung disease, which our country explored several decades ago in connection with exposure to toxins such as asbestos and the development of lung disorders. The most consistent finding to date in occupational cardiology is that workers in jobs with low control have a significantly increased risk of experiencing premature death from cardiovascular disease, even after adjusting for all other known behavioral and biomedical risk factors.

Work stress has been linked to a greater risk of developing musculoskeletal disorders, such as carpal tunnel syndrome and chronic back pain. Work stress also can increase the risk for chronic mental illness. High-demand and low-control jobs can often result in workers experiencing depression and alcohol dependence. And, of course, lack of control at work and low levels of work-related social support are important contributing factors in burnout.

So, the natural question for women in the paid labor force is, how does work affect you in relation to stress? Following are two self-assessments: a general assessment about work and stress, and an exercise to determine whether you are a workaholic.

Does Your Job Cause You Stress?

What are your specific job stressors and how do you tend to respond to them? In addition to looking over your responses on the Job-Stress Inventory that follows, reflect back over your recent experiences at work. I also want you to consider what you say to yourself about your job stress, and what you do in response to it.

Job-Stress Inventory

. . . .

Read each statement and choose the response that best describes you. Then add up your scores for each section.

1 = Strongly disagree
2 = Disagree
3 = Neither agree or disagree
4 = Agree
5 = Strongly agree

Degree of Control

The following items assess your perception of the degree of *control* you have on your job.

1. I have accountability but lack the authority to get the job done. __

(continued)

. . . .

2. I feel trapped in a situation without influence or real options for change. __

3. I am unable to influence decisions that affect me. __

4. There are a lot of arbitrary requirements that get in the way of my doing certain tasks. __

5. I don't have discretion to use or acquire skills in the execution of my job. __

Understanding Your Score

5–11: Lack of control or the authority to do your job is probably not contributing factors in job stress or strain. You are fortunate. If you are in a position of leadership, let this knowledge influence your strategies for those beneath you.

12–18: You have limited control, such that you are dissatisfied with your job and may often feel that your hands are tied. You can either address the issue or continue to suffer in silence. It may be that you can identify specific issues and come up with solutions that can improve the bottom line of productivity, personal performance, and ultimately organizational performance. Make a decision and take action, so that your performance does not suffer further, making you resent the organization more.

19–25: You have a serious lack of control in the workplace. "Control" here means your ability to make decisions on the job and to decide which skills are needed to execute your job. This control issue can be real or perceived. First, look around and try to assess how much of the problem is built into the culture of the organization, as opposed to being about you personally. Think about whether this job is really a good "fit" and congruent with your skills and your interests. Assess whether you can improve your situation by acquiring new skills or knowledge or whether you simply need to find a new job. But proceed carefully. Even CEOs do not have ultimate control. They are accountable to a board of directors!

Rewards for Your work

The following items assess your perception of the *rewards* for your work. (Rewards include monetary compensation, status, and security.)

(continued)

Job-Stress Inventory (continued)

1. I feel that my salary is fair compensation for my work. __
2. I feel that my job title accurately reflects my work. __
3. I am secure that my job will not disappear in the next six months. __
4. I am respected by my peers and by those above and below me. __
5. I have real opportunities for increasing my income in six months. __

Understanding Your Score

5–11: You feel you are lacking fair rewards for your work and/or you feel a lack of job security. If these concerns are constant, I suggest that you be proactive. First, realize that there is no such thing as absolute job security in the current technological and global economic environment. No whining. You must become what Cathy Black, the president of Hearst Communications, calls the "essential employee." This holds for all levels in the organization. Next, reassess the fair market value for your work in your region. Then, assess the demand and the need for your particular skills. This may or may not be the best time for you to make a move. If you feel that the situation involves bias or discrimination, carefully assess the pros and cons of taking formal action. Starting down this path can change the complexion of your work relationships forever. Finally, consider that often, and particularly for women, the reason we don't receive the things we want is that we don't ask for them. If you are doing your job well and you aren't being compensated fairly, simply speak up or put this on the agenda for your next performance review.

12–18: You are not fully satisfied with your rewards or you have some doubts about your ability to increase your income or position in the organization, contributing to an underlying resentment. Take a self-assessment: Are you happy? Is this position worth fighting for? Make a decision. Act on it. Move on.

19–25: You are likely to be comfortable with how you are rewarded at your job.

Information and Communication

The following items assess your perception of how much *information* and *communication* you do or don't have that directly relate to your ability to be an essential employee.

1. I am unsure about the responsibilities of my job. __
2. I don't have enough information to carry out certain tasks. __

(continued)

Job-Stress Inventory (continued)

. . . .

3. I am underqualified for certain tasks I'm expected to do. __

4. Others I work with are not clear about what I do. __

5. I don't understand the criteria that are used to evaluate my performance. __

Understanding Your Score

5–15: It is unlikely that you are experiencing job stress because of an information gap. Now may be a good time to review the current job description for
your position. Also, be sure to make a note of all ongoing communications
that contain information you are expected to be accountable for.

16–25: You are lacking crucial information that is necessary to perform your job.
You need to determine whether the problem is that the information does not
exist or it is not being made available at all or in a timely manner, whether the
information is vague or ambiguous, or whether the information reaches you
in a manner that makes it difficult to understand. If you want to reduce your
stress, be proactive. What connections or relationships do you have that you
can use to improve the flow of information down to you? Some information may
be available on the Internet. Sometimes you have been on a job so long, the
details have changed and you have not seen information that new employees
in your role are receiving. Performance criteria can usually be made available
to you in advance if you ask. I recommend going to Human Resources if you
are uncomfortable with approaching the individual who performs the review.

Conflict

The following items assess the presence of *conflict* as a source of stress in your job.

1. I work with people who are difficult to get along with. __

2. I disagree with my coworkers often. __

3. I disagree with my supervisor often. __

4. I am caught in the middle and can't get my job done. __

5. I feel that I am being sabotaged on my job. __

Understanding Your Score

5–15: You may be having problems with a single person or situation in
which there is conflict; however, overall you are able to do your job without
conflict-generating, ongoing stress.

(continued)

Job-Stress Inventory (continued)

16–25: It is likely that you are experiencing some degree of conflict on a daily basis in your job. You need to ask yourself several questions: Am I difficult to get along with? Are my disagreements related to interpersonal issues, or are they truly connected to the work? What is the political climate? Are these conflicts the natural result of some temporary crisis in the organization? Is someone really trying to harm me?

Your Fit in Your Job

The following items assess your *fit* in your job. Do you feel like an alien in your workplace?

1. I experience little meaning in my work. __
2. I feel unsupported by my coworkers or boss. __
3. My values seem at odds with those of the management. __
4. The organization seems insensitive to my individuality. __
5. I find that I cannot be myself at work because I feel different from my coworkers. __

Understanding Your Score

5–15: You are likely to be part of the "in crowd" on the job. This is good, and you are fortunate. This may be a good time to look around you and provide a little support to those who are not.

16–25: You have a genuine problem with the fit of your job. It is likely that your job is not aligned with your life's purpose. Perhaps this goes without saying, but if your circumstances allow you make a change, make it, and make it fast. You might have taken the job knowing it was a bad fit, however, or chosen to stay in it once you realized the problem. Sometimes you have to do what it takes to get by, either for economic reasons or because of some other factor beyond your control. You can reduce your stress in this kind of situation by acknowledging and accepting the dissonance. Once you've made that choice, you owe it to yourself and the company to work hard anyway and seek to be an essential employee. Reassess your unique contribution to the organization's performance. This is the only level of your "individuality" that is relevant in the workplace. Get over it! But we all do need support. This is a good time to continue to nurture and seek relationships with people outside your workplace. You are okay—and so is the job opportunity at this time. Lack of support on the job may be due to many things. Long term, reassess your work setting and work toward a more aligned environment or self-employment.

(continued)

Job-Stress Inventory (continued)

. . . .

Perception of Overload

The following items assess your perception of *overload* related to your work.

1. I have too much to do and too little time in which to do it. __
2. I take on new responsibilities without letting go of any of the old
   ones. __
3. My job seems to interfere with my personal life. __
4. I must work on my own time (during breaks and lunchtime, at home, and
   so on). __
5. The size of my workload interferes with how well I do my job. __

Understanding Your Score

5–15: Overload affects most of us. You may not be in crisis mode now, but it
   can happen quickly. Read chapter 8 to find specific suggestions for living in
   the BestStress Zone.

16–25: You are clearly overloaded, and it might be at a crisis level. The sense of
   overload may spill over into your nonwork life, making you feel out of balance
   all of the time. You need to make a major overhaul. Here is a simple approach.
   Identify four key responsibilities that are creating overload on your job. Choose
   the one that requires the greatest degree of mental work (creativity, decision
   making, problem solving), one that simply takes time, one that is mindless
   but recurring, and one that is just unpleasant but an essential part of your job.
   Next, determine which of these tasks draw on your unique knowledge,
   training, and/or skills, and thus can be done only by you. Realistically determine how much time it takes to get these done. Go to your supervisor, lay
   out the details of your situation, and then offer a plan to reduce your stress,
   improve your productivity, and ultimately make a better contribution to the
   organization. Be clear and be firm, and don't leave room for argument. This is
   just the quick-and-dirty approach, of course. Go back and look through
   this chapter again for other tips and strategies for reducing stress related to
   overload.

Physical Work Environment

The following items assess your *physical work environment.*

(continued)

Job-Stress Inventory (continued)

1. I find my work environment unpleasant. __
2. I lack the privacy I need to concentrate on my work. __
3. Some aspects of my environment seem hazardous. __
4. I have too much or too little contact with people. __
5. I have to deal with many little hassles. __

Understanding Your Score

5–11: You have a great degree of control over own your work environment, and it structurally and aesthetically meets your needs. You have the right amount of privacy, and your physical boundaries are respected by others.

12–18: Identify the specific element of your work environment that you can control and do so. There may be some design issues that you can't influence. You may need to identify a place on site where you can go for a respite during the workday, for breaks or pauses to refresh yourself.

19–25: Your work environment needs immediate attention, in order to reduce stress. Determine whether the problem relates to noise, comfort, convenience, lighting, or some other factor. There are simple things you can do to improve your physical space and so improve your mood and productivity. If there are safety issues, you should report them to the appropriate person in the organization. (Don't worry, this doesn't make you a whistle-blower. This is an obligation.) Develop a specific strategy for dealing with people who take up your time with interruptions.

Workaholic Addiction Risk Test

This exercise will help you determine whether you are a workaholic. Read each statement and choose the response that best describes your work habits. Then add up your responses.

The higher your score (the highest possible is 100), the more likely you are to be a workaholic; the lower your score (the lowest possible is 25), the less likely you are to be a workaholic.

(continued)

Workaholic Addiction Risk Test (continued)

. . . .

1 = Never true
2 = Sometimes true
3 = Often true
4 = Always true

1. I prefer to do most things myself rather than ask for help. __
2. I get impatient when I have to wait for someone else or when something takes too long. __
3. I seem to be in a hurry and racing against the clock. __
4. I get irritated when I am interrupted while I am in the middle of something. __
5. I stay busy and keep many irons in the fire. __
6. I find myself doing two or three things at one time, such as eating lunch and writing a memo while talking on the telephone. __
7. I overcommit myself by biting off more than I can chew. __
8. I feel guilty when I am not working on something. __
9. It's important that I see the concrete results of what I do. __
10. I am more interested in the final result of my work than in the process. __
11. Things just never seem to move fast enough or get done fast enough for me. __
12. I lose my temper when things don't go my way or work out to suit me. __
13. I ask the same question over again without realizing it, after I've already been given the answer once. __
14. I spend a lot of time mentally planning and thinking about future events, while tuning out the here and now. __
15. I find myself continuing to work after my coworkers have called it quits. __
16. I get angry when people don't meet my standards of perfection. __
17. I get upset when I am in situations in which I cannot be in control. __
18. I tend to put myself under pressure from self-imposed deadlines when I work. __
19. It is hard for me to relax when I'm not working. __
20. I spend more time working than socializing with friends or engaging in hobbies or leisure activities. __

(continued)

Workaholic Addiction Risk Test (continued)
. . . .

21. I dive into projects to get a head start before all of the phases have been finalized. __

22. I get upset with myself for making even the smallest mistake. __

23. I put more thought, time, and energy into my work than I do into my relationships with loved ones and friends. __

24. I forget, ignore, or minimize celebrations, such as birthdays, reunions, and anniversaries or holidays. __

25. I make important decisions before I have all of the facts and have a chance to think them through. __

   25–54 = Not work addicted
   55–69 = Mildly work addicted
   70–100 = Highly work addicted

Those scoring in the lowest range (25–54) are not considered workaholic. If you scored in this range, you probably are a hard worker instead of a workaholic. You needn't worry that your work style will negatively affect you or others.

Those scoring in the middle range (55–69) are considered mildly workaholic. If you scored in this range, there is hope. With acceptance and modifications, you and your loved ones can prevent lasting negative effects.

People scoring in the upper third (70–100) are considered highly workaholic. If you scored in this range, it could mean that you are on your way to burnout, and new research suggests that family members may be experiencing emotional repercussions as well.

Like any addiction, workaholism should be treated with a multipronged approach that may include counseling, behavior modification, hypnotherapy, lifestyle changes, and family intervention. If your score is above 54, here are some steps you can take to address your addiction.

- Get the support you need. Counseling will help you focus on the big picture and shift your energy from work to rest, relaxation, wellness, and recreation.
- Schedule leisure activities for yourself that cannot be canceled. Put your workouts, movie nights, and other leisure activities in your calendar and consider them appointments, just as you would events for your kids or a meeting with a client or a customer.

(continued)

- Make an effort to identify the real underlying issue. Could anxiety or a lack of confidence be driving you to prove something to yourself or others? Low self-esteem and the need to overachieve are often at the core of workaholism.
- Set boundaries. Leave the office at 5 p.m. and don't bring work home. This requires focused self-discipline, or perhaps a coach or a colleague who will hold you accountable may be helpful.
- Learn to delegate. Most workaholics believe that they are the only ones who can do the job right (perfectionism). Learning to let go and eliminating the need for control are two powerful strategies to set yourself free from the dysfunction of workaholism.

Adapted with permission from Bryan Robinson, Chained to the Desk: A Guidebook for Workaholics, Their Partners and Children, and the Clinicians Who Treat Them *(New York: New University Press, 1998), pp. 52–54.*

Final Thoughts

Overall, work is good for your health, despite the fact that contemporary work environments, in which most of us spend the majority of our waking hours, are increasingly characterized as demanding, constraining, and highly stressful. If we can recognize the situations and settings in which work can be toxic, having both short- and long-term harmful effects, we can prevent these situations from hurting us. In this chapter, you learned how stress, especially when it's work-related, can damage your health. You will want to use the information from the self-assessment when you focus on your own life in the BestStress Zone in chapter 8.

Finally, here are some specific tips you can use, regardless of your environment, to reduce the harmful effects of a stressful work environment:

- Remember that you always have choices.
- Women's work lives tend to be nonlinear for a variety of reasons but most commonly because of their caretaking responsibilities. Don't feel that you are less accomplished or less committed to your company because you need to devote time to your family or

to other personal commitments. Jobs may come and go, but your child's fifth-grade play will occur only once in a lifetime.

- Organizations of all sizes are in a continual economically driven hurricane. Don't be swept off your feet. Moreover, be prepared to calm yourself with the thought that it's okay not to know where you'll be three years or five years from now. After all, who knows whether the organization will even exist in its current form?

- To your own self be true. Nowhere is this idea more important than in today's work environment. You must identify and control elements of your job that you can control. The number one goal should always be to improve your skills, knowledge, and competence. You'll surely receive many performance reviews in your job, but the one that matters most is your review of yourself. It should be ongoing. Every day, think about whether you can learn something or acquire a new skill.

- Educate yourself about the social, economic, and political factors and environments that influence your company and your industry. It's important to have a clear understanding of how your company fits into the big picture. Take time to visit the Web to see how your company presents itself to the public and how the public perceives it. Read what the leaders have to say. Read the quarterly reports. Do the same thing for companies that compete directly with yours or that are somehow related or connected.

- Step up to the plate. In times of perpetual rightsizing, downsizing, mergers, and acquisitions, you can help alleviate the stress of job insecurity by making yourself invaluable. This is not about brownnosing but is simply a matter of practical economics. Learn new skills. Cross-train when possible. Take on one task that others may be reluctant to attempt. Most important, whether you are the least-skilled member of the team or its leader, always give credit for success to the entire team.

- Reach out and help others on your team or across teams. Acknowledge and compliment others liberally. If the opportunities exist to be a mentor and you feel you have something to offer to the next generation, do so. This can be a component of your "attitude of gratitude."

- Integrate some form of relaxation into your day's routine. Maintain a sense of humor. Use any organizational resources for physical activity. Avoid caffeinated drinks. Maintain an ergonomically fit environment. Reward yourself for small successes throughout the day.

- Establish a mental and physical transition routine for when you go from the workplace to your home and car. Do this even if you work in your home. Leave work in the workplace. Make a clean break. Apply a technology policy to let everyone know that you are now available and receptive and are not a slave to your e-mail or cell phone. Consider engaging in physical activities when you connect with your family members at the end of the day. How about taking a walk with your children or your partner for physical activity and conversation before dinner? This will also help reduce your appetite.

- Finally, reexamine your motivation. Most of us are motivated primarily by a need to earn an income. But remember item number one: you have choices. It may take some time to identify all of the factors that influence how you feel when the alarm clock goes off and you prepare for the workday or worknight. Promise yourself to appreciate your job, or make a plan for transition and/or change. Rest your mind and be grateful for the opportunity to do what you do.

4

what is causing you stress

At this point in the book, I hope you've come to accept the inevitability of stress in your life and understand that stress isn't necessarily something to fear. You should feel comfortable with knowing that the stress response is a natural aspect of life that fundamentally protects your health.

In this chapter, we will consider two conditions: anxiety and worry. Each can be both a cause and an effect in the stress process. Each plays a major role in what causes many women to experience stress. Next, you will complete a comprehensive inventory to uncover specifically what is causing you stress right now. Identifying what is causing you stress is a small but important step toward discovering your BestStress Zone. Finally, you will learn about the major styles of coping and consider which style is best for you in any particular situation.

Anxiety and Worry

I have observed two moods, or conditions, that are common to women who lead complex lives: anxiety and worry. Let's talk first about anxiety. Often, even though you feel you have a good understanding of a situation or an event or of people in your life, you find that they still leave you feeling anxious. According to the *Diagnostic and Statistical Manual of Mental Disorders*, published by the American Psychiatric Association in 2000, the essential feature of generalized anxiety disorder (apprehensive expectation), also known as GAD, is at least six months of "excessive anxiety and worry" about a variety of events and situations. Generally, *excessive* can be interpreted as more than would be expected for a particular situation or event. According to the Anxiety Disorders Association of America and the Centers for Disease Control, anxiety affects more than 25 percent of adults. That translates into some forty million people in the United States, age eighteen or older, who suffer from one form of anxiety disorder or another. The condition is believed to cost the U.S. health-care system more than $42 billion a year, or roughly a third of the total expenditures on mental health in this country per year. The actual illnesses that fall under the anxiety grouping include such things as generalized anxiety, panic disorder, post-traumatic stress disorder, and a host of others. Dealing with the condition often depends a great deal on the exact type of anxiety disorder at hand.

As widespread as anxiety disorders are, they are not well understood. At present, scientists and physicians believe that this disorder is caused by genetics, brain chemistry, and environmental factors, such as the death of a loved one, stress, and even withdrawal from certain addictive substances. Anxiety can look and feel like so many things, but diagnostic criteria for GAD require the presence for most days over the previous six months of three or more (only one for children) of the following six symptoms:

1. Feeling wound-up, tense, or restless
2. Fatigue
3. Problems with concentration
4. Irritability
5. Significant muscle tension
6. Sleep difficulty

In order for a person to be diagnosed with GAD their symptoms cannot be related to another medical issue or mental diagnosis and they must cause "clinically significant distress" or problems with functioning in daily life. Deciding what is "clinically significant" is up to the treatment provider, whose judgment is, of course, subjective. Usually, this level of anxiety will cause most people to seek professional help, but some people can cope with several of these symptoms at once and continue to function at a high level.

Anxiety that is not clinically significant (meaning that it doesn't interfere with day-to-day functioning), which most of us appropriately have from time to time, can help us cope or focus our attention for learning, problem solving, or even self-defense. Severe anxiety, however, can be a disabling medical condition; it may cause intense fear, disturb your thinking and reasoning, create abnormal biological responses, and make you hostile and angry. Ongoing anxiety often leads to addictive behaviors involving alcohol, food, sex, drugs, shopping, or any other activity that you indulge in to an extreme. Even more problematic, you develop anxiety about these behaviors, which turns the pattern into a vicious cycle and deepens your overall level of anxiety.

Often when you are anxious, you simply need reassurance that you are okay. You might be a well-adjusted individual with a strong sense of psychological well-being and an internal locus of control. *Internal locus of control* refers to a belief that your destiny is controlled by you and not primarily by external forces such as fate, God, or powerful others. Often, however, feelings and emotions short-circuit and bypass your belief in yourself and your rational approach to living. Most of us absolutely and unequivocally are okay. The anxiety we experience is not uncommon, and it is not a signal of some deeper problem or disorder. Sometimes anxious feelings that become problematic are caused by a conditioned reflex that is simple to eliminate with the proper motivation and practice. Here is way of thinking about how anxiety works.

In the mid-1990s, Dr. Joseph LeDoux, a researcher at New York University, devised a radically different model for how we perceive the world. Prior to his work, the common understanding was that information goes to the "thinking centers" (cortex) of the brain, where it triggers specific biological processes and behavior. Dr. LeDoux's research demonstrated that a biological pathway exists between our senses, which provide raw information, and our thoughts, emotions, and anxiety. This pathway creates an automatic, instantaneous response and is mediated by a structure in the brain called the amygdala. The amygdala stores emotional memories and works in conjunction with another brain structure, the hippocampus, which stores contextual memory (who, what, where, and when) to form the complete memory center.

I'm sure you remember where you were when you first heard about the tragedy on 9/11. Your amygdala created an emotional memory, so that now when you see anything related to the tragedy on television or even read about it, your brain automatically compares this new information with the stored emotional memory of the actual event. When someone "pushes your buttons" at work, at home, or in your interpersonal relationships, you experience the activity of the amygdala. Without consciously thinking, your brain generates an emotional response and an action. This, however, is not necessarily a bad thing. What if you had to stop and think about how to respond to a shadowy figure rapidly approaching you in the dark of night as you leave the subway? The important point here is that the emotional processes operate much faster than conscious thought processes do, and they often bypass the mind's reasoning process entirely. Of course, your conscious thought processes can give rise to an emotional response, but many times emotions are triggered by unconscious associations in the amygdala. The good news is that these two separate but interacting processes—rational and emotional—are in regular communication within the brain. They communicate by chemical and electrical messengers. Living in the BestStress Zone requires that you develop an understanding of what's in your emotional memory bank, or amygdala. The amygdala processes information that is received from the senses and seeks to match that information with mental, emotional, and physical responses and habits, even if those responses and habits are harmful to your health, well-being, or behavior. This is why anxiety can often be self-perpetuating and self-reinforcing. Don't be alarmed, though. You can interrupt the cycle and develop new patterns, new emotional memories, and new biochemical responses, all of which will allow you to deal with life's challenges in a much more healthy way. You can and will make these changes if you are ready to accept responsibility for managing your emotions. Otherwise, you're stuck with letting your emotions manage you! You will learn specific techniques in subsequent chapters.

Another separate but related issue is *worry*, which can be paralyzing. Have you ever asked yourself whether you worry too much or whether your worrying is okay? Here are two comments about worry as a part of stress.

> *Stress means worrying. Stress means juggling a crazy work schedule and parental duties. Stress means worrying about not having enough time to keep the house in order, the bills paid, and, needless to say, have any time with the spouse.*
>
> —Janice, 34, food service manager

> *Stress to me is the change that I and my family have faced. I am worried all the time. My oldest son is serving in Iraq as a medic, my middle son is finishing high school and leaving for college, and my youngest son is turning thirteen and entering his teenage years. My husband has started a new job and career last week. Change is all around me, and I worry about it all.*
>
> —Tina, 47, customer support call center supervisor

According to author Matthew McKay, Ph.D., a professor at the Wright Institute in Berkeley, California, who is an expert on anxiety and depression, worry is a natural response to life's circumstances. You can worry about your personal safety or the safety of your children, about interpersonal relationships, about promotions and job security, or about the threat of terrorism. It's only when worry interferes with your day-to-day functioning and your decisions are no longer guided by reason or by a true understanding of your emotions that worry becomes a problem. McKay described six markers that you can use to determine whether your worrying is out of control and getting in your way. Do you do the following?

1. Chronically worry about future dangers or threats?
2. Consistently make negative predictions about the future?
3. Often overestimate the probability or seriousness of bad things happening?
4. Endlessly repeat the same worries over and over and over again?

5. Escape worried thoughts by distracting yourself or avoiding certain situations?
6. Find it difficult to work constructively to produce solutions to problems?

The main quality that distinguishes healthy worry from unhealthy worry is *focus*. Your worry can produce catastrophic thinking, or it can force you to focus on problem solving. Unhealthy worry leads to your imagining terrifying worst-case scenarios when you are confronted with challenges and thus creates negativity. In contrast, healthy worry focuses your mind on problem solving and the need for positive action. Healthy worry looks to the future, while unhealthy worry leaves you stuck in the seemingly unfixable present. If this sounds all too familiar to you, or you think the quality or intensity of your worry is unhealthy, it may help if you shift your focus away from the problems themselves and concentrate instead on the solutions.

Worry is closely related to guilt. I believe it's one of those instincts that we women seem to have programmed right into our genes. Guilt gives rise to several interrelated phenomena that can sometimes build on one another, creating unhealthy worry:

- *Overcaring.* It is right and natural, especially for women, to nurture and to care for others. (Remember "tend and befriend"?) The term *overcare* was coined by Doc Childre, a visionary businessman and scientist who founded the Institute of HeartMath. He described overcare as the condition that results when you are unable to put limits on the level of care for others that you assume as your personal responsibility. If you make yourself responsible for behaviors or situations that are in fact beyond your control, you inevitably become frustrated, angry, and exhausted.
- *Overattachment.* An offshoot of overcaring, overattachment develops when you become afraid of losing the thing you care so much about.
- *Overcontrolling.* Overcaring and overattachment can drive you to repress people you love by imposing your will over theirs in hopes of achieving your desired outcome. You get caught up

in the belief that your chosen outcome for others will determine your own personal inner peace and security.

- *Overidentifying.* A natural result of any of the above might be your inflexible commitment to a certain position in a situation or a particular outcome or individual. As with any of the previously listed characteristics, such identification becomes unhealthy when it controls you, rather than the other way around.

Overattachment creates a vicious cycle. Your overdependence on other people's approval starts to sap them of energy. The draining cycle begins when you overidentify with a position, a situation, an issue, or a person you care about. You begin to overcare and want things to go a particular way. You become overattached to how you want things to turn out. More important, you're unable to see other options. You are less able to let go of that issue, that situation, or that person. When you overattach, you become obsessive. The irony is that what results is usually just the opposite of what you want to occur. You get fired instead of promoted, or the person you want to bring closer to you will want to avoid you. This self-destructive cycle is worsened when you yourself don't understand what you are experiencing, because, after all, you cared so much!

All of these attitudes or behaviors are defined by degree. Caring, attachment, and commitment can be useful and positive attributes. It is only when you allow them to take over that you run into trouble. Ultimately, you could be wrestling with a case of obsession, a self-destructive cycle that is exceedingly unhealthy.

Take a Worry Break

I've found that most women, especially you seasoned multitaskers out there, can do yourselves a lot of good by actually scheduling worry time and worry exposure. By training yourself to worry only at specific times, you can limit the affect of worry on your day-to-day life. Schedule a thirty-minute worry appointment on your calendar to assure yourself that you have the space and time to worry, and be sure to keep the commitment. A good time to do this is at the end of your day as you prepare for bed. Keep a pad and pen beside your bed and allow yourself five to seven minutes to write down a situation that is really worrying you. Consider whether the worry is related to the overcare phenomenon. Determine whether the worry is healthy or unhealthy. Next, consider problem-solving strategies for those worries for which problem solving is appropriate. Don't settle on the first answer that comes to mind. Brainstorm for as many alternatives as you can. List all of the possible things you can do to improve or correct the situation. Evaluate each idea. Make a contract with yourself that includes specific dates to take an action.

Specific Sources of Stress

The stress response requires a trigger. In this section, I want you to identify those triggers and quantify the effects of these stressors in your life. If you are familiar with the work of the productivity guru David Allen, author of *Getting Things Done: The Art of Stress-Free Productivity*, you'll know that one of the tenets of eliminating stress is to get rid of clutter. Oftentimes we hold on to things in our mind unnecessarily. Consider this an opportunity to reach into the corners of your mind and identify the demands, challenges, or situations that may be causing you worry or anxiety. At this point, I don't want you to think about how you are going to solve anything, just acknowledge what is going on in your life. This will motivate you to go through the work of discovering your BestStress Zone in chapter 7. I want you to consider your life in terms of seven dimensions established by the husband-and-wife team of psychologists Drs. Jane E. Myers and Thomas J. Sweeney, of the University of North Carolina at Greensboro, who are the authors of *Counseling for Wellness: Theory, Research, and Practice.* We'll look at each of the seven dimensions in greater detail later. They are

1. family;
2. work;
3. self-care;
4. friendship;
5. spirituality;

6. love/romance; and

7. leisure/play.

First, we'll consider the seven dimensions in broad terms (in the following assessment), then we'll identify the possible demands and challenges of each.

Next, we will take this to the next level and identify specific chronic and acute stressors and ordinary daily hassles that are bothering you. Acute stressors are a disruption. They may be predictable (the death of a ninety-eight-year-old relative) or unpredictable (you unexpectedly stayed at work to meet with a client and now are late for an important family event). Chronic stressors are disparities—the difference between what you want and what you have. The detailed exercises that follow provide an opportunity to choose from listed stressors or come up with your own for each of the seven dimensions of your life.

Overall Stress Assessment

In this exercise, choose the response that corresponds to your experience of stress in each of the seven dimensions. In which of these areas do you feel a lack of satisfaction or recognize a source of triggers for the stress process? Note that the number represents the absolute *presence* of stress in this dimension of your life *and* the *intensity* of associated stressors.

0 = Does not apply
1 = No stress
2 = Minimal stress
3 = Moderate stress
4 = Extreme stress

Family __   Work __   Self-care __   Friendship __
Spirituality __   Love/romance __   Leisure/play __

Family

We all define *family* differently, so be clear in your own mind if your definition goes beyond your nuclear family to include any other people whom you consider to be a part of your kinship. In this dimension, the goal is to feel that you are able to care for and nurture others and maintain mutually enjoyable relationships.

Healthy families provide the most positive source of individual wellness. More important, healthy families can be either biological or families of choice. Yet although you intuitively know how important a satisfying family life is, it may be difficult to achieve in this high-pressured modern world. Following are some first-person accounts of women who are struggling with the stress of many demands on them as they try to maintain happy family lives.

- "When the kids are sick or you are holding up your end of the family duties and work is calling you, the juggling act becomes difficult. Not being able to fully leave one area of your life and move completely into another causes stress for me."
- "Although I greatly enjoy the variety of work and people, the pace is sometimes so fast that I am not able to keep track of 'to-dos' and end up falling behind. This all leaves me wiped out on the weekends, when I have other home-related jobs to complete and a family that expects other things from me. Work-related stresses cause me to take home work on weekends, nights, and sometimes over vacations, which affects the time I have with my family. Also, for the last two years I did not take much vacation time due to my workload and I missed my sister-in-law's funeral. I feel that I need to keep going at this pace to do quality work, to be recognized within my own group, and to continue to receive opportunities. Now my stress is increased because I need to leave work at 5:30 p.m. to pick up my son at school and I can't stay later as I did before—which gives me less time to do the work overall."
- "My daughter and my husband had a falling out more than a year ago, and for a long while they didn't talk when she came home to visit from school, but both of them told me what they

thought and felt, when they should have been talking to each other instead. I want peace and harmony in my family. Finally, the situation is now rectified. Both of them talked out their opinions and feelings (it was more like yelling at each other), and now they are talking and enjoying the summer. I am, too, but before this was corrected, I found myself trying to avoid the subject because I felt caught in the middle. My daughter was right about how she felt and my husband was right about her respecting his position as her father."

- "Stress in my daily life means trying to get as much work done as possible, yet still see my kids in the mornings, at night, and on the weekends. Stress is juggling a constantly moving schedule and demanding clients and still trying to maintain somewhat of a normal life at home and participate in my children's lives. The stress was so much lower before I became a mom because I could work as much as I needed to on a given day or I could take the assignment or a complex client and give it my all. Now that I am a mom, I have to manage both my career and my home life and think of what various career moves will do to my kids. This creates stress for me."

- "Stress typically takes the form of guilt in the context of my not being able to get home at a reasonable time to be with my family in the evenings and for dinner."

- "Getting married at age forty, moving, and working on high-level projects at my job was an incredible adjustment for me over the past three years. Balancing a lot of change and needing to do well in all areas is stressful."

- "My mom only lives about forty-five minutes away from me, but finding the time to visit with her becomes challenging, so guilt is one of my stressors, even though it is self-imposed and not at all brought on by my mother."

- "Witnessing domestic violence in my home as a child has definitely been a source stress for me throughout my life."

- "Dealing with my aunt's and mother-in-law's deaths in the same year was a stressful time, as was providing emotional support to my husband during his time in law school and comforting him when he learned he failed the bar exam."

Self-Assessment: Family

. . . .

Read each statement and choose the response that best indicates how often during the last six months an issue or a situation has created stress for you. Please respond with your first impression. For "other," include any personal issue or situation not represented by any of the statements.

0 = Never
1 = Seldom
2 = Sometimes
3 = Often
4 = Frequent
5 = Constant
6 = Does not apply

1. The health of my parents or significant elders in my life __
2. My child/children or significant young dependents in my life __
3. Problems with my in-laws __
4. Problems with the dynamics in my blended family __
5. Loss of a family member __
6. Managing home responsibilities __
7. Coping or problems with single parenting __
8. Child care and management of my children's school __
9. Inadequate help from my spouse or partner with household tasks or children __
10. Frequent problems with my children or teenagers (verbal, legal, school) __
11. Injury or a chronic health problem of a family member __
12. Problems with my relatives __
13. Finding "quality" time __
14. Paying attention to one another's needs __
15. Showing affection __
16. Providing mutual support __
17. Too much travel time away from my family __
18. Conflicting views of child rearing between me and my spouse or partner __

(continued)

Self-Assessment: Family (continued)
. . . .

19. Other: __
20. Other: __
21. Other: __
22. Other: __
23. Other: __

If you chose 3, 4, or 5 for three or more items, you are at risk for significant NetStress Load.

Work

This dimension may include more than you first think. Any paid activity that promotes your well-being is relevant if it contributes to your financial resources, your self-esteem and satisfaction, a feeling that your skills are used appropriately, a sense of job security, and a feeling that you are appreciated for your efforts and contributions.

It's easy to define ourselves through our work. This is not entirely wrong or inappropriate, but you must remember to keep work in perspective, by realizing that it is not everything that you are but rather is only one of the many dimensions in your life. Following are various women's comments about stress and work.

- "Stress for me means two things. One, did I make the right decision, did I give the right answer to a client on a technical matter? The second one would be, will I get everything done that I need to do? The first situation is much more infrequent, but when I'm in it, it is all consuming and incredibly immobilizing. The second one happens every single day and makes it really, really hard to turn the job off; I'm always checking my e-mail, voice mail, and so on. It's hard to enjoy vacations and time with my family when work looms over me."
- "Dedicating 100 percent to work, 0 percent to my husband, and 0 percent to my kids has been very stressful to me this year

and has negatively affected both my personal and my professional life. With respect to work, it was *not* worth it because in the end the results were not fully accomplished. Unfortunately, they were out of my control and depended on others to achieve them."

- "During my six-month review, my manager said she was a little concerned about my performance. She cited certain examples, and I knew I had been 'caught.' In a way, I felt very relieved. I told her I had noticed the same thing and that I had been concerned about it but wasn't exactly sure why I was having lapses in my performance. I thought it wasn't happening in my personal life, but as she and I continued to converse, I realized that I was having these same lapses in my personal life. The problem was much broader. I ended our meeting with a greater awareness of my personal situation and with some ideas on to how to fix it. I also felt great relief that I no longer had to hide or cover up my feelings of inadequacy."

- "I grew up with two alcoholic parents, so that speaks for itself with regard to stress related to chronic disruption (moving), abandonment, and neglect. My first profession as a professional opera singer was very stressful (albeit a combination of positive and negative stress). Making a recording in Europe was one of my most memorable stressful situations in this career because of the pressure to demonstrate a high level as a lead soloist in an opera, while recording under time limitations."

- "Work at my company is always two hundred miles per hour. God, how I wish I could get over to the right-hand lane!"

- "I work part time and take care of two small boys, so stress is always having too much to do and constantly worrying about the things I'm missing (such as paying bills). I continue working after the kids have gone to bed, and I'm always tired."

- "Once my kids started kindergarten, I decided to focus on my career. This was very stressful as I did not want to be perceived as caring less about my children or have them feel that my job had become more important than them. Finding that balance between career and family continues to be difficult. My husband continually questions what is more important to me, which makes it even more stressful."

Self-Assessment: Work

Read each statement and choose the response that best indicates how often during the last six months an issue or a situation has created stress for you. Please respond with your first impression. For "other," include any personal issue or situation not represented by any of the statements.

0 = Never
1 = Seldom
2 = Sometimes
3 = Often
4 = Frequent
5 = Constant
6 = Does not apply

1. Concern about job security __
2. Work overload, being responsible for more than can be done well __
3. Change in immediate leadership __
4. Change in organizational/company leadership __
5. Lack of time to maintain professional competencies __
6. Too much travel time to and from work __
7. Too much work-related travel out of town __
8. Lack of adequate development of relationship/mentorship opportunities __
9. Experience of gender discrimination or bias __
10. Organizational gender discrimination or bias __
11. Experience of ethnic/racial discrimination or bias by individuals __
12. Organizational ethnic/racial discrimination or bias __
13. Lack of value for my work in my organization __
14. Influence of politics on my job __
15. Ambiguous job responsibilities __
16. Unreasonable employer/organizational demands __
17. Conflicting expectations about what I am to accomplish __
18. Difficulty with subordinates __
19. Lack of ability to be involved in decisions that affect my job __
20. Physically unhealthy work environment __
21. Unsafe work environment __

(continued)

Self-Assessment: Work (continued)

. . . .

22. Conflict between my personal values and those of the organization __

23. The organization does not use my abilities to its best advantage __

24. Concerns about promotion __

25. Dissatisfaction with my salary and benefits __

26. Working excessive hours __

27. Lack of control over my work hours __

28. Chronic problems with communication with some coworkers __

29. Angry or tense relationships within my department __

30. Lack of mutual respect among fellow workers __

31. Frequent need to take work home __

32. Lack of adequate resources to optimally perform my job __

33. Face-to-face meeting time __

34. Not having at least one person who is interested in my growth and well-being __

35. Difficulty with internal customers __

36. Difficulty with direct supervisor __

37. Difficulty with the internal staff __

38. Uncertainty about promotions __

39. Increasing height of the performance bar __

40. Competition with key businesses __

41. Competition with key products __

42. Competition with pricing of key products __

43. Conflicts between my personal values and the values of the enterprise __

44. Technology speeding up the pace of work __

45. Inability to say no __

46. Lack of appreciation by those around me at work __

47. Lack of time to step back and process or reflect on the work being done __

48. Too many tasks to work on at the same time __

49. Too many interruptions during the workday, making it difficult to get work done __

(continued)

Self-Assessment: Work (continued)
. . . .

50. Having to deal with work-related matters outside normal work hours __

51. The BlackBerry . . . aka the "Stressberry" __

52. Need to do work-related activities when on vacation __

53. Lack of savings __

54. Financial investments __

55. Other: __

56. Other: __

57. Other: __

58. Other: __

59. Other: __

If you chose 3, 4, or 5 for ten or more items, you are at risk for significant NetStress Load.

Self-Care

Self-care means making proactive efforts to live long and live well and taking responsibility for your personal wellness through habits that are preventive in nature. It includes engaging in sufficient physical activity to stay in good physical condition, eating a nutritionally balanced diet, avoiding overeating, getting adequate sleep and regular relaxation, and performing some sort of ongoing self-assessment of your coping resources, as well as of your ability to set limits and to organize and manage resources such as time and energy.

Following are first-person accounts by women who have difficulty finding time to take care of themselves.

- "I know that I am stressed when I can't get time for myself or can't sleep through the night. To me, stress means being pulled in a million directions and, even after working eighty hours per week, still feeling like I am behind."
- "I'd like to get pregnant again, but I'm in my early forties and still want to be a partner at my firm. I wonder if getting pregnant

will be too overwhelming from a health perspective, as I am currently overweight. I believe that overeating and underexercising are exacerbated by work demands and work-related stress."

- "My health was affected two years ago from overwork and an extended lack of sleep due to pressure to meet a client deadline. It all culminated with me becoming ill at the client's location and needing to be hospitalized for several days."

Self-Assessment: Self-Care

Read each statement and choose the response that best indicates how often during the last six months an issue or a situation has created stress for you. Please respond with your first impression. For "other," include any personal issue or situation not represented by any of the statements.

0 = Never
1 = Seldom
2 = Sometimes
3 = Often
4 = Frequent
5 = Constant
6 = Does not apply

1. Not having guilt-free quiet time with myself __
2. My own recent injury or chronic health problems __
3. Having to be pleasant no matter how you feel __
4. Recent change in living conditions or home __
5. Desire to do everything perfectly __
6. Feeling of a lack of success __
7. Feeling that others are better than me __
8. Fear of having hot flashes at inconvenient times __
9. Discomfort with growing older __
10. Discomfort with my physical appearance changing with age __
11. Lack of adequate sleep __
12. Lack of adequate exercise __

(continued)

. . . .

13. Lack of time to eat __

14. Eating too much __

15. Overuse of alcohol __

16. Being overweight __

17. Eating disorder __

18. Use of tobacco __

19. Use of illicit drugs __

20. Abuse of prescription drugs __

21. Lack of sense of control over important aspects of my life __

22. Lack of sense of meaning in my day-to-day life __

23. Lack of optimism in general __

24. Other: __

25. Other: __

26. Other: __

27. Other: __

28. Other: __

If you chose 3, 4, or 5 for five or more items, you are at risk for significant NetStress Load.

Friendship

This dimension is, somewhat obviously, about connectedness with others in a nonsexual manner. Friendship is a two-way street. We all need access to social support, as well as a confidante for tangible, emotional, and informational support, but the satisfaction that comes from being able to provide that same support to others is also essential to your well-being. True, deep, and open friendship means not feeling lonely and frees you from any potential sense of conflict in social situations.

Friendships and intimate relationships do enhance the quality and length of your life. Isolation, alienation, and separation from others are generally associated with all manner of poor health conditions and a greater susceptibility to premature death, whereas in multiple studies social support remains the strongest identified predictor of positive mental health over a person's life span.

Following are some first-person accounts about the importance of friendship in women's lives and how the lack of friends' support causes stress.

- "In the last three months, graduating from college, moving to a new city, and my overall introduction to the 'real world' have contributed to my stress. I have no friends here."
- "My husband has always been my best friend and a source of support. He has been unemployed since last year, and I have all of the financial responsibility, even though I realize that he helps me a lot in dealing with my eighty-six-year-old father and a mentally retarded sister (which are my next stressful life situations). Probably my biggest conflict is to deal with and accept the fact that he is not a provider, but on the other hand, he gives a lot of support in the other aspects of my life."
- "I currently live in a state where I was not raised and do not want to be anymore. My husband and I willingly relocated with our company nearly ten years ago and then again about six years ago. Then, we both left the company and now find ourselves living in an area that has little to offer us in terms of friends, emotional networks, fun, and so on."
- "I am still in shock over the death of my older sister that left me without my best friend. I turned to her for support, understanding, love, and amusement. I felt deep pride in her as well."

Self-Assessment: Friendship

Read each statement and choose the response that best indicates how often during the last six months an issue or a situation has created stress for you. Please respond with your first impression. For "other," include any personal issue or situation not represented by any of the statements.

0 = Never
1 = Seldom

(continued)

Self-Assessment: Friendship (continued)

2 = Sometimes
3 = Often
4 = Frequent
5 = Constant
6 = Does not apply

1. Lack of someone with whom I can confide my true feelings __
2. Lack of time for hanging out or visiting with friends __
3. Lack of energy for visiting with friends __
4. Lack of time to communicate with friends __
5. Current lack of friends who would do almost anything for me __
6. Lack of at least one close relationship that is secure and lasting __
7. Lack of friends and/or relatives who would provide help if I were in need __
8. Other: __
9. Other: __
10. Other: __
11. Other: __
12. Other: __

If you chose 3, 4, or 5 for two or more items, you are at risk for significant NetStress Load.

Spirituality

Perhaps the best way to define the spiritual dimension is that it concerns your personal and private beliefs that arise out of your recognition that you are more than the material aspects of your mind and body. More specifically, spirituality might include a belief in a higher power; hope and optimism; a practice of worship, prayer, and/or meditation, alone or through organized religious and spiritual practices with others; a purpose in life; compassion for others; moral values; and transcendence (a sense of oneness with the universe).

Spirituality, not religiosity, has positive benefits for longevity and quality of life. It fortifies your existential sense of meaning, purpose, and hopefulness about life.

Following are some first-person accounts of how spirituality has strengthened women in times of crisis.

- "I was diagnosed with breast cancer in 2001. Unfortunately, it took this event to allow me to rediscover my beliefs. They are the foundation of my life now. I'm happy to report that I've been in remission for four-plus years, but the possibility of the cancer reoccurring is always on my mind. After beating that, other issues don't compare, and my beliefs in a higher power sustain me now."

- "I am a single woman and have lived in Washington, D.C., for twelve years. I've been in my job position for a little over three years. I have my sister and her family in the area and have a huge network of friends. I'm also on the board of a nonprofit organization. My family and my religion are the most important parts of my life, even though they sometimes cause me stress."

- "Finding my purpose is really what I need to do at this stage of my life. I make really decent money, but I find that financially I'm out of control. I have used money like food, as a way to quiet my insides, but both of these methods cause me stress and have had long-term negative effects on my life. I grew up in a religious family. I don't need the building, but I need something more."

- "The most recent challenge or stress-inducing situation in my life is child rearing. How to handle this person you love but who gives you grief, is disrespectful, and knows so much more than everyone else. I have been thinking about getting involved in a spiritual community. Help! But this too shall pass, as the child grows to be an independent adult. (Hopefully, I'll survive that long!)"

- "My mother became ill with breast cancer when I was sixteen, then got ill again five years later, and died when she was sixty-one and I was thirty-one. I was very close to her, and the loss was tremendous. My faith was challenged, but ultimately it was strengthened. My church remains a cornerstone of my life."

Self-Assessment: Spirituality

Read each statement and choose the response that best indicates how often during the last six months an issue or a situation has created stress for you. Please respond with your first impression. For "other," include any personal issue or situation not represented by any of the statements.

0 = Never
1 = Seldom
2 = Sometimes
3 = Often
4 = Frequent
5 = Constant
6 = Does not apply

1. Lack of time to formally worship __
2. Desire to build more spirituality into my daily life __
3. Not living up to the tenets of my faith or belief system __
4. Family members do not share my beliefs or religious tradition(s) __
5. Have moral conflicts with some practices in my workplace __
6. Not as involved as I would like to be in my spiritual/religious community __
7. Searching for a spiritual/belief system to guide my life __
8. Other: __
9. Other: __
10. Other: __
11. Other: __
12. Other: __

If you chose 3, 4, or 5 for two or more items, you are at risk for significant NetStress Load.

Love/Romance

This category includes the ability to be intimate, trusting, and self-disclosing with another person; the ability to express affection with a significant other and to accept another's affection without conditions; being able to convey unpossessive caring that respects the uniqueness of another individual; ideally, having at least one relationship that is secure and lasting, and for which there is a mutual commitment; having concern for the nurturance and growth of others; experiencing physical and emotional satisfaction with your sexual life; having a family or a familylike support system characterized by shared spiritual values; and, with a significant other, being able to solve conflict in a mutually respectful way, solve problems together, be committed to each other, maintain healthy communication styles, enjoy shared time together, have the ability to cope with stress, and have mutual appreciation.

I have yet to meet a person who is completely happy without love, as shown by these statements.

- "I've been single for a number of years and recently embarked on a new relationship. The challenge and stress is, how do I fit him into my already-busy life?"
- "My intimate relationship with my husband suffered greatly after the birth of our second daughter. She was born with a birth defect that made breast-feeding difficult. I felt that my husband was not very supportive of my efforts to try to breast-feed her, so I 'punished' him by being 'romantically difficult.' He noticed, and we had a lot of stress during our intimate moments."
- "I found out that my husband of more than thirty years had an intermittent but ongoing affair (for seventeen years!) with a woman who was known to me. A number of my friends knew about this situation, but no one told me anything about it, and, in fact, some had helped sustain the affair through invitations to parties, and so on, when all of us would be present. I had suspicions for years but no confirmation. I was shaken to my core. This is the first time in my life that I've seen a psychiatrist to get prescription drugs for anxiety and depression."
- "I feel stressed by the addition of children to my marriage and having to balance the demands of my job with that of my husband's needs. He had always been number one in my life, and I love him dearly. Then there is my in-laws' role in my life postchildren and my husband's resulting handling of those situations—I have boundary issues with my in-laws; they don't partner with

me as a mother but make their own decisions on what they think is best for my children. Although my husband may agree with my views, he (a conflict avoider) will refuse to sit down with his folks and discuss this as a family."

- "My husband had an affair while I was working on getting a promotion at work. I guess the exchange was career advancement for the loss of my marriage. It was difficult to for me stay focused on my work and the new responsibilities I had taken on, knowing that the man I had spent twenty years with was wrapped in the arms of his assistant. I thought I would lose my mind. Work was a curse and a blessing, and this recent promotion at work has added huge amounts of stress to my life."

- "Dealing with infertility has put a strain on my marriage. While we are now blessed with a son and a daughter, our relationship during all of this was the most stressful and hopeless situation that I have dealt with in my life."

Self-Assessment: Love/Romance

. . . .

Read each statement and choose the response that best indicates how often during the last six months an issue or a situation has created stress for you. Please respond with your first impression. For "other," include any personal issue or situation not represented by any of the statements.

0 = Never
1 = Seldom
2 = Sometimes
3 = Often
4 = Frequent
5 = Constant
6 = Does not apply

1. Lack of adequate time for spouse/partner/significant other __
2. Problems with dating (time, interest, availability of potential partners) __
3. Personal problems with sexual functioning __
4. Loss of a spouse/partner/family member/friend through death __

(continued)

. . . .

5. Coping with separation/divorce __

6. Chronic health problems of your partner, spouse, or significant other __

7. Problems with being single __

8. Inadequate emotional support from spouse/partner __

9. Lack of substantive communication with spouse/partner __

10. Lack of trust between self and spouse/partner __

11. Spouse/partner's loss of job due to firing or retiring, or experiencing work problems __

12. Disagreements over how to spend money __

13. Other: __

14. Other: __

15. Other: __

16. Other: __

17. Other: __

If you chose 3, 4, or 5 for three or more items, you are at risk for significant NetStress Load.

Leisure/Play

This category includes physical, social, intellectual, volunteer, and creative activities that have a positive effect on your self-esteem and perceived wellness. Life satisfaction is influenced by leisure congruence, which is defined as the selection of leisure activities that are consistent with your personality type. Leisure activity choices, like vocational choices, are an expression of your personality. The meaning and quality of leisure activities may contribute more to your well-being than participation in the leisure activity itself. Participating in leisure activities may help reduce stress and may provide social support. It is important to feel satisfied with your recreation and leisure time activities and to have at least one activity in which "you lose yourself and time stands still."

Leisure is essential to the concept of wellness. Learning to become totally absorbed in an activity during which time stands still helps you not only cope with but also transcend life's problems. Leisure opens up pathways to growth in both creative and spiritual dimensions.

Following are some first-person accounts that relate how leisure and play help to create a life worth living.

- "Getting rid of stress would mean turning off work when I am supposed to! I used to swim, which was a real joy for me. I still have a hard time and feel guilty when I think about swimming. There have been times when I fell asleep in my home office because I couldn't stop working. As for the guilt factor, it hits me the most when I see the next morning that the boss sent an e-mail after hours, and colleagues who were logged on late into the night responded then. But I could only respond the next morning because I wasn't logged on at 9 p.m. And I never take time just to do something fun."

- "Managing two small children, a demanding job, and a horse farm all contribute to my serious lack of sleep. I feel as if I don't get enough time with my children or with my passion of training horses. I can conquer the world if I can find time to ride every day; the problem is I don't have the time and I start to fall apart without my stress releaser—riding."

Self-Assessment: Leisure/Play

Read each statement and choose the response that best indicates how often during the last six months an issue or a situation has created stress for you. Please respond with your first impression. For "other," include any personal issue or situation not represented by any of the statements.

0 = Never
1 = Seldom
2 = Sometimes
3 = Often
4 = Frequent

(continued)

Self-Assessment: Leisure/Play (continued)

. . . .

5 = Constant

6 = Does not apply

1. Lack of time to pursue hobbies or leisure activities __

2. Lack of fitness to participate in physical individual or team activities __

3. Limited recreation areas or facilities that are convenient for my use __

4. Lack of skill to get involved in organized play/sports/games __

5. Lack of awareness of resources to pursure leisure activities __

6. Feeling guilty when I put my work aside for leisure/play __

7. Other: __

8. Other: __

9. Other: __

10. Other: __

11. Other: __

If you chose 3, 4, or 5 for two or more items, you are at risk for significant NetStress Load.

More about Coping

Finally, in this chapter, I want you to think about how you are currently coping with all of the demands and challenges in your life. The good news is that whatever you're doing, it's all okay. Coping is not an inherited or unconscious trait, and styles vary. Nor is it purely adaptive versus maladaptive. How anyone copes must be evaluated on a "person-by-situation" basis. There are several approaches and mechanisms but two broad types of coping styles: problem-focused coping and emotion-focused coping. In general, problem-focused coping refers to a response that is aimed at eliminating a perceived threat. It has been related to higher levels of well-being and therefore to fewer psychological symptoms. Emotion-focused coping aims to lessen the emotional discomfort triggered by a situation, and it has been suggested that it is less effective than problem-focused coping.

As you read about each coping style, consider which one you use most often.

- *Problem-focused coping* addresses the specifics of the stressful situation itself. It includes taking charge of changing the environment or developing an action plan that you hope will lead to a solution. This style of coping (planning actions, personal growth, self-adaptation, engaging in positive thinking) has been found to decrease emotional distress and reduce the risk of depression.
- *Emotion-focused coping* represents your attempts to process the feelings and reactions that are associated with a stressful event or situation. Emotion-focused coping can be good or bad. Common negative emotion-focused coping strategies include rumination, self-blame, and wishful thinking. Positive emotion-coping strategies include reappraisal, relaxation, seeking a forum to express your emotions, or talking with a friend. Talking with a friend works unless the level of support is less than what you need or is not at the level of intimacy that you expect. Then it will only serve to exacerbate the negative effects of your feeling a lack of control, thus further increasing your risks of experiencing harmful effects.

Several studies have contrasted the differences between men and women in their use of coping mechanisms. For example, some studies show that women use emotion-focused coping more than men do. More specifically, as far as social support coping is concerned, women request and receive more support than men do. Women are also more influenced by social context, and their coping involves interpersonal relationships more than their male counterparts' coping does. Women also have the additional "tend-and-befriend" coping style that was described in the previous chapter.

With regard to problem-focused coping, there is no consistent evidence about gender differences. Some studies point out that men use this coping style more than women do, whereas other studies find the opposite, and still more do not find any difference. Several studies suggest that this inconsistent evidence could be the result of differences in status, power, and the types of jobs held by women and men. Solid research has demonstrated that if these variables are controlled, few differences are found.

Wrapup

Before you move on to the next chapter, take a moment to think about the many common scenarios and situations we've explored in this chapter—situations that women often find themselves in and that often make us ask ourselves, "Am I okay?" The truth is that there are so many possible explanations for why we feel the way we do. Furthermore, each of us is unique, not only in terms of our life experiences and stressors but also in the way we perceive and react to those experiences and stressors. I hope you will come away from this discussion with new insights and information about what is causing you stress.

5

what's really important in your life

defining your purpose, passions, and priorities

In the last chapter, you had the opportunity to examine the issues, demands, and challenges that you face on a daily basis. It is likely that these challenges are what stand between you and what you may describe as *balance*. One of my core beliefs is that to live a life in the BestStress Zone, a person needs to feel that her life is in balance. What I call *balance* starts with a deep understanding of all of the dimensions that make us whole. In addition to our physical well-being, the psychological, social, emotional, biochemical, and spiritual dimensions—all interrelated and interdependent—combine to make us who we are. The common threads binding these dimensions together are your core values: your purpose, passions, and priorities, or the 3Ps. This chapter provides an opportunity for you to go through a self-assessment process and hopefully give some shape and clarity to those core values. For some of you, it may be a time to revisit what you may have done consciously or unconsciously in the past. But I know so many women who feel disconnected from their deepest dreams or from the ideas or ideals they hold dear. Over and over again, my clients talk about how their lives seem to have grown up around them, without any conscious design, and how they feel as if they're constantly in *reaction* mode, simply putting out fires or putting one foot in front of the other. These women discover that what's missing is a sense of focus or direction,

Some of the questions you'll encounter in this chapter may concern issues you haven't thought about for a while, and it may take some genuine introspection before you arrive at comfortable answers, but you can do it. Think about it. You assess yourself every day. When you get up in the morning, you assess how you feel. When you look into the bathroom mirror, you may assess your appearance. The assessment you'll do in this chapter goes a little deeper, of course, but it may be the most important step you'll take as you discover your BestStress Zone. I want you to make a deliberate and conscious assessment that includes identifying your personal likes and dislikes, your true strengths and weaknesses. This knowledge will allow you to live in the BestStress Zone effortlessly. You will be able to see challenges and problems in the context of your core values and larger purpose in life. You will be able to immediately recognize attitudes, feelings, and behaviors that undermine your performance, vitality, and health. A clear vision of, and a commitment to, your 3Ps can give you the courage and the tools to address problems decisively and to accept the negative things that can't be changed. It can lead you to strengthen your personal effectiveness and stay healthy. When your values, purpose, passions, and priorities are aligned, you are intuitively able to give and receive from others. You will experience clarity, energy, health, and happiness.

We associate the emotion we call *happiness* with feelings that range from contentment and satisfaction to bliss and intense joy. Research has identified a number of factors that are interrelated with happiness. These include religious involvement, parenthood, marital status, age, and income. In his book *Authentic Happiness*, Dr. Martin Seligman, one of the founders of positive psychology, describes happiness as consisting of "positive emotions" and "positive activities." He further categorizes emotions as connected to either the past, the present, or the future. Positive emotions relating to the past include satisfaction, contentment, pride, and serenity. Positive emotions relating to the future include optimism, hope, and trust. He divides positive emotions about the present into two categories: pleasure and gratifications. Bodily pleasures and other higher pleasures are "pleasures of the moment" and usually involve some external stimulus. When the pleasurable situation ends, we quickly lose our positive feelings. Gratifications, however, involve our full engagement, the elimination of self-consciousness, the blocking of felt emotions, and what we described earlier as flow. When a gratification comes to an end, we will continue to feel positive emotions. This is what is often lacking in superficial relationships.

We derive a feeling of *authenticity* from the gratification and the positive emotions that come from simply being our best selves. The most profound sense of happiness is achieved through experiencing a meaningful life—by being fully engaged in a purpose greater than one's own immediate goals. Both happiness and authenticity are important components of life in the BestStress Zone.

Happiness depends, in large part, on living a life that fulfills your personal sense of purpose or meaning. As an introduction to the exercises that follow, I want you to recall and reflect on situations in your life, perhaps even extreme experiences, of great satisfaction, positive emotion, and happiness. What were you doing? What was the circumstance? I also want you to recall a time when you were occupied in an activity during which you lost all track of time, when you were so engaged that you missed your normal meal and sleep times without realizing it. Try to remember not only the activity itself but also the way you felt at the time. This is an excellent first step toward discovering the core of who you are and what is important to you.

The exercises in this chapter are not designed to bring about some fundamental change in who you are. The goal is to get rid of any confusion you might feel about your purpose, direction, or identity. If you're hard-driving and aggressive, this exercise won't make you serene and complacent. During the course of reading this chapter, I want you to be able to recognize and feel comfortable declaring what you really want in life. But simply putting a label on your 3Ps isn't enough. You'll see that being honest and open about them makes it possible to embrace them fully—to make a deeper commitment to the life you want and to take responsibility for fulfilling that commitment, including effective management of the stress that is inevitably associated with fulfilling that commitment.

These exercises will reveal to you where you are right now. Most of you will feel that you know and honor your 3Ps. I want you to evaluate how closely you are currently living your 3Ps by taking the quick self-analysis that follows.

Self-Assessment:
My Purpose, Passions, and Priorities

Read each statement and choose the response that indicates how strongly you agree or disagree. Then add up your score.

1 = Strongly disagree
2 = Disagree
3 = Uncertain
4 = Agree
5 = Strongly agree

1. I know what makes me happy. __
2. I am crystal clear about the greater meaning that shapes all of my life. __
3. I feel "on track" in my day-to-day life. __
4. My education or career path reflects my deepest values and purpose. __
5. I feel I am making a positive contribution to my family and community through my day-to-day activities. __
6. My day-to-day life allows me to be my best self. __
7. I am excited about my life most days. __
8. I have defined what success means to me. __
9. I am comfortable receiving love, support, and pleasure. __
10. I feel nourished and fulfilled in my personal and/or work- (school-) related relationships and am aligned with my purpose. __
11. I regularly reach out to and seek the company of others on a path to living out their life's purpose. __
12. I self-monitor to ensure I am "on track" with my purpose on a day-to-day basis. __

(continued)

Self-Assessment: My Purpose, Passions, and Priorities (continued)

· ·

13. I have consciously decided how I measure my life: longevity, legacy, material wealth, achievements. __

14. I schedule regular time with the important people in my life to give me feedback and suggestions for keeping my career and personal paths aligned with my purpose. __

15. My home physically provides a sanctuary for my soul, and all of the people in the household (including children) are honored in body, mind, soul, and individual purpose. __

Scoring

15–39: Congratulations! Today is the beginning of your new life. Even if you feel less than great about your responses, it's all good. You're here now, ready, willing, and able to realign your life. Keep at it!

40–54: Congratulations! You are a living a life strongly influenced by your 3Ps. You are well positioned to take the last, big step toward living up to your highest possibility through working carefully with the material in this chapter.

55–75: Congratulations! You are living a life that is solidly guided, whether consciously or unconsciously, by your purpose. Your everyday activities reflect your values, gratitude, and use of your natural talents.

What Is Your *Purpose?*

Early in my career as an ER doctor, I pulled the chart of the next patient waiting to be seen. As is often the case, I decided to prepare for the patient encounter by reviewing the online problem list from this patient's prior visits to the ER. I was intrigued to note that two of the "conditions" noted in the problem list were unemployment and "ineffective use of leisure time." This diagnosis of ineffective use of leisure time is, in fact, a legitimate billing code physicians can use to get reimbursement for their services. But this was the first time I had ever seen the code, and I laughed out loud. At that time in my life, all that I wished for was more leisure time, whether effective or ineffective! The triage nurse had listed the man's chief complaint for that particular ER visit as "fatigue and possible infection." This was a distinct possibility, based on the stench emanating from behind the drape around the gurney in Treatment Bay 6.

John was in his mid-forties, thin, unshaven, and wearing dark glasses and a hat that covered most of his head. I felt a little uncomfortable around him but began with the usual questions: "Why are you here today? How can I help you?" Without hesitation, he said he had an infection from where he had "shot up" two days earlier. He had purchased street antibiotics, but they hadn't worked. "What do you think, doc?" John did indeed have a huge infection near the site where he attempted to inject heroin into his veins. He had missed the vein and infected the surrounding tissues. The pus, swelling, redness, enlarged lymph nodes in his armpits, fever at 104 degrees, and subsequent lab tests suggested that an infection had spread throughout his entire body. He was critically ill. I explained that he would need to be hospitalized to receive appropriate treatment.

"How long, doc?" he asked. "How long do you think I will need to be here?"

Without thinking, and clearly from an entirely different life view, I responded abruptly, "Why does it matter? Do you have something more important to do?"

"Yeah, doc. I always got something to do. No matter what, every day, every minute, I got one thing on my mind: how am I gonna get my next hit? If I have to rob my mother or shoot you, I'm gonna get it or die trying. So I need to know how long you want me holed up here in the hospital. I got a decision to make."

Suddenly, I realized there was no way this man should be labeled as using his time ineffectively. He had a specific life's purpose, driven by his conscious or unconscious values. He made strategic choices based on his priorities, and, in pursuit of that, he used his time with uncommon effectiveness. In fact, it made me pause to think about my own purpose and priorities.

John's story exemplifies the life of someone who ascribes to the philosophy of James Allen, the inspirational British author who in 1902 penned *the* classic self-help book *As a Man Thinketh*. Allen wrote, "All that a man achieves and all that he fails to achieve is the direct result of his own thoughts." Purpose informs thoughts, consciously or unconsciously.

While you can argue with the origins of addiction or about the quality and the societal affect of John's thoughts, they were indeed driven by his current life's purpose.

Purpose provides a focus. It is a drive that is unique and innate in each of us if we choose to capture it and make it ours. The fact is that only when you are aware of your purpose can you live a life that is intentional and congruent and that allows you to be your best self. You will feel as if you are in alignment. Purpose is the key to self-mastery, enabling you to live up to your highest possibilities. Purpose allows you to live with your personal truth, rather than according to someone else's plan, even that of someone you love. The media bombards you with messages suggesting who to be and why. As you discover your purpose—your truth—you will have greater integrity and authenticity. Knowing your purpose is empowering because it can integrate who you are with what you do. When life's circumstances force you to acknowledge unhappiness, lack of fulfillment, or dissatisfaction in some dimension of life, you find yourself searching for a deeper sense of meaning or knowing. You don't have to wait for some unfortunate circumstance to trigger those bad feelings. Let's begin the process of determining your purpose right now.

So, what is your purpose? No doubt, you can name the last time someone asked you, at some gathering, "What do you do?" But can you recall anyone ever asking you, "What is your purpose?" Your identity is tied up with the role you fulfill and your job in society. You often label this your "purpose," but you are so much more than this. Just as with John, your life is already an expression of your purpose, whether you're consciously aware of it or not. If you are driven by a purpose but only on an unconscious level, this exercise is an opportunity to revisit and refocus on your motivation.

You are about to discover your real purpose in life. I'm not talking about your job, your daily responsibilities, or even your long-term goals. I mean the real reason why you're here at all—the very reason you exist. Purpose gives clear direction and momentum to your life. Purpose gives you a reason for *being*, rather than just *doing*. With clarity of purpose, you can answer the question "Who are you?" as easily as you answer the question "What do you do?" You don't need permission to determine your own purpose. No boss, personal or professional partner, parent, or friend can decide this for you. Purpose has nothing to do with sacrifice, approval, guilt, or conforming to someone else's idea of the correct way to live. Your purpose may or may not have a grounding in a spiritual belief system or a structured religion. It does not mean giving up something you like or that "feels good" in exchange for something that might be considered more worthy or important. Living in the BestStress Zone requires you to maintain a conscious awareness of your purpose. On a practical level, this allows you to set specific goals and strategies for day-to-day living.

Although these exercises will lead to your creation of a "statement of purpose," I want you to build it with due diligence. It may be helpful for you to think about a "statement of work" as a component of a proposal. This is no different. It is a blueprint to help you execute your life! Here are what I believe to be the ten core building blocks of your purpose statement.

1. Your purpose allows you to be your best self in service of a larger cause.
2. Your purpose is how you live and what you do.
3. Your purpose communicates your core values.
4. Your purpose governs the quality of your thoughts.
5. Your purpose builds on your natural talents.
6. Your purpose enriches you, your relationships, and society.
7. Your purpose defines personal possibilities and defines your epitaph.
8. Your purpose is unmistakable to everyone from your verbal and nonverbal communications.
9. Your purpose nourishes you with fulfillment and joy.
10. Your purpose in action is gratifying.

Don't hold back. In reflecting on these building blocks, don't limit yourself to thinking that your purpose relates to only one dimension of your life. This involves *all* of the dimensions we have discussed. Finally, keep in mind that purpose is not static. You may not be living your purpose at this very moment, but it evolves as you discover it.

To get to that statement of purpose, you first need to explore some of the component building blocks. The exercises in this chapter can help you along the path of self-discovery, relating to your purpose. Let's start with values.

What Do You *Value?*

People seem to talk a lot about *values.* Politicians certainly make a fair amount of noise about values. And yet not only are we occasionally confused about what our values are, but sometimes it feels as if the word itself has been used so much that it has begun to lose meaning. (Kind of like the word *stress!*)

Stop and think about the things in life that you hold most precious. Clarity about your values will enable you to make choices that make you happy, because you know what's best for yourself. First, let's be sure you know what we're talking about when we mention values.

- A value defines what you cherish in life, whether it's an idea, like commitment to family or community engagement, or a goal, such as financial security or professional success, or something tangible, like your physical surroundings or possessions.
- You choose your values freely. They should not—in fact, they *cannot*—be forced on you.
- You are proud of your values, and you are able and willing to articulate them publicly.
- You are willing to defend your values against criticism.
- Values may change or evolve over the course of your life, but your commitment to them should not.

At the same time, you accept the fact that others may not value what you do and you may have to accommodate someone else's values without compromising your own. Ideally, you live according to your values but are able to grow and change as you adapt to different circumstances in your life. The relationship of values to the BestStress Zone is dynamic. Reassessing your values on a regular basis will enable you to continue living accordingly, without experiencing conflict between the old and the new.

Examining Your Values

. . . .

Values Clarification Exercise

This first exercise consists of three rounds and should take you no more than fifteen minutes to complete. In round one, place a checkmark beside the ten values that are most important to you. For round two, narrow those ten values down to five. In round three, narrow the values further to three and number them in order of importance. For "other," please fill in values important for you that are not listed.

- Accumulation of wealth __
- Financial security __
- Respect from others (those who know you) __
- Recognition—to be well known to other people __
- Personal freedom and independence __
- Family structure and cohesiveness __
- Spirituality and faith __
- Organized and clean structure of surroundings __
- Organized structure of personal routine and schedule __
- Punctuality __
- Efficient use of time __
- Desire for personal solitude __
- Power over others __
- Personal creativity __
- Accumulation of knowledge __
- Appreciation by others __
- Good health __
- Taking on challenges __
- Experiencing excitement and adventure __
- Competitiveness __
- Productivity __
- Feeling inner peace __
- Experiencing love and affection __
- Interaction with others __
- Service to others __
- Gaining wisdom and insight __
- Cultural activities __

(continued)

- Intimate, truly honest, close relationships with others __
- Other: __
- Other: __

Select the one value that is of greatest significance to you and write it down.

Values in Action Exercise

Now let's examine your values more closely. This exercise also helps you transform words into actions. The following is a list of values in action. Read each value and rate how your actions over the last six months have been congruent (harmonious) with each one.

    1 = Low congruence
    2 = Medium congruence
    3 = High congruence

It is important to me that:

1. I am proactive in actively maintaining good health. __
2. I have many close friendships. __
3. I have a large family. __
4. I have a fulfilling career or job. __
5. I have a stable marriage, partnership, or committed relationship. __
6. I have at least one truly intimate friendship. __
7. I live a financially comfortable life. __
8. I have independence. __
9. I have the ability to demonstrate creativity. __
10. I participate in an organized religion or spiritual activities. __
11. I have children in my life who are a source of fulfilment for me. __
12. My family is cohesive. __
13. I experience love and affection. __
14. My children are high achievers. __
15. I can have variety of interests. __
16. I have the freedom to create my own lifestyle. __
17. I acquire and/or sustain wealth. __

(continued)

Examining Your Values (continued)

18. I am in a happy and loving relationship. __
19. I contribute to my community. __
20. I have an organized structure in my personal routine and schedule. __
21. I have an organized and clean structure in my environment. __
22. I have an abundance of leisure time. __
23. I use time efficiently. __
24. I have personal solitude. __
25. I am appreciated by others. __
26. I experience excitement and adventure. __
27. I experience inner peace. __
28. I am a successful competitor. __
29. I have a stable life. __
30. I have a life without stress. __
31. I am able to live my spiritual and faith values. __
32. I have the opportunity to make social changes. __
33. I will be remembered for my accomplishments. __
34. I can help those in distress. __
35. I have the freedom to live where I wish. __
36. I take time for myself. __
37. I take time to enjoy art, entertainment, and cultural activities. __
38. I have a life with many challenges. __
39. I have a life with many changes. __
40. I have the opportunity to be a leader. __
41. I can accumulate knowledge. __
42. I can accumulate wisdom. __
43. I create or maintain a good physical appearance. __
44. I live an exciting life. __
45. I have a chance to get into politics. __
46. I live according to strong moral values. __
47. I have the opportunity to teach others. __
48. I am able to write something memorable. __

(continued)

Examining Your Values (continued)
. . . .

49. I have a chance to become famous. __

50. I am able to help others solve problems. __

51. Other: __

Of the items that you rated "high congruence" (the ones most important to you), select the top three and write them down.

Next, you must combine the values from both exercises into a single value sentence (which may or may not include words or phrases from the values themselves). You can, and no doubt will want to, come back and revisit this exercise as you reflect on the meaning of your value sentence. If you are reading this book sequentially, I want you to write your value sentence before moving on to the next chapter: *The single most important value that is the core foundation in my life is __.*

What Are Your *Gifts?*

Now that you have articulated your core values—the foundation of your purpose statement—let's examine the next component, your *gifts.* Don't lose sight of the fact that this work is essential to build the self-awareness that is necessary to cope with the stressors in your life. You are identifying and shaping not only *what* you think but *how* you think. Your gifts and talents are the natural abilities that come easily to you and enable you to produce extraordinary results. They are as natural as your laughter and come just as easily as taking a breath. Yet they are often overlooked because they require so little thought or effort. Often, you fail to see them as special and valuable and to consciously consider them as you create a purpose statement. Each of your gifts and talents represents an ability to do, sense, be aware, or know something. It's conceivable that you never had the chance to feel good about these gifts; sometimes they are the qualities or abilities for which you were chastised as a child and that you learned to downplay in your life. If you were lucky, though, a mentor or a friend helped you understand the true value of these gifts. You may not have had the opportunity to list your gifts and abilities in the past. Now is the time.

In this exercise, I want you not simply to identify or reconsider your talents but to put them in the context of action. Reflect on the best "gift" you can give to others (family, friends, society) in the present, as well as what will remain later as your legacy. One way to get clarity about your gifts is to try to imagine the experience that people have when they are around you on a day-to-day basis.

Gifts and Talents Exercise

Complete the following sentences.

1. When I was growing up, people admired and recognized me as having a talent or a gift in:
2. It is as easy and natural as breathing when I am engaged in:
3. What amazes me about myself and what I can do without even trying is:
4. If I had the resources, I would pay to be able to work daily at:
5. Family, friends, and colleagues commonly think I am awesome at:
6. If I could retire today, I would:

Review your responses. Next, merge and purge to complete this sentence: *I am naturally great at and can function at my highest level of possibility when I _____.* There is no single best answer. You may list up to three alternatives.

What Do I Want to *Give*? What Do I Have to Be *Grateful* For?

Gratitude is a balanced response to a life filled with highs and lows. A key component of a purposeful life is the capacity to give back and incorporate gratitude into your daily routine. Research demonstrates that people with a well-developed sense of gratitude tend to be more happy, helpful, and forgiving and less depressed than people who don't feel grateful. According to these researchers, a life of gratitude is composed of three parts:

1. A sense of purpose in our lives
2. An appreciation for the lives of those around us
3. A willingness to take action to show the gratitude we feel

Gratitude is expressed through the big things in life—major events, decisions, and choices—but also and often more importantly through the small things. Living a balanced life of gratitude requires that your family and other close relationships are in order. This often comes into focus for me in my work in the emergency room, where every day patients and family members have to confront an unexpected illness, a scary diagnosis, or worse. The way my colleagues and I speak to family members, the ability to pick ourselves up and face the next crisis and the next, and even the choice to recycle instead of throwing everything in the trash can depend on my loving all aspects of work, enjoying at least most of them, and staying focused on the knowledge that we are contributing to something greater than ourselves. It's empowering and uplifting to feel as if every decision, no matter how large or how small, truly matters.

Gratitude is not the same as indebtedness. While both are related to receiving help, indebtedness occurs when a person perceives that he or she is under an obligation to repay the kindness or help that was received. Also, gratitude is not all about rewards or money, but that's certainly a piece of it. The way we handle our money reflects how we feel about other people and our lives in general. Therefore, an important part of living gratefully usually includes a commitment to regularly help others with our financial resources. If you don't have a strategy for giving to charity, I recommend that you create one by reviewing your finances and identifying a few organizations that are worthy of greater support. Then set up automatic donations to those organizations so that you won't forget about sending in the money. The process of outwardly showing more gratitude (by investing your money in others' lives) will create an inward feeling of gratefulness. It's a win-win relationship.

Gratitude must be regularly cultivated, even when times are hard. If you spend time every day expressing gratitude in a way that is meaningful to you, it will quickly become an integral part of your life.

Like anything else, the more we practice it, the more natural and habitual it becomes. We can cultivate gratitude through prayer, meditation, writing, and other expressions of art.

Gratitude Survey

Read each statement and choose the response that best indicates how strongly you agree or disagree. Then add up your score.

1 = Strongly disagree (never true)
2 = Disagree (rarely true)
3 = Agree (true some of the time)
4 = Strongly agree (true most of the time)

1. I take time to stop and enjoy my life for what it is. __
2. I think it's really important to "stop and smell the roses." __
3. I'm really thankful for friends and family understanding that nothing is permanent. __
4. Thinking about dying reminds me to live each day to the fullest. __
5. I use personal or spiritual/religious practices to remind myself to be thankful. __
6. I reflect on how fortunate I am to have basic things in life like food, clothing, and shelter. __
7. If I had to list all that I am grateful for, it would be a very long list. __
8. Every day I see many things to be grateful for. __
9. The saying, "I am where I am because I stand on the shoulders of others before me" applies to me. __
10. Very little time goes by without my feeling grateful for something or to someone. __

Scoring

10–18: You currently believe that there is nothing in your life to express gratitude for. Doing the work in this book will help you overcome that belief.

(continued)

Gratitude Survey (continued)

. . . .

19–29: Although to some degree you express gratitude for the things and people in your life, you may want to consider finding more opportunities
to express gratitude.
30–40: It is probable that you express gratitude on a regular basis and are
likely to experience greater health and well-being because of this.

   This survey is based on the teachings of Dr. Martin Seligman, also known as the
"father of positive psychology."

Gratitude Exercise

. . . .

Think of three things that you have gratitude for in your life.

   Imagine the "gift" you wish to leave for yourself, your family, and society. You
may think of this as the single word that would be on a marker or a tombstone
after you pass away. The word you choose will be the solitary message communicating this "gift" and reflecting your life's purpose.

   Here lies [your name]. She leaves behind to a grateful world the gift of _____.

You have completed a deep exploration of the components I feel
are important for describing your purpose. It's now time to assemble
everything you've learned and put it to use. The following exercise
addresses the issue of achievement. You will use this information and
the knowledge you unearthed about yourself in the previous exercises
to write your purpose statement. This statement is invaluable as your
guide to living in the BestStress Zone.

Purpose and Achievement:
The Ladder of Life Exercise

. . . .

For highly driven women in the competitive workforce, it is common to confuse
purpose with achievement. The following exercise should provide some clarification. Imagine a ladder with ten steps. The steps on the ladder stand for ten pos-

(continued)

Purpose and Achievement: The Ladder of Life Exercise (continued)
. . . .

sible steps in your life. The tenth step stands for the *best* possible way of life for you, and the first step stands for the *worst* possible way of life for you. Keeping in mind that step ten represents your best way of life and step one represents your worst way of life, apply the number that applies best to each question.

1. What step number best describes where you are *now*? __
2. What step number best describes where you were when you were *twenty-one years old*? __
3. What step number best describes where you would *like* to be next year? __
4. What step number best describes where you *expect* to be next year? __
5. How disappointed would you be if you found out that you would never reach the step you identified in question 3?

   Very disappointed
   Fairly disappointed
   Slightly disappointed
   Not at all disappointed

6. Which of the following would keep you from getting to the step you identified in question 3? (Chose as many as are applicable.)

   Lack of ability
   Lack of opportunity
   Lack of effort
   Bad luck
   Your religion or ethnicity
   Your gender
   An act of a higher power
   Other:

   Review your answers carefully. I want you to recognize from this exercise that career success, bumps, delays, and off and on ramps are parallel to but independent of your true purpose. As driven and intentional as you may be in your professional work habits, at the end of the day it is just a job.

Purpose Statement

. . . .

Find a quiet place for contemplation. Close your eyes and focus your attention on completing your quest to define and describe your true purpose. I want you to feel positive about simply being you and excited about the opportunity to write your statement. Write, in three sentences or less, your purpose statement. I'll get you started.

My life is meant to serve the purpose of _____.

What Are Your Passions?

What brings you to tears? What do you absolutely love to do, see, be a part of, or experience? These are your *passions*, and whatever they are, as long as they are legal and healthy, you need to know them and understand how they function in your life. Passion is fuel. Passion can give you energy, provide your body and mind with the capacity or ability to do work. For so many people, at the core of stress is a lack of energy. You find yourself feeling exhausted, as if you're swimming against the current of life instead of enjoying the flow. If this sounds familiar, chances are you are not in tune with your passions. Passion is a force—sometimes uncontrollable—that infuses life with meaning, joy, and sometimes even outrage. Passion can foster commitment and determination. It is an urge that consistently calls us to action, sometimes radical action. Passion can be used or misused. Passion has energy and force, but you must provide the direction.

Passion is that compelling emotion that enables you to go places where others are afraid to go, to try things that others will not, and to be the kind of person others dare not be. It can create the energy and drive that are required to do what others may think impossible. Often, when you speak with people who love their work, what you hear is not that they chose their careers, but that the careers chose them. They can't imagine their lives without their passion. Passion can push you to do your best, to remain steadfast and strong in the face of adversity, and to feel the freedom to pursue your desires. Passion keeps you going when everyone tells you to give up.

So often, we experience passion vicariously, through the passions of others, such as actors, athletes, and musicians. We are avid consumers of "people" shows and magazines. Their passions reinvigorate us. But what about your own world, your own experiences? What excites you? Who energizes you? What and whom do you love? Recognizing your passions enables your self-regeneration.

The good news is that passion is a natural state of being. We often say, "I want to find my passion," as if it is something we expect to stumble across in the shopping mall. Passion is not a commodity; it is the by-product of taking time to reflect and listen to your inner voice. Passions may change over the years, but they can surface and flourish only through your honest self-exploration.

In order to listen to your heart, you need to shut out the day-to-day noise and confusion and seek a clearer, wider perspective on your life. Do whatever you need to do—take a quiet walk or listen to your favorite music. At some point, you will need to sit down, breathe deeply, and try to relax. Then answer these basic questions.

- What specific ideas, issues, and concerns preoccupy your mind, intruding on whatever else you need to think about?
- What do you find yourself unconsciously drawn to and really obsessive and excited about? What one subject can you enjoy talking about for many hours?
- What makes you feel good and gives you pleasure (that is also legal and healthy)?

Look to the past, the present, and the future for clues to your passion. Remember your childhood and any activities that excited or intrigued you. You may have abandoned them only because you thought it was practical to do so, not because you lost your passion for them. Then examine the present. Consider the things you look forward to from day to day—the aspects of your work you enjoy or the activities or thoughts in your life that really thrill you.

Next, examine your surroundings—the things you fill your home with, the ways you spend your time, the people you like—for insights into yourself. I want you to be able to complete the following sentence: *I am passionate about* _____.

What Are Your Priorities?

Prioritizing means determining what needs to get done and in what order. Your priorities should flow directly out of your values, purpose, and passions. This isn't where I teach you how to manage your to-do list. Here we are taking the wide-angle view, for life in the BestStress Zone. Remember that life is dynamic and has phases; each phase enables you to reassess, make new choices, and set new priorities.

Your priorities will help create your perspective, inform your analysis of stressors, and guide your decision making on a daily basis. Commit yourself to your priorities, recognizing that you will likely have to adjust them over time, just as you do with your purpose and your passions. All three should be regularly reassessed. I strongly suggest that you consider how taking care of yourself (i.e., eating healthfully and exercising) can be integrated into your life. Without a healthy mind and body, you can't enjoy the benefits of life in the BestStress Zone. Without good health, you will not have the ability to enjoy your friends, work, family, and leisure activities.

Priority-Setting Exercise

This exercise asks you to consider priorities across the seven dimensions of life that we discussed in chapter 4. Take into account the following as you respond.

1. *Use the Pareto Principle (the 80/20 rule).* Recognize that 20 percent of your focus is likely to provide 80 percent of your personal satisfaction, so focus on identifying your top priorities. Ask yourself, "Am I doing the things that are aligned with my values and purpose?"

(continued)

Priority-Setting Exercise (continued)
. . . .

2. *Identify priorities by the absolute necessity for your involvement.* Your focus and your energy should go toward priorities that cannot be delegated.

3. *Determine the future effect.* High-priority items will have a big effect on the future, whereas low-priority one will have no or a negligible effect.

Following are lists of qualities across the seven dimensions of life. Read each one and rate how important is in your life at this time.

1 = Low priority
2 = Medium priority
3 = High priority

1. Family: children, life partner, parents, siblings, extended and nontraditional family members __

2. Work: career, paid employment, school __

3. Self-care: optimal wellness and health, nutrition, fitness __

4. Friendship: nonromantic relationships __

5. Spirituality: faith, belief, religion, individuality __

6. Love: intimate and romantic personal relationships __

7. Leisure: leisure activities, hobbies, talents __

It may be easy to set priorities, but it is harder to live them. How you spend your time reflects your values and contributes to stress.

Self-Assessment: Your Priorities
. . . .

In the first column, indicate what percentage of your time you believe you allocate to each of the seven dimensions listed. In the second column, indicate what percentage of your time you would like to spend on each dimension. In the third column, indicate the percentage gap between how you currently spend your time and how you ideally want to spend your time. In the fourth column, have a person you value and trust (your spouse or partner, your child, or one of your parents) give his or her perception of the time you allocate to each of the seven dimensions. Then reflect on the six questions that follow the chart.

(continued)

Self-Assessment: Your Priorities (continued)

	A	B	C	D
	Your Perception of Current Time Allocation (%)	Your Ideal Time Allocation (%)	Gap (%)	Perception of Your Time Allocation by Valued Person* (%)
Family	___	___	___	___
Work	___	___	___	___
Self-care	___	___	___	___
Friendship	___	___	___	___
Spirituality	___	___	___	___
Love	___	___	___	___
Leisure	___	___	___	___
Total	**100%**	**100%**		**100%**

1. Is there a high degree of congruence between who you are, what you have formally prioritized as of high importance in the Priority-Setting Exercise, and how you spend your time on a day-to-day basis?
2. How do you manage the time requirements and conflicts in your life?
3. Currently, what are the most important aspects of your family life?
4. What is the role of friendships in your life?
5. How does "giving back" work for you on an ongoing basis?
6. What is the most difficult choice or trade-off between various aspects of your life that you have made in the past? What would you do differently in the future?

* Valued person is a partner, spouse, child, or parent.

What's Really Important?

In this chapter, I've provided some tools to help you figure out what you really want, by developing greater clarity about your purpose, passions, and priorities. There are a few simple concepts I want you to take away with you. Your values may shift and evolve slightly throughout your life; mine certainly have and continue to as I age. But values are the bedrock of the belief system that supports and serves your purpose. It's your purpose, however, that provides the real driving force. Only with purpose can you align your values and beliefs into a plan. It is my belief that each of us wants personal fulfillment and to live a life that is about being our best selves and our vision of the best world. Knowing your purpose allows you to do that. In fact, if you aren't living out your purpose, you'll sap the energy out of your life a little bit at a time. Knowing your purpose gives you a blueprint for your life, but it is your actions that will determine your destiny. You must decide to make a move.

Questions to Reflect On

1. Is your life right now consistent with your personal values, purpose, priorities, and passions? If not, why not?
2. What are your *purpose* or main focus and the driving force(s) in your life?

Let's return to James Allen and *As a Man Thinketh*:

Cherish your visions. Cherish your ideals. Cherish the music that stirs in your heart, the beauty that forms in your mind, the loveliness that drapes your purest thoughts, for out of them will grow all delightful conditions, all heavenly environment, of these, if you but remain true to them your world will at last be built. Until thought is linked with purpose there is no intelligent accomplishment. . . . A man should conceive of a legitimate purpose in his heart, and set out to accomplish it. He should make this purpose the centralizing point of his thoughts. . . . He should make this purpose his supreme duty, and should devote himself to its attainment, not allowing his thoughts to wander away into ephemeral fancies, longings, and imaginings. This is the royal road to self-control and true concentration of thought. Even if he fails again and again to accomplish his purpose (as he necessarily must until weakness is overcome), the strength of character gained will be the measure of his true success, and this will form a new starting-point for future power and triumph.

I hope you are now informed and inspired enough to do the following deceptively simple exercise. Commit to spending no more than ten minutes to complete the following sentence: *More than anything else in life right now, I want _____.*

If this chapter helped you create a list of what you want in life, the next chapter will help you address the obstacles in the way. Later, in part II of this book, we'll use all of this information to establish your personal BestStress Zone.

6

what is in your way

change, emotions, and putting it all together

Before we launch into the second part of this book, in which we set up your personal BestStress Zone, I want you to have a clear picture of what is going on in your life right now. In this chapter, we separate the truths from the myths about your current life and level of stress.

The idea of change intimidates most of us, and that fear often prevents us from trying anything new. It's true that change—even positive change—can trigger stress, but I don't want you to think that learning about and living in the BestStress Zone requires making radical changes in your life. Because it's useful to understand how we generally manage change, I want you to look at a model that can help you grasp the process of conscious change.

The Stages of Change Model

The stages of change model (SCM) was originally developed in the late 1970s and early 1980s by James Prochaska and Carlo DiClemente at the University of Rhode Island, when they studied how smokers were able to give up their habits or addiction. The SCM model has been applied to a broad range of behaviors, including weight loss, injury prevention, and alcohol and drug problems, among others.

The idea behind the SCM is that people tend to progress through different stages on their way to a successful change in behavior. Each of us progresses through the stages at our own rate. This model is consistent with wellness philosophies, which emphasize decision making and intentionality as the foundation for successful change. After I describe the model, I'll provide self-assessment tools to help you gauge whether you're ready to initiate change around the issues that are creating stress in your life.

The six stages of change are:

1. *Precontemplation*—not yet acknowledging the existence of a problem that needs to be changed
2. *Contemplation*—acknowledging that there is a problem but not yet convinced of the need or desire to make a change
3. *Preparation/determination*—getting ready to change
4. *Action/willpower*—the process of changing behavior
5. *Maintenance*—maintaining the behavior change
6. *Relapse*—returning to older behaviors and abandoning the new changes

Stage 1: Precontemplation

I am a "list" person and try to manage all of my responsibilities on a daily to-do list. It works for me, and I don't see any problems so far. It can be extremely helpful and gratifying when most of the tasks get completed. However, it can also get extremely stressful, when at the end of the day little or nothing has been accomplished. I have had issues with my health because of stress, but overall, I think I have it under control.

—Gloria, 58, hospital administrator

In the precontemplation stage, you have not begun to think seriously about changing and are not interested in any kind of help. In this stage, you don't acknowledge that a behavior is problematic and tend to be defensive in the face of efforts to pressure them to quit. Are you in the precontemplation stage? No, because the fact that you are reading this shows that you are beginning to recognize that your stress is out of control and you want or need to change.

Stage 2: Contemplation

I do not have positive coping mechanisms, and I know this is a problem. I get home too late to prepare a nutritionally balanced meal, but because my stress level is so high, I am not interested in cooking a proper meal anyway and end up eating sugary snacks, which makes me feel worse. I can't seem to break this vicious cycle.
—Gigi, 41, systems analyst

In the contemplation stage, people are more aware of the personal consequences of their habits or issues. Although they are able to consider the possibility of changing, they tend to be ambivalent about it. In this stage, people weigh the pros and cons of quitting or modifying their behavior. They compare the negative consequences of their bad habits against the benefits of changing them and may conclude that the long-term benefits associated with, for example, quitting smoking will outweigh the short-term costs. There's no telling how long it might take each person to get through the contemplation stage. (In fact, some people think and think and think about giving up their bad habits and may die without ever getting beyond this stage.) On the plus side, people in this stage of change are more open to educating themselves and reflecting on their own feelings and thoughts concerning their bad habits.

Stage 3: Preparation/Determination

My husband and I nearly split up—until we realized that we could face all of these stresses either as a team or alone (and divorced). We concluded that we still loved each other and that we ought

to support each other and do the best we could under these very trying circumstances. Just acknowledging that life had dealt us some difficulties and that we were a team was the turning point that got us on the path to reducing the stress.
—Oksana 29, graphic designer

In this stage, people have made a commitment to make a change. When people say things like "I really ought to do something about this . . . ," you know they are in the preparation/determination stage, which involves taking steps toward change, such as doing research and gathering information about what they will need to do to change their behavior.

Too often, people skip this stage and try to move directly from contemplation into action. These folks tend to fall flat on their faces because they haven't adequately researched or accepted what it will take to make this major lifestyle change. Reading this book is essential for your work in preparing to change how you deal with stress in your life.

Stage 4: Action/Willpower

On the relationship side, I signed up for several dating services in an effort to be proactive and also made it clear to several people that I was again single and open to dating. I also made a concerted effort to work out more as that is a significant way for me to release stress.
—Katherine, 34, marketing and PR executive

We take action only when we believe we have the ability to change. This stage requires various amounts of time for different people and different behaviors. When taking action, we mostly depend on our own willpower. It's important to review your commitment and develop plans to deal with both personal and external pressures that may lead to slips. You may use short-term rewards to sustain your motivation and enhance your self-confidence. People in this stage tend to be open to receiving help and are also likely to seek support from others, which can be critically important to successful change.

Stage 5: Maintenance

I constantly work at communicating better with my son and trying different approaches. It's paying off—he's doing better and I'm not always crying. In my career, I'm trying to learn as much as I can and encourage my team to perform optimally. I talk to myself a lot about personal commitment.

—Katiana, 40, industrial hygienist

The goal of the maintenance stage is to maintain the new status quo, avoiding any temptations to return to the bad habit. You can benefit, in this stage, from reminding yourself of how much progress you have made. Remain aware that you are striving for something worthwhile and meaningful. Be patient with yourself and recognize that it often takes a while to let go of old behavior patterns and practice new ones until they are second nature. People in this stage constantly reformulate the rules of their lives and acquire new skills to deal with challenges and avoid relapse. They are able to anticipate the situations in which a relapse could occur, and they prepare coping strategies in advance.

Stage 6: Relapse

Remember, it is normal and natural to regress, to attain one stage, only to fall back to a previous stage. Even in the course of one day, you may go through several different stages of change. This is just a normal part of making changes in your behavior. Along the way to reducing a negative behavior or stopping it altogether, most people will have a relapse, and probably more than one. Although a relapse can be discouraging and can trigger feelings of failure, it's normal. Most people cycle through the five stages several times before achieving a stable lifestyle change. Rather than giving up in the wake of a relapse, use it as a learning opportunity. Analyze what could have caused the relapse, and consider changes to your strategy for the next time. Relapses can contribute to your understanding, and they can empower you. Immediately get back on the horse that threw you, but don't go all the way back to the precontemplation or contemplation stage. Restart the process again at preparation, action, or even the maintenance stage.

People who have relapsed may need to learn to anticipate high-risk situations (such as being with their families) more effectively, control environmental temptations (such as being around drinking buddies), and learn how to handle unexpected episodes of stress without returning to their bad habits. This gives them a stronger sense of self-control and the ability to get back on track.

The Outcome

Eventually, if you stay in the maintenance stage long enough, you will reach a point where you will be able to work with your emotions and understand your own behavior and view it in a new light. This is the stage of transcendence, as you are moving beyond your old life to a new one. In this stage, not only is your bad habit no longer an integral part of your life, but to return to it would seem atypical, abnormal, even weird to you. When you reach this point in your process of change, you will know that you are truly becoming a new you and no longer need the old behaviors to sustain yourself.

Are You Ready for Change?

Which of the following statements most closely corresponds to your feelings about reducing the stress in your life today?

1. I have not thought about changing or reducing the stress in my life at all.
2. I'd like to change and have less stress in my life, and I've thought about it some.
3. I'm thinking about changing. In the last few weeks, I have thought quite a lot about what it would be like to have less stress in my life.
4. I am actively trying to change things to have less stress in my life right now.
5. I have changed and feel that I'm currently living with less stress. I need to work on maintaining the changes I've made.
6. I've made all of the changes in this area that I want to right now. There's no problem for me in dealing with stress at all.

If you are still reading at this point, you must have selected a level of readiness other than statement six. If this is the case, you are right where you need to be. Let's turn our attention to identifying and assessing what I call your "stress traps." Based on my research, these are the common barriers, whether conscious or unconscious, that prevent you from dealing effectively with stress.

The common traps that I have experienced personally and see in many of the clients I work with fall into six general areas:

1. Emotions
2. Negative thoughts
3. Control
4. Guilt
5. Generational priorities
6. Role versus identity

Stress Trap 1: Emotions

The meeting was not what I expected, and I was completely caught off guard. My ideas and approach for our new project were being presented by the "alpha male" in our group as though it was his original concept. It was just too much for me, and everyone knew it by the time I finished letting him have it. I have never let my emotions get so out of control.

—Adrienne, 36, human resources training director

"If I were not so emotional, I could handle stress better." I hear women talk this way all the time. It reveals a pernicious and unhealthy level of self-blame. There is no such thing as being too emotional. Our emotions are our internal GPS; we might think we know the way, but we're more likely to find the route to happiness by being honest about what really feels good and right to us. Emotions are a fundamental component of the overall stress response. In fact, I counsel clients to embrace their emotions, to listen and learn from them. *Emotional intelligence* is the term used to describe the ability, capacity, and skill needed to identify, assess, and manage the emotions of ourselves and others.

What are emotions? The answer to this question might be simpler if we limited our discussion to *primary* or *universal* emotions: happiness, sadness, fear, anger, surprise, or disgust. It is important to note, however, that numerous other conditions and behaviors have roots in your emotions. These include so-called *secondary* or *social* emotions, such as embarrassment, jealousy, guilt, pride, and what are called *background* emotions, such as well-being or malaise, or being calm or tense. Some people use the term *emotion* to describe certain drives and motivations and the states of pain and pleasure.

Biology underlies all emotions. Here is how it works: Classical thinking in medicine proposed that a specific area of the brain, the limbic system, generated emotions. Research led by Joseph LeDoux, of New York University, described the pathway that involves a part of the brain called the amygdala. The amygdala serves as our emotional memory bank and takes in deposits starting from the day we are born. The programming that takes place when we are infants influences us throughout our lifetime. Until recently, it was thought that the unconscious, conditioned reflex responses that we feel—the "knee-jerk responses" or the "gut instincts"—come directly through the amygdala.

We now know differently. Dr. Candace Pert, at the National Institutes of Health, described how emotional states or moods are produced by biochemicals called neuropeptides. These "molecules of emotions" communicate with the cells in the brain and throughout the body simultaneously. Her work led to the discovery of the mechanism for the feel-good neuropeptide endorphin. Natural substances like endorphins are now synthetically manufactured to simulate and produce mind-altering states and a variety of emotions.

We no longer consider the source of emotions to be confined to the amygdala. Although this region of the brain plays an important role, we now know that the body itself, with all of its receptor mechanisms, is the true "unconscious mind." Emotions constantly regulate what we experience as reality. Childhood experiences and what we learn in our early years influence our emotions on both a conscious and unconscious level. Each of us is unique, but the basic regulatory function is always the same. Take, for example, what happens when you see a shadowy figure when you are walking down a street alone at night. Unconsciously, you immediately appraise the event. Your appraisal will be influenced by past emotional memories (stored in the amygdala) and your rational thoughts, and you instantaneously take the appropriate action.

In short, emotions are not a dispensable luxury but rather are powerful forces rooted in the brain and are necessary to the mind and body. Emotional responses are quicker and in some ways purer than thoughts (cognitive responses). You need emotional integrity, which is the ability to trust your feelings so that they can be understood and appreciated. Emotions tell you about what you truly value, and they can focus your attention on the things that stimulate you. And, of course, emotions can motivate you. Emotions are your friend. We all need to learn how to recognize and experience adverse feelings and to tolerate and express them productively, rather than suppress them or express them in a destructive manner.

Emotional awareness means knowing how and when feelings are contributing to behavior, whether your own or that of others. It is closely related to emotional literacy, which means being able to label feelings with specific feeling words. At its highest level, emotional awareness means being able to predict feelings in advance. Initially described by Dr. Richard Lane, the six levels of emotional awareness are:

1. *Knowing that an emotion is present.* You become "aware" of the feeling when you first think about it or realize that you feel something at that moment. Example: You walk into a meeting. You are the only woman. Another person enters. At first you don't see him or her, but you hear a new noise. You turn and then you see the person and become aware of this individual in the room.

2. *Acknowledging your emotion.* To continue the example of the person in the meeting room: After you have become aware that there is someone in the room, you might acknowledge that person by nodding or saying hello. You may not know exactly what the feeling is, but if you notice and acknowledge that you have *some* feeling, you have taken the next step. Nature has given you a sophisticated guidance system in your feelings. Your negative feelings, for example, call your attention to things that are not healthy for you. They tell you when you are out of balance. If you feel lonely, for example, you need more connection with other people. The literature on emotional intelligence points out that

your feelings direct you to what is important to think about. Through thought, your feelings can point you to the causes of your negative feelings and to possible solutions. But if you fail to acknowledge your negative feelings, you won't be able to focus your attention on the problem that needs to be solved. For nature's inner guidance system to function, you must acknowledge your feelings. Many people try to stop themselves from feeling their negative emotions. They may use drugs or alcohol, entertainment or distraction. They may simply try to deny the existence of their negative feelings. Even education, memorization, or intellectual or religious pursuits can prevent you from acknowledging your feelings. All of this defeats nature's purpose in supplying you with negative feelings.

3. *Identifying and labeling the emotion.* Like anything else, the more you practice identifying emotions, the better you get at it. Each time you identify an emotion and assign a label to it, the brain's cognitive and emotional systems work together to remember the emotion, the label for the emotion, and the circumstances in which you encountered it. The simple act of naming a feeling helps you feel better for several reasons. First, people have a natural fear of the unknown. When you label your feeling, you move it from the unknown to the known, and thus you help make it less scary and more manageable. Second, when you label it, you begin to move it from the emotional center of your brain to the rational center. Finally, by beginning to think about your feeling, you are also taking the next step toward solving your problem. When your thoughts are clear, you feel more in control and empowered.

4. *Accepting your feelings.* Once you have felt, acknowledged, and identified your feelings, the next step in emotional awareness is to accept the feeling. Sometimes you might think that you shouldn't feel the way you do, but this is only because you've given in to restrictions imposed by others. One of the primary benefits of a highly developed emotional intelligence may be that it helps you become more independent from the opinions and beliefs of others. Instead, you can listen to your own inner voice, a voice that speaks to you through your individual emotions.

5. *Reflecting on your feelings.* Reflecting takes place at two different levels of emotional awareness. First, at a low level of emotional

awareness, you might reflect on your feelings only after the fact. You might lie awake at night, thinking about an event during the day and your feelings about that event. This might help you identify your feelings more quickly in the future. I believe, though, that when your emotional intelligence is highly developed, the process of feeling your feelings and identifying them takes place quickly enough for you to reflect on the feeling nearly instantaneously. The sooner you can accurately identify the feeling and reflect on it, the sooner you can take actions that are in your best interests.

6. *Forecasting your feelings.* If you are in tune with your emotions, you will be better able to predict how you might feel in future situations. You can improve this ability by weighing alternative courses of action and considering how each will make you feel. The value of this ability cannot be overstated. The ability to predict your emotional response will enable you to make the decisions that can lead to your long-term happiness.

Dr. Ronald Bergman developed a very useful model for consideration of what he calls "emotional fitness." In his book *Emotional Fitness Conditioning*, he explores why some people handle stress and challenges better than others do. Based on a review of the literature and on his clinical experience as a psychologist, he identified four universal core components of emotional fitness.

1. *Feelings identification and tolerance* refers, first, to the ability to label or identify your feelings specifically and accurately, and, second, to the ability to withstand and channel or express your emotions productively. Feelings identification and tolerance involves delayed gratification, patience, self-control, frustration tolerance, and impulse control.

2. *Empathy* is the ability to accurately identify and relate to the feeling state of another person with tolerance and understanding. To have empathy is to identify with the entire range of human feelings, including joy and satisfaction, as well as sorrow, fear, and insecurity.

3. *Insight,* in this context, means understanding the psychological and emotional forces that produce your thoughts, feelings, and behaviors. It means learning to connect your past to your present and

understanding the impact and legacy of your experience and heritage. Insight also includes the ability to look beneath the surface and recognize the underlying reasons for your behaviors and emotions.

4. *Assertiveness* begins with a reasonable view of legitimate rights and entitlements and using that to balance a confident and well-defined attitude, behavior, and pursuit of your goals.

Following is a self-assessment for the most crucial components of emotional fitness—feelings identification and tolerance. This assessment will help you better understand your current level of emotional fitness. Starting from whatever point you are at today, you can get better.

Self-Assessment:
Feelings Identification and Tolerance

Respond to each statement with either true or false.

1. I practice procrastination or avoidance too often. __
2. I often find myself reacting strongly to a given situation without really knowing why. __
3. I'm generally perceived as impatient or intolerant. __
4. I don't believe it's good to feel things too intensely. __
5. I like to be in control most of the time. __
6. Strong feelings usually make me uncomfortable. __
7. It's usually better for me to make decisions with my head and not with my heart. __
8. It's usually safer to keep my feelings in check and toned down. __
9. I've been known to have a problem with my temper. __

Four or more true answers indicate a need to work on feelings identification and tolerance. The higher the number of true answers, the greater the need to work on this.

You want to develop the ability to recognize, label, and understand the full range of your feelings without judgment or denial, and then to accept them and

(continued)

Self-Assessment: Feelings Identification and Tolerance (continued)

function in a healthy way. This is a core part of embracing your stressors for life in the BestStress Zone. Use the following short exercise to begin to come to terms with your emotions:

1. List all of the emotions and feelings that made you uncomfortable in the past week.
2. State how they have affected you.
3. Describe how you could and will channel that energy differently in the future.

Adapted with permission from Ronald Bergman and Anita Bell, Emotional Fitness Conditioning: An Action Plan for Lifelong Emotional Health *(New York: Penguin Press, 1998).*

Emotional Cachet

This questionnaire is for you if you work outside the home. Reflect on your experience in the workplace over the last six months. For each statement, choose the response that best reflects how accurately or how frequently the statement applies to you. Then add up your score.

1 = Least applicable
2 = Neutral
3 = Most applicable

1. I act like nothing bothers me, even when others at work make me mad or upset. __
2. I have to act the way people think a person in my job should act. __
3. I work hard to keep myself in a positive mood at work. __
4. At work, I have to appear to be concerned, even when I don't feel like it. __

(continued)

Emotional Cachet (continued)

. . . .

5. I want my boss, coworkers, and clients to think that I'm always calm and in control. __

6. I give my all at my job, and there's nothing left at the end of the day. __

7. My job requires constant helping or relating to people who need my expertise. __

8. My job requires me to make decisions that are in conflict with my personal values. __

9. My job and my family life often interfere with each other. __

10. I can't depend on my friends or family for emotional support when things get tough. __

Scoring

24–30: Your job places extraordinarily high demands on you emotionally and likely contributes to your NetStress Load. You need to reassess the root causes and make some changes as soon as feasible.

17–23: You have to put forth a moderate amount of effort emotionally in the workplace. It may be of value to examine specific sources that are draining you.

10–16: You are very fortunate. You are able to maintain emotional integrity in the workplace.

Keeping the following ideas in mind can help you avoid the falling into emotional traps.

- Feelings are neither right nor wrong. They are messages to be interpreted.
- Listening to feelings is like tapping into an added resource—your intuition.
- Intuition is as important as logic when making decisions, such as how and with whom you want to spend your time, your career path, or where you are going to live.
- Intuition warns you of trouble looming and of exciting opportunities.
- Observe your physical responses throughout your emotional journey on a daily basis.

Stress Trap 2: Problematic and Negative Thoughts

I was dating an old friend as an experiment. We decided to remain friends rather than take things further. While I know we will still be the best of friends, I initially felt a significant sense of loss. Since then I automatically have negative thoughts about every guy I meet, before I really get to know them. The search for a life partner remains one of my most stressful issues as a woman.

—Carlita, 34, administrative assistant

"I think too much about things. That's why I am so stressed." This is a common statement. Interestingly, thoughts can be a trigger and also part of the response in the stress process. Acute stress can result from your immediate perception of a situation, a demand, or a challenge, as well as your appraisal of whether it represents a threat to your well-being. Your instantaneous decision either triggers or aborts the stress response.

Self-awareness refers to a conscious awareness of your own thought processes. Neuroscience confirms that emotion and thought can best be considered separate but interacting systems. I believe the key to successfully integrating the thoughtful component of the mind and emotion relies on increasing the harmony between the two. There is an intricate two-way communication between thoughts or cognition and the emotional systems that is hardwired into the brain. (We discussed this in detail in the last chapter.) This goes a long way toward explaining the tremendous power of emotions, in contrast to that of thoughts alone. The path that links thoughts to stress has been described by four prominent psychologists, whose work has combined to form the field of cognitive therapy. The first three researchers, Drs. Albert Ellis, Aaron Beck, and David Burns, focus on the *presence* of maladaptive assumptions and beliefs as the cause of stress. The work of the fourth psychologist, Dr. Donald Mitchenbaum, focuses on the *absence* of maladaptive thoughts and actions as the cause of stress.

First came the work of Dr. Albert Ellis in the 1960s. Ellis was a psychoanalyst who became interested in *learning theory* and developed a rational approach to helping patients answer the question "Am I okay?" Ellis worked from the premise that human beings are uniquely rational, and that irrational or distorted logical thinking results in problems. In fact, from this perspective, irrational beliefs often trigger your knee-jerk reactions to demands and challenges. Think about it: have you ever encountered a situation that made you immediately assume the worst, yet the situation did not turn out to be as tragic as imagined?

Ellis believed that each of us has a set of underlying beliefs and assumptions that guides our lives. I call this your standard operating procedure. We all have stereotyped perceptions of certain situations that tend to make us absolute and dogmatic about our expectations and behavior in those situations. We can recognize in ourselves or in our interactions with others particular needs or demands, as opposed to preferences. Ellis suggested that there are core beliefs that lead to stress. These beliefs may be irrational, but they are ingrained in our society and form the basis for many thought processes that create stress in our lives. The irrational beliefs he identified that most of us hold are the following:

- It is essential that a person be loved or approved of by virtually everyone.
- A person must be perfectly competent to be considered worth-while.
- Some people are bad and deserve to be blamed or punished.
- Unhappiness is caused by outside circumstances, and a person has no control over feeling unhappy.
- It is a terrible catastrophe when things are not as a person wants them to be.
- It's easier to avoid certain difficulties and personal responsibilities than to face them.
- A person should be dependent on others and should have someone strong on whom he or she can rely.
- Past experiences and events determine present behavior.
- A person should be upset over other people's problems and disturbances.
- There is always a right or perfect solution to every problem, and it must be found at all costs.

The good news is that Ellis's findings became the basis for the form of cognitive or thought therapy called rational emotive therapy (RET). The framework for RET can be understood using the A-B-C-D-E model. We will explore this further in the chapter on living in the Best-Stress Zone, but for now here are the basics.

A: There is an *activating* experience event (something happens).

B: There is a *belief* about the event, which leads to.

C: There is a *consequence*, which may be emotional or behavioral.

D: To overcome irrational beliefs, one must *dispute, debate, discriminate,* and *define* automatic thoughts.

E: An individual can acquire a new *effect* or philosophy, which helps him or her think more rationally and constructively.

The second important researcher in this area was Dr. Aaron Beck, a physician, psychoanalyst, and behavioral therapist. Have you ever asked yourself whether you need a "reality check" when coping with a challenge or a demand? In the 1970s, Beck extensively studied and described what *reality check* really means. He based his work on the commonsense notion that what people think and say about themselves is relevant and determines their emotions and behavior. The defining feature of his work was the notion of *automatic thoughts*. He maintained that on a moment-by-moment basis, our thoughts and actions represent a continuous stream of self, revealed through speech and occurring outside of our immediate level of awareness. These thoughts are often rapid and automatic. More important, these thoughts tend to be self-evaluative and anticipatory in a negative way, rather than related to the specific momentary experience. This can get us in trouble. According to Beck, we tend to repeat our behaviors—to act consistently in similar situations. But our behavior may not be appropriate to a situation, because the automatic thoughts and actions are driven by so much more than that particular situation.

Automatic thoughts share two characteristics.

1. *Personalization.* Objective judgments tend to be replaced by subjective or egocentric views. We're apt to interpret events around

us as applying for a set period. For instance, you might assume that the frown on the face of a stranger is a direct reflection on some behavior of yours. Another form of personalization is the tendency to compare yourself to other people, usually in an irrational way that renders your evaluation of yourself inappropriate and unflattering.

2. *Polarization.* We often take extreme views of situations that impinge on sensitive areas in our lives. We interpret events as being all good or all bad, with no middle ground. Other errors in thinking that lead to polarization are *selection* and *abstraction.* We might focus on a detail out of context and miss the overall significance. Other common traps are *arbitrary inferences*, or jumping to conclusions with insufficient evidence, and *overgeneralization*—making an unjustified generalization based on a single incident.

Often our stress response can be triggered by the anticipation of a certain situation—a particular e-mail sender, a certain phone number that appears on our cell phone, or the goverment's announcement of the "Orange Alert" status. These are typical triggers of automatic thoughts. Automatic negative thoughts can fuel what Dr. Herbert Benson called the *negative stress cycle.*

Automatic negative thoughts are easy to identify. Listen carefully to yourself and see whether any of the following words crop up in your thoughts or conversations on a day-to-day basis; they often indicate automatic thoughts:

- Always
- Must
- Never
- Ought
- Should

More fully formed automatic thoughts might sound like this:

- Oh, no
- Why me?

- I can't stand this!
- I'm not good enough.
- Nothing will ever change.
- This always happens to me.
- I'll never get everything done.
- How could I be so stupid?
- I should have done better.

I'd like you to try to identify circumstances that trigger your specific automatic negative thoughts.

What Are Your Automatic Negative Thoughts?

Trigger	Automatic Negative Thought
You and your husband have a disagreement.	Nothing will ever change between us.
Your manager criticizes your work performance.	I'm so stupid; I'll never get promoted now. I'll be stuck in this dead-end job forever.
You're stuck in traffic and late for an important appointment.	Why does this always happen to me? I'm always running late and I'm unreliable.

More recently, Dr. David Burns, noted psychologist and author of the bestselling book *Feeling Good: The New Mood Therapy*, extended the work of Dr. Ellis. Burns described ten broad categories of *distortions* in our thinking that are listed here.

1. *Filtering.* You take the negative details and magnify them, while filtering out all positive aspects of a situation.
2. *Polarized thinking.* You see things as only black or white, bad or good. You are either perfect or you're a failure. There is no middle ground.
3. *Mind reading.* You think you know what people are feeling and why they act the way they do, even without their telling you. In particular, you are able to divine how people are feeling toward you.

4. *Catastrophizing*. You expect disaster. You notice or hear about a problem and imagine worst-case "what-if" scenarios.
5. *Control fallacies*. You see yourself as a helpless victim of fate and external circumstances. The fallacy of *internal control* has you responsible for the pain and happiness of everyone around you.
6. *Fallacy of fairness*. You feel resentful because you believe you know what is and isn't fair, but other people don't agree with you.
7. *Shields*. You have a list of ironclad rules about how you and other people should act. People who break the rules anger you, and you feel guilty if you violate the rules.
8. *Fallacy of change*. You expect that other people will change to suit you if you pressure or cajole them enough. You need to change people because your hopes for happiness seem to depend entirely on them.
9. *Being right*. You are constantly on trial to prove that your opinions and actions are correct. Being wrong is unthinkable, and you will go to any lengths to demonstrate your rightness. You don't listen well.
10. *Heaven's reward fallacy*. You expect all of your sacrifice and self-denial to pay off, as if someone were keeping score. You feel bitter when the reward doesn't come.

The fourth researcher I want to mention in the area of the mind-body connection as it relates to stress is Donald Mitchenbaum. Unlike Beck's and Ellis's, Mitchenbaum's background was nonmedical. He was a psychologist who developed a model to explain how verbal control can affect our interpretation of events. His work really was an extension of the work of child psychologist Dr. Alexander Luria, who in the 1960s described three stages of assistance to children with attention deficit disorder. In the first stage, a therapist or an adult uses verbal cues to direct a child's behavior. In the second stage, the child's own speech becomes a regulator of his or her behavior. Finally, the child's inner voice or speech becomes self-governing. Adults tend to follow the same sequence in learning a new behavior or skill. Mitchenbaum refers to this as our *internal dialogue* or *internal speech*. Later, when I discuss how to stay in the BestStress Zone, we will take a more detailed look at the key role of our internal dialogue. At this point I want you only to take a moment and try to identify what might be playing on that perpetual loop in your brain that creates stress.

One final thought component contributes to stress in our lives: cluttered thoughts. Despite the many organizing devices and reminder systems most of us have in place, from the simple refrigerator magnet to the latest handheld electronic device, most of us still keep too much in our heads. We use our minds unnecessarily as information clearing-houses. According to author Sally McGhee in her book *Take Back Your Life*, we all underestimate how much we use our minds as a collecting point. We specifically underestimate the negative impact of this effort on our daily focus and our ability to be "present." Think about it. You're at a meeting and suddenly remember something you need to do, so you immediately start to think about how you're going to accomplish the new task. Or you worry about things that have to get done that are out of your control, which in itself is not productive and can generate stress. Your conscious mind has a limited amount of space and can track only a certain amount of data at any time. Carrying lists of incomplete tasks in your mind can create enormous emotional, as well as physical, stress. When you run out of room in your conscious mind, things go to your unconscious mind, and, unfortunately, that part of your brain often gets active when you least need it to—like at two in the morning when you can't fall asleep!

Now you have the underlying basis for thinking about thinking! Let's summarize some skills you can learn to keep your own thoughts from getting in your way.

- *Mindfulness.* Mindfulness consists of paying attention to an experience from moment to moment—without drifting into thoughts of the past or concerns about the future or getting caught up in "thoughts" or opinions about what's going on.
- *Mindshifting* (cognitive restructuring). The goal of mindshifting is to change your feelings and actions by changing how you think! It's helpful to be aware of your automatic thoughts, which are usually negative and problematic thoughts. Replace distorted, emotionally damaging thoughts with accurate, emotionally healthy thoughts.

Mindshifting allows you to challenge thoughts that trigger or reinforce unhealthy states. The important steps in mindshifting are:

1. Identify a problem or a challenge (people, situations, issues, demands).
   - Is it associated with your 3Ps (purpose, passions, and priorities)?
   - Is the problem avoidable? Is it solvable?
2. Audit and record thoughts as you experience this challenge. Do they fall into either of these general categories?
   - Automatic negative thought: personalization or polarization
   - Problematic thought: rapid, automatic, self-evaluating, or anticipatory
3. Challenge the thought (define, debate, and dispute your assumptions and preconceived notions).
   - Is the thought true?
   - Did I jump to a conclusion?
   - What is the evidence?
   - Am I exacerbating a negative aspect of the situation?
   - Am I catastrophizing?
   - What is the worst-case scenario, and is it really that bad?
   - Is this hurting me?
   - Can this issue be thought about differently?
4. Make the shift.
   - Examine the thought.
   - Re-create it to make it less harmful.

Stress Trap 3: Control

I know I am stressed when my life is out of control! I have so many things to do, so many places to be. And I don't mind doing them and I don't feel guilty about them. The issue for me is control. I feel like at any moment, things could just fall apart. That's the feeling that affects my head and my stomach constantly.

—Farideh, 28, machinist

A wide variety of theorists have emphasized the importance of perceived personal control and have suggested that the desire to control the world around us is a fundamental characteristic of human beings. If that sounds like you, don't worry—you are okay. Most of us either consciously or unconsciously equate our stress level with the amount of control we believe we have over our own lives. We tend to believe that less control means greater stress, and vice versa. That actually may or may not be completely true, but the truth is you probably have more control than you think.

Consider the different types of potential control: behavioral, cognitive, decisional, and informational.

- *Behavioral control* means the opportunity to make choices about your behavior in various situations. For example, if you're stuck in traffic, you can choose to switch from an all-news station, with lots of stories about crime and war and natural disasters, to a station that plays calming music.
- *Cognitive control* refers to the freedom of interpretation. Some situations are stress triggers only because you've chosen to perceive them in a specific negative way, but a change in focus or perception can reduce the potential stress. Cognitive control also encompasses the level or the amount of *attention* you give to a potential stressor.
- *Decisional control* is the control you have to make choices within a framework of available options. For example, you can choose to take advantage of flextime scheduling to attend your child's regularly scheduled sporting events, or you can choose to stay in the comfort zone of regular, predictable work hours and remain stressed because of the missed opportunities with your child.
- Last, *informational control* refers to your ability to reduce the intensity of a stressor by learning more about it. We've all heard the expression "the fear of the unknown," and we all know someone who responds to stressful situations by learning everything possible about the stressor and thus removing the element of surprise. An example of this might be the research you do on the Internet about an upcoming outpatient procedure or the

phone calls you make to friends who have been through the procedure previously.

The concept of internal locus of control was developed originally by Dr. Julian Rotter in the 1950s and refers to the extent to which you believe you can control the events thataffect you. Individuals with a high *internal* locus of control believe that events result primarily from their own behavior and actions. Those with a high *external* locus of control believe that powerful others, fate, or chance primarily determine the outcome of events.

As you will see, being able to tap into this broader definition of *control* is crucial for living in the BestStress Zone. It allows you to maintain an internal locus of control in situations that might appear to be uncontrollable or unchangeable. This concept is made indelible in Reinhold Niebuhr's famous prayer, adopted by Alcoholics Anonymous: "God grant me the serenity to accept the things I cannot change, courage to change the things I can, and the wisdom to know the difference."

The following self-assessment is widely used in social sciences and health sciences to discern patterns of perceived control of the self and the environment. Take a moment to see how you're doing in this area.

Self-Assessment: Control

Read each statement and choose the appropriate response. Then add up your score.

1 = Strongly disagree
2 = Mildly disagree
3 = Neither disagree nor agree
4 = Mildly agree
5 = Strongly agree

(continued)

Self-Assessment: Control (continued)

1. I have very little control over what happens to me in the future.__
2. Sometimes I feel like I'm being pushed around in life. __
3. There is no way I can solve some of the problems that I have. __
4. There is little I can do to change the important things in my life. __
5. I often feel helpless in dealing with the problems of life. __
6. Murphy's Law seems to rule my life: "Anything that can go wrong will go wrong." __
7. I don't believe I can do anything I set my mind to. __

Scoring

26–35: You have a high external locus of control, meaning that you currently do not feel that you are in control of your life. This is likely to be a serious source of stress for you.

15–25: You have traits and beliefs that point to a mixture of having internal and external locus of control.

7–14: You have a high internal locus of control. Congratulations!

Stress Trap 4: Guilt

When it was clear to me that my daughter needed my time and emotional energy to the degree that it was clearly going to affect my career significantly, I felt stressed. My decision to change my role at work to accommodate her needs was viewed by some of my peers and supervisors as a career mistake. When my performance rating was lower than it had ever been, I felt it was because of the conscious decision I made to spend more time and energy on my family. I feel my choice was the best one, but sometimes I feel guilty about the mentor who helped me reach my position at work.

—Isabella, 32, senior associate at a law firm

Formally, we can define *guilt* as an emotional and cognitive experience caused by your perception that you have violated a personally relevant moral or social standard. Often, for women, guilt is a constant state of mind. Sometimes guilt is triggered by the simple conflict between what you *want* and what you think is *right*. You might feel regret over having done something that you feel you shouldn't have or, conversely, not having done something that you believe you should have. Feelings of guilt, which are driven by conscience, are not at all easy to shake.

Guilt often finds its way into explanations of the dynamics between normal and deviant personalities or behaviors. In principle, guilt can have both adaptive and maladaptive consequences. On the one hand, guilt experienced at moderate levels can serve a positive social function, by inhibiting abnormal behavior or, in the event of transgression, by stimulating the impulse to seek forgiveness and make amends. On the other hand, excessive or inappropriate guilt can result in dysfunctional and disruptive experiences and, in some cases, clinical psychological disorders. The phenomenon of guilt is relevant to a variety of everyday experiences, and, as a concept, it is important to statements regarding morality, personality, and adjustment.

Guilt has been described in research studies in three different ways:

1. The way you feel after violating a personal or societal moral standard
2. An enduring personality trait
3. Readiness to experience guilt based on one's values or upbringing

Studies show that most women tend to feel guilt more often than most men do. Women are more at risk for what is called "false guilt," which means taking responsibility for situations even when they are not to blame and when the circumstances are beyond their control. It has been said that women's guilt is often inappropriate, deenergizing, and even paralyzing. My female clients repeatedly describe themselves as feeling guilty, and I believe our society has virtually made an industry out of women's guilt, encouraging us to take personal inventories and find ways to improve ourselves or to seek more balance, as if we're all starting with the premise that our inventories are lacking, that we need improvement, or that our lives are by nature out of balance. It sometimes feels as if the goal is to make us take on an extra burden of guilt. The ways in which women are urged and prodded to better themselves plays right into our own natural inclination to tend, to provide care, and to fix what can be fixed, but this propensity for self-blame is very bad medicine. It can easily become a vicious cycle, in which the very effort to improve our situation actually highlights our feelings of guilt or frustration and thus only adds to our stress. And, of course, once women become mothers, we suffer from the mother of all guilt, blaming ourselves for everything that happens to our children. That "guilt gene" naturally gets passed on in an endless chain from mothers to daughters, almost as if it were a badge of honor—proof that we take the role of mothering seriously.

So, here is the real deal. Guilt often boils down to two factors. First is our interpretation of how other people perceive who we are or how we live our lives. Second, our gendered society has essentially institutionalized guilt in women. The important thing for you to remember is that you are okay! Don't let the self-improvement industry convince you that you have to start changing who you are. As you go through the BestStress Zone discovery process, you will explore how to rid yourself of debilitating and all-consuming guilt.

The following exercise will allow you to assess your current level of guilt in your day-to-day life.

Self-Assessment: Guilt

Read each statement and choose the appropriate response that reflects your current feelings about guilt in your life. Then add up your score.

1 = Strongly disagree
2 = Mildly disagree
3 = Neither disagree nor agree
4 = Mildly agree
5 = Strongly agree

1. If I could live my life over, I would do many things differently. __
2. Guilt and remorse have been a part of my life for as long as I can recall. __
3. I often have a strong sense of regret about issues related to communication with my parents, my partner, or my children. __

(continued)

Self-Assessment: Guilt (continued)
. . . .

4. I have recurring guilty feelings about a brief lapse in my behavior as it relates to my personal moral code. __

5. I feel a constant internal conflict between equally significant areas of my life. __

Scoring

19–25: Your level of guilt is extremely high. You need to examine the sources of your guilt and work toward solutions.

12–18: You have a moderate amount of guilt that likely contributes to the stress in your life.

5–11: Your level of guilt is very low and is unlikely to be a significant source of stress in your life.

If your assessment suggests that guilt may be contributing to your stress, you need to take action. Oftentimes it's simply a matter of being able to say no. Let this self-assessment guide and strengthen your ability to not merely say no without guilt, but to believe in that no. The other common source of extreme guilt is not being able to forgive yourself. You are solely accountable and responsible for your prior actions. However, it is likely that you did the best you could with the information you had at the time. Whatever the case, it's time to let it go. If you believe in a higher power, seek forgiveness, believe you have attained it, and move on. If you feel an obligation to demonstrate some level of service or gratitude for what you have labeled as transgressions, do so. Then move on.

Stress Trap 5: Generational Priorities in the Workplace

Stress for me is about coping with people. I am a great problem solver, and I actively enjoy running my business, making decisions, juggling a hectic schedule, multitasking, and so on. I am a type A personality, and for us type As, stress is about those things we cannot control or have little influence upon. In this category I would put the behavior

of members of my staff members who are from the Y generation.
They don't get it! The workplace has rules and they just don't get it!
—Janet, 64, entrepreneur in the entertainment industry

There are four specific groups that we can identify in the workplace.

1. *Traditional workers* (those born before 1946). They value loyalty and discipline, and they respect authority and hierarchy. These workers played key roles in their companies when economic development was strong.
2. *Baby boomers* (those born 1946–1960). They joined the work force in the mid-1960s through the 1970s. This generation of workers had access to more formal education than the previous generation, and expectations for their success and loyalty to their employers were high. Currently, the baby boomer generation occupies positions of the highest corporate responsibility and has the largest population of workaholics in history.
3. *Generation X* (those born 1961–1979). The children in Generation X often grew up in families where both parents worked, and while this may have led to a financially comfortable upbringing, many saw firsthand their parents struggle with job security as companies downsized to become more competitive. Generation Xers favor a more informal work environment and a more horizontal and flexible organizational structure as opposed to the hierarchal structure that traditional workers and baby boomers worked under.
4. *Generation Y* (those born in 1980 and later). Generation Yers have the distinction of having lived their entire lives in a technology-driven world. Like members of Generation X, they had mostly comfortable childhoods, but job security and layoff fears touched their families, too. They are more individualistic than the previous generations and demand autonomy in their opinions and behavior. There's also more of an emphasis on meaningful work and personal satisfaction among Generation Yers.

Business environments require teamwork, but I often hear "laptop-ers" and seasoned leaders comment that their teams "just don't understand." This was highlighted in a study called "Generation of Differences in the Workforce." It presents insights into our practices that we can use to prevent a major potential stress trap. In the study, women and men in successive generations were asked the same questions regarding their attitudes toward work and lifestyle. In 1977, the generation polled was the group we now label traditional workers (who are now over age sixty-three); in 1992, it was the baby boomers (who are now forty-nine to sixty-three); in 1999, it was the Generation Xers (who are now thirty to forty-eight); and in 2002, it was the Generation Yers (who are now younger than twenty-nine).

Here are some results from the most recent study in 2002. It's not surprising that a "work-centric lifestyle" (placing a higher priority on work than on family) was noted by 54 percent of traditional workers, 22 percent of baby boomers, and only 12 percent of Generation Xers and Yers. "Family-centric" lifestyle prioritization was noted by 50 percent of Generation Yers, 52 percent of Generation Xers, and 41 percent of baby boomers. The study also found that fewer women wanted jobs with more responsibility than women did in 1992 (57 percent vs. 36 percent). Promotable employees were found to be less ambitious, largely because of the negative effect of their jobs on their family lives.

Understanding the potential issues of conflict and the mind-sets of diverse generational groups can minimize the trap of generational differences in the workplace by using these tips to shape dialogue, policy, and practice.

- Recognize that each individual prioritizes work and family in his or her own way, and that no one way is inherently right or wrong.
- Allow a team of workers of various age groups and at different levels in the organization to establish a statement of the organization's values and how those values can be used to measure performance.
- Provide opportunities for workers of various age groups and at different levels in the organization to interact in social settings. There is much to be shared among generations that goes beyond on-the-job knowledge. Formal and informal mentoring programs can be very effective.

- Understand that humility is a virtue. Before you judge the actions or words of a member of another generation, ask yourself, "What if this were my mom/cousin/daughter?"

Stress Trap 6: Role versus Identity

Stress is trying to balance being a working woman, wife, and mother. Stress in having to "play the game" at work and not lose sight of who I am or my values. Stress in being there for my family when they need. Stress in taking care of myself and not feeling selfish for doing so.
—Chris, 27, human resources director

In and of itself, the effort to achieve more balance can trigger the stress response. The contemporary reality is that most corporate structures, cultures, and practices continue to be designed as if "face time" represents the highest level of commitment. Do not fall into the trap of thinking that a comfortable integration of your work and personal life is a luxury. As organizations restructure fundamental practices and processes beyond the Band-Aid remedies of flextime and parental leaves, you must reexamine your personal practices, roles, and contributions.

I want to emphasize the importance of differentiating your *roles* from your *identity*. A role is usually defined by the tasks that we perform as a part of an organization, a system, or a team. As women, we often pride ourselves on simultaneously wearing multiple hats, reflecting our level of engagement in work, family, community, or spiritual teams.

In most instances, my clients have the knowledge and the skills to fulfill many different roles across the various dimensions of life, from their roles as corporate executive vice president to organizer of the carpool. Triggers can and will occur, but a lack of clarity around your evolving identity often creates the most harmful stress traps. What is most important is your identity—defined as the essential values and qualities that give you pleasure and provide meaning in your life. It is through a clear connection with your 3Ps that you are able to derive meaning from your daily activities by shifting and maintaining your fundamental identity. For example, work does not have to be a role that generates stress if you don't let it detract from your identity as a nurturing parent, or vice versa.

Here are two ways to avoid the trap of the perceived conflict between your role and your identity.

1. List your roles and identities at work and at home to clarify your commitments.
2. Assemble teams at work and home. Evaluate roles and responsibilities, including a list of expected actions.

Resilience

Finally, I want you to think about whether you are resilient. Many studies cite resilience as a necessary component of the successful adaptation to stress. We often talk about resilience, but you may not be clear about its true meaning. Resilience is akin to being hardy. You can comprehend the attitudes and skills of a hardy personality by thinking of the three Cs.

1. *Commitment.* Your chosen life activities are those that you engage in with full attention, imagination, and effort.
2. *Control.* Resilient people have an attitude and a belief that personal efforts can influence outcomes. You positively influence the outcomes of the changes going on around you. You determine which aspects of a situation are open to change and gracefully accept those outside of your control.
3. *Challenge.* Resilient individuals accept change as normal and acceptable in life and as an opportunity for personal development. When faced with demands, you first try to understand them, then to solve problems as you learn from them. Being open to change allows you to approach life with openness and optimism.

Self-Assessment: Resilience

Read each statement and choose the appropriate response.

0 = Strongly disagree
1 = Mildly disagree

(continued)

Self-Assessment: Resilience (continued)

. . . .

2 = Mildly agree

3 = Strongly agree

1. Trying my best at work makes a difference. __
2. Trusting to fate is sometimes all I can do in a relationship. __
3. I often wake up eager to start on a day's projects. __
4. Thinking of myself as a free person leads to great frustration and difficulty. __
5. I would sacrifice financial security in my work for a really challenging job opportunity. __
6. It bothers me when I have to deviate from the routine or schedule I've set for myself. __
7. An average person can have an impact on politics. __
8. Without the right breaks, it is hard to be successful in my field. __
9. I know why I'm doing what I'm doing at work or school. __
10. Getting close to people puts me at risk of being obligated to them. __
11. Encountering new situations is an important priority in my life. __
12. I really don't mind when I have nothing to do. __

Calculate your scores according to the following formula:

Control score (add the scores together that you assigned to statements 1 and 7, then add the scores together that you assigned to statements 2 and 8, and, finally, subtract the second score from the first score)

Commitment score (add the scores together that you assigned to statements 3 and 9, then add the scores together that you assigned to statements 4 and 10, and, finally, subtract the second score from the first score)

Challenge score (add the scores together that you assigned to statements 5 and 11, then add the scores together that you assigned to statements 6 and 12, and, finally, subtract the second score from the first score)

Total hardiness score (control + commitment + challenge) = __

Clinical psychologist Susan Kobasa, from the City University of New York, has suggested that the following holds true:

- A score of 10 to 18 represents a person who has a high hardiness
- A score of 0 to 9 represents moderate hardiness
- A score below 0 is low hardiness

Last Words

In this chapter, I've tried to give you some ways to explore and understand what may get in the way of your ability to handle stress in your life, and I've identified common traps you are likely to encounter. You are now armed with knowledge of what your stressors are and how they affect you. You also have insight into your current level of resilience. You are ready for part II of this book: discovering your BestStress Zone.

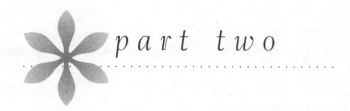

part two

optimal stress: living in your beststress zone

discovering your best-stress zone and achieving the beststress balance

N ow, let's take everything you've learned about yourself in the first part of the book and make it the foundation of a new and better way to manage stress in your life. The Best-Stress Zone is a dynamic framework for preventive stress maintenance that is anchored in your purpose, passions, and priorities. It is a state of mind. The BestStress Zone is like a virtual space and state of mind where you can organize and shape your world. It can make you resilient and able to respond in a healthy way to the inevitable challenges and demands in your life. Discovery of your *personal* zone arises out of a deep understanding of how the stress process works for you. You will learn how to analyze and address situations and challenges and transform them into opportunities for strengthening your resilience, hardiness, satisfaction, health, spirituality, stamina, and performance. You will be in a position to solve problems creatively and maybe even head them off before they become problems. In your BestStress Zone, you can be mindful of your beliefs, attitudes, and feelings, and also the day-to-day behaviors that undermine your well-being and productivity. It will require courage and self-knowledge, plus the ability to give and get from others the social support and encouragement you need to advance your relationships at work, at home, and in your community. With luck and determination, at the end of this process you will understand the importance of embracing the stresses associated with what is really important to you—in other words, your optimal stress. You will also have a strategy to transform stressful situations into opportunities to learn and renew yourself.

In this chapter, I'll take you through a series of steps to help you discover your BestStress Zone, beginning with a review of the stress law. Next, we will briefly revisit the stress process, because your BestStress Zone is created out of a personal analysis of each element of the stress process. Finally, you will learn how to embrace specific stresses within the boundaries of your personal BestStress Zone.

In earlier chapters, I explained how stress hormones and other components of the stress response are necessary for happiness, performance, creativity, and other peak experiences. Remember the stress law, which holds that we must experience some amount of stress in order to achieve our maximum potential. The body and the mind are equipped to shift into a heightened state of readiness when faced with a challenge or danger. But beyond a certain level, the stress hormones become counterproductive, negatively affecting performance and concentration, triggering anxiety, and potentially leading to the development of medical conditions such as diabetes, coronary heart disease, hypertension, obesity, and depression. When you have maximized the effects of good stress and reached that "tipping point," you must be able to avoid or eliminate what has now become bad stress. This principle was researched and described in 1908 by psychologists Robert M. Yerkes and J. D. Dodson. (See the illustration on page 183.)

What if you could live a balanced life, in which you performed at an optimal level while remaining immune to the toxic effects of the workplace and free of the potential traps of guilt and control? What if your blood pressure could stay normal or become normal and the added risk of developing heart disease due to stress was eliminated in your life? What if you could live a full and complex life, embracing the stress that provides you with forward momentum, yet knowing how

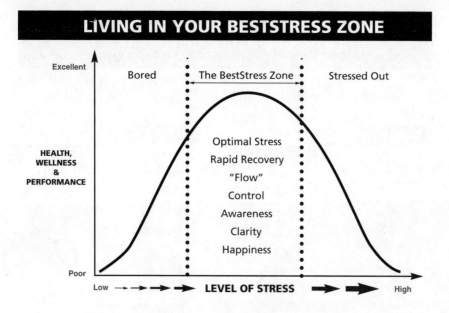

LIVING IN YOUR BESTSTRESS ZONE

Excellent

Bored   The BestStress Zone   Stressed Out

Optimal Stress

**HEALTH,
WELLNESS
&
PERFORMANCE**

Rapid Recovery

"Flow"

Control

Awareness

Clarity

Happiness

Poor

Low ➞ ➞ ➞ ➡   **LEVEL OF STRESS**   ➡   ➡   High

to recognize when your stress starts working against you. This is what living in the BestStress Zone is all about.

Step 1: Understand the BestStress Process

The first step toward discovering and living in your BestStress Zone is to understand stress as a process (see the illustration on page 184). The stress response occurs when there is a triggering situation, demand, or challenge. Your perception or interpretation of the triggering event sets into motion a series of responses. Your perception is unconsciously and consciously influenced by your 3Ps. There are four levels, or types, of responses in the BestStress Process: emotional, thoughts, biological, and behavioral. Factors such as genetics, personality traits, and buffers can modify and even mitigate these responses. Living with optimal stress in the BestStress Zone is about learning how to deal on a day-to-day basis with the inevitable stressors in your life.

Viewing stress as a process is the key to managing stress effectively in the BestStress Zone. In this chapter, we are going to consider each

THE BESTSTRESS PROCESS

The Ultimate Mind-Body Connection

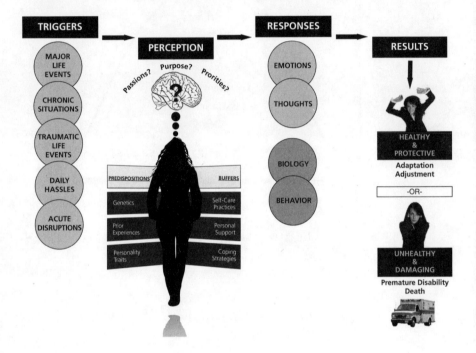

step of this process very carefully. By the end, you will have the knowledge and skills to establish your own personal BestStress Zone. Let's get started!

Using the BestStress Process

This exercise will help you appreciate that you have many options for managing stress when you view stress as a process. You will learn that even though stress is inevitable, it doesn't "just happen."

(continued)

Using the BestStress Process (continued)

. . . .

Do the following:

1. List up to three specific stressors that you are currently dealing with (they can be traumatic life events, everyday hassles, or chronic problems).
2. Choose at least two of the following approaches that you believe will lead to less stress:

Reduce or eliminate a trigger

Change your perception

Modify your response

Try a new coping strategy

Step 2: Consider the Stressors and Triggers in Your Life

For the next step in discovering your BestStress Zone, consider the stimuli or the causes of the stress. Without a trigger, there is no activation and no stress response. You know that a stimulus or a trigger may be internal or externally generated. Examples of externally generated stimuli include the threat of a terrorist attack, your car breaking down, caring for an aging parent and your children, and hitting a traffic jam. Internal stimuli include experiencing a crisis of confidence at work, indecisiveness about the stability of a personal relationship, or an illness. Stress triggers can range from the very physical, such as a lack of air supply during an asthma attack, to purely psychological or emotional, like a sudden fear response to a shadowy figure when you're walking alone down a city street late at night, or the sudden realization that you forgot to buy a key ingredient for a recipe.

Triggers can be acute or chronic. The American Psychological Association defines an acute stressful trigger as one that has an affect or a response of less than four weeks. Chronic stress triggers—for which the affect is longer than four weeks—include ongoing interpersonal conflicts, work overload, constant arguing with a teenage child, caretaking responsibilities for elderly parents, self-care for a chronic illness, a lack of help around the house, a difficult boss, or financial worries. As you prepare your list of triggers, you are likely to find that many of them are actually composites: daily hassles (acute stressors) that are connected in some way to deeper ongoing issues (chronic stressors).

Think about this concept as it relates to the types of problems that most Americans seek professional psychological help for. It turns out that people most commonly cite relationship issues as the primary reason for seeking therapeutic help. In more specific terms, unresolved interpersonal conflict appears to hold the greatest stress potential.

Living in the BestStress Zone requires that you recognize and accept the stressors that bring you closer to your 3Ps. Your goal is to eliminate, or at least minimize, the stressors that move you in the wrong direction away from your 3Ps. In this section you will list up to three triggers in your life that are in some way associated with your purpose, passions, and priorities. Include at least one recent stressor that was acute and those that are constant or chronic. Be sure to consider all of the domains of your life (work, family, self-care, friendship, spirituality, love/romance, and leisure/play) that are affected by your 3Ps. It may be helpful to refer to chapter 4. If you initially have difficulty labeling a stressor, look inside yourself for your personal body-mind signals of the stress response: sleeplessness, irritability, headaches, upset stomach, constipation or diarrhea, backaches, sadness or depression, high blood pressure, lack of appetite or binge eating, increased use of alcohol or cigarettes, or other dangerous behaviors.

Think carefully about how each trigger is related to your 3Ps. Ask any three individuals what their 3Ps for the next year include, and you'll get three very different answers. Caren may want to focus on creating a stable and nurturing environment for her newborn infant and toddler. Kayla may have more pragmatic professional priorities, such as achieving partnership in her professional service organization. Jenna's primary goals may be providing a safe care environment for her recently widowed mother and launching her own entrepreneurial IT company. Each of these three women has potential and real challenges/ triggers. What are yours? Use the following exercise to determine at least one trigger for two of the seven major domains in your life: work, family, self-care, friendship, spirituality, love/romance, and leisure/play. This exercise may be difficult at first, but be persistent. You are investing in yourself.

Determining Your Stress Triggers

1. Choose the two domains for which you will explore a specific trigger: work, family, self-care, friendship, spirituality, love/romance, leisure/play.

2. Describe in detail the demand/challenge (stressor) and isolate a specific event, situation, or factor (trigger) that caused you to feel stressed for each of the two domains.

3. For each trigger, specifically address each of the following points (examples given in parentheses).

- Context—describe the situation in general terms (e.g., getting up and out of the house in the mornings).
- What was the actual trigger that activated the entire stress process (e.g., your daughter initiated an argument)?
- How is this stressor related to your ultimate 3Ps (e.g., nurturing a cohesive family)?
- How did you feel, both physically and emotionally (e.g., tired, frustrated)?
- What did you think about at the time you recognized that the trigger was being pulled and activation of the stress process had begun (e.g., you resented your daughter's lack of appreciation of your love and commitment to her)?
- What were your behavioral responses (e.g., you yelled and left the room)?
- What did you do to cope or feel better (e.g., nothing, developed a headache)?

Step 3: Clarify Your Perception of Stressors and Triggers

Remember that your personal appraisal or *perception* of the challenge determines the potential magnitude of the stress response. Traditionally, the common understanding of perception involves your senses gathering information from the environment, and the information then flows to the higher centers of your brain, where you process and analyze the information and initiate your responses to it.

I want you to consider an alternative way of thinking about your perception in the BestStress Zone. It requires that you have an ongoing conscious awareness of what author Deepak Chopra describes as your *being*. Chopra says that the mechanism of manifestation, or creating the change we want in our lives, is attention and awareness. Your perception, attention, and conscious thought processes enable you not only to acknowledge the situations, events, and relationships that are potentially harmful or negative but also to work toward the positive things you want and need. Intentional focus and a capacity for acceptance create what Chopra calls the "thinking body." This powerful connection between the mind and the body must be a part of your personal BestStress Zone. I believe that knowing and embracing your stressors is a way to give attention to the demands and challenges that serve your life's purpose and will enhance your *being*.

Consider the stressors and the triggers you listed in the previous step in light of this insight. At the moment you perceived an acutely stressful situation or trigger, your mind instantaneously and unconsciously tapped into your emotional memory bank (the amygdala) to recall similar episodes. That automatic input, combined with your conscious mind, created a perception, which in turn influenced your next step. Your mind assessed whether you had the immediate resources or capacity (speed, competence, skill, energy, tolerance, and so on) to deal with the stressor. At this stage, you know that in the BestStress Zone, your 3Ps should guide your perception. What are the current 3Ps that may influence your perception of the stressors in your life?

Assessing Your Perception: Your Current Purpose,
Passions, and Priorities

. . . .

Complete the following statements.

1. I know that my personal BestStress Zone is a very special place, which is dynamic and should be reassessed periodically. Currently, and for the next six months, my top three priorities are: __
2. My purpose, which will be driving my focus and efforts and will provide meaning for my day-to-day activities, can best be described as: __
3. The passion and energy that I bring to these endeavors can best be described as my love for: __

Step 4: Sort and Categorize Your Stressors and Triggers

Often clients describe some of their most troubling and stressful situations as making them feel out of control. Research confirms that the less control or predictability we feel in connection with a potential stressor, the more likely it is to trigger the stress response, so, next, let's take the triggers you identified in step 1 and categorize them based on these factors.

Predictability, actual control, and your belief systems about your ability and need for control are key characteristics that determine whether a trigger leads to a harmful stress response. It makes sense that a predictable stressor will trigger less of a stress response than will something random and unpredictable. First, you can prepare for predictable stressors or make the effort to avoid them altogether. For example, you might bypass a traffic jam by getting up five minutes earlier and listening to a radio traffic report. Or, if you know a confrontation is coming with someone at work, you can anticipate the other person's arguments and responses and actually prepare what you want to say or try to prevent the confrontation from occurring. Second, predictable triggers arouse your biological systems less than unpredictable triggers do. A disapproving glare from your mother-in-law may have seemed much more shocking and serious during the first year of your marriage than in the seventh year.

Living in the BestStress Zone enables you to have predetermined responses and strategies for predictable triggers.

Now let's look at the stress triggers you listed in the Determining Your Stress Triggers exercise in step 2, with an eye toward assessing the level of control and predictability inherent in each trigger.

Making that determination of controllability may not always be easy, but it will help you remain clear in your own mind about what you really believe to be controllable about any situation. So, for instance, people who suffer from depression often feel helpless in their own lives, meaning that they perceive a very low level of personal control. On the other hand, aggressive men tend to believe that virtually all situations in their environment and even most people are controllable, making these men somewhat less prone to depression. A realistic understanding of your level of control in any given situation is essential to minimizing potential stress triggers. It also helps you to keep from trying to exert control where none is actually possible will frustrate and exhaust you and will actually contribute to an even stronger stress response. Think about the marriage therapists who listen to repeated reports of complete failure from people who are constantly trying to remake their spouses into the people they believed or wished they had married.

The final key component of control is the ability to distinguish between independent, external triggers and those that we generate ourselves—or exaggerate—in our own minds. An external trigger might be a neighbor who drives you crazy with loud music every Friday night. You know, stuff happens. Expensive equipment breaks down and usually at the worst moment. Nasty viruses will find their way into your computer. Companies go under, jobs are lost, and people in your life will die. You can only control what you can control, and your health depends, in part, on knowing that.

Following is an exercise that will help you define and categorize your stress triggers.

By sorting your stressors into those four groups, you've formed part of the foundation for your BestStress Zone. Here are some guidelines for taking further action regarding the stressors in each group.

Sorting Out Your Stress Triggers

. . . .

Sort the stressors you identified in step 2 ("Consider the Stressors and Triggers in Your Life") into the appropriate categories. Determine whether each stressor is related to something important in your life, meaning that it potentially stands in the way of your living according to your 3Ps, and whether the stressor is controllable, perhaps like quitting smoking, or not, such as a natural disaster.

Category A: Related to the 3Ps and controllable (e.g., an argument with your partner, problems with your boss, difficulty in meeting job deadlines, quitting smoking)

Category B: Related to the 3Ps and uncontrollable (e.g., the death of a loved one, losing your job, a serious illness, a natural disaster

Category C: Not related to the 3Ps and controllable (e.g., unnecessary meetings at work, irritating phone calls, errands, chores)

Category D: Not related to the 3Ps and uncontrollable (e.g., someone spilling food on your clothes, neighbors' opinions, bad weather, traffic jams)

Category A: Related to the 3Ps and Controllable

The parts of your life that you determine are controllable (meeting job deadlines, sticking with a self-care plan, quitting smoking) are important to identify because the simple act of taking action on these issues will reduce the stress associated with them. Because these are a part of your 3Ps that you can control, you often know exactly what to do to alleviate these stressors. Remember to consider the definitions of what's controllable in the previous exercise. Many triggers in your life are indeed controllable with some deliberate consideration. The best way to deal with these issues is to take action. Just do it!

Here are some additional ideas to consider as you build your Best-Stress Zone regarding these stressors.

- Learn how to say no. Know your limits and stick to them. Whether in your personal or your professional life, refuse to accept added responsibilities when you're already functioning near full capacity. You may need to negotiate or delegate, but even in times when you are required to do more with less, you must be firm about setting limits. Don't take on more than you can handle for extended periods of time. Keep in mind that when you do something once that stretches you and you are successful, you are a hero. Do it twice and it becomes an expectation. You may need to think about resetting people's expectations of you in all dimensions of your life.

- Avoid people who stress you out. If someone in your life consistently triggers a stress response and you can't turn the relationship around, limit the amount of time you spend with that person or end the relationship entirely.
- Take control of your environment. If the evening news makes you anxious, turn off the TV. If traffic's got you tense, take a longer but less-traveled route. If going to the market is an unpleasant chore, do your grocery shopping online.
- Avoid hot-button topics. If you get upset over religion or politics, cross them off your conversation list. If you repeatedly argue about the same subject with the same people, stop bringing it up or excuse yourself when it's the topic of discussion.
- Pare down your to-do list. Analyze your schedule, responsibilities, and daily tasks. If you've got too much on your plate, distinguish between the "shoulds" and the "musts." Drop tasks to the bottom of the list if they aren't truly necessary or eliminate them entirely.

Category B: Related to the 3Ps and Uncontrollable

These stressors are the most troubling and the most likely to generate a harmful response, ranging from frustration to hopelessness, from anxiety to insomnia. No matter what you do, you can't cure a disease in your loved one, stop your company from merging with another one, change someone's difficult personality, or bring a family member back from the dead. Hurricanes will come whether we want them to or not, and painful memories never go away.

Though you may not be able to change the entire situation, you do have some ability to control your thoughts and reactions to it. You can use mindshifting skills to reduce your anxiety about problems. Step back and reconsider the situation objectively. If you can identify *any* aspect of the situation that you might be able to do something about but haven't tried, then it doesn't qualify as uncontrollable. For example, you can't control the cutback in your hours and how it will affect your finances, but you can sit down and create or re-create a realistic budget that takes into account your new realities.

Here are some additional ideas to consider as you build your Best-Stress Zone regarding these stressors.

- If you can't change the situation/stressor, change yourself or your response. You can adapt to these situations and regain your sense of control by changing your expectations and attitude.
- Even when a stressor may appear to be uncontrollable and unavoidable, there may be some elements of it that you can alter or control in some way. Figure out what you can do to change things so that the problem is avoided in the future. Often, this involves changing the way you communicate and operate in your daily life.
- Express your feelings instead of bottling them up. If something or someone is bothering you, communicate your concerns in an open and respectful way. If you don't voice your feelings, resentment will build, making the situation seem like it's getting worse, even as it remains basically unchanged.
- Be willing to compromise. When you ask someone to change his or her behavior, be willing to do the same. If you both are willing to bend at least a little, you'll have a good chance of finding a happy middle ground.
- Manage your time better. Poor time management can cause a lot of stress. When you're stretched too thin and running behind, it's hard to stay calm and focused. But if you plan ahead, you can avoid these stress-inducing pitfalls.
- Reframe problems. Try to view stressful situations from a more positive perspective. Rather than fuming about a traffic jam, look at it as an opportunity to pause and regroup, listen to your favorite radio station, or enjoy some alone time.
- Look at the big picture. Get some perspective on the stressful situation. Ask yourself how important it will be in the long run.

Will it matter in a month? A year? Is it really worth getting upset over? If the answer is no, focus your time and energy elsewhere. Moreover, when you look at a problem in the context of the rest of your life, perhaps you'll be able to see how it stacks up against other ongoing stressors. Sometimes you can see other areas to reduce the stress in your life, thus making more room to accommodate the unchangeable stressors.

- Adjust your standards. Perfectionism is a major source of avoidable stress for stressors in this category. In fact, adjusting your attitude might enable you to convert an uncontrollable stressor into a controllable one. Stop setting yourself up for failure by demanding perfection. Set reasonable standards for yourself and others, and learn to be okay with "good enough."

Category C: Not Related to the 3Ps and Controllable

You may also want to not immediately deal with stressors that are unimportant (not related to the 3Ps) and controllable. If it is fun or empowering for you, however, go ahead and address them. It can be especially useful to handle a small but controllable problem on a day when you're facing a larger one. Besides being good practice, it can boost your confidence about problem solving and prepare you to tackle the bigger problem.

As you build your BestStress Zone, here are some additional ideas to consider regarding category C stressors.

- Develop a contingency plan or a triage plan. Even when a trigger is expected, its timing may be unpredictable. You might know all of the right moves for dealing with a particular crisis, but it can create anxiety, anyway, if it occurs in conjunction with another crisis, if other people who are involved are reacting as if it's an emergency, or if for some reason you aren't as well prepared as you expected to be.
- Focus on the positive. When stress gets you down, take a moment to reflect on all of the things you appreciate in your life, including your own positive qualities and gifts. This simple strategy can help you keep things in perspective.

- Be optimistic and exercise your ability to be assertive when necessary. Don't take a backseat in your own life. Deal with problems head-on, doing your best to anticipate and prevent them. If you've got a strict deadline for a project and a friend stops by to talk, focus on what the project means to you, trust your friendship to survive, and limit the amount of time you have to talk.

Category D: Not Related to the 3Ps and Uncontrollable

If the problem truly is uncontrollable and not related to your 3Ps, then you can label it as unimportant. This can be liberating, because then the best solution is to let it go. It may have surprised you to find, after careful consideration, that one of the stressors you identified in step 2 really belongs in this group. Everybody, no matter how privileged and perfect his or her life seems to be, has to deal with little daily hassles. That's just the way life is, and if you try to change that fact or pretend that life should somehow be different, I can guarantee that you'll only end up creating more stress for yourself. Starting now, give yourself permission to let go of these concerns.

On the other hand, if you really can't let go of one of these stressors, then it should be moved to your list of important stressors. It is probably related to your 3Ps. Sometimes a problem that may appear trivial can represent something much more profound. As you build your BestStress Zone, here are some additional ideas to consider regarding these stressors when you have clarified that they are truly category D stressors.

- Accept these hassles for what they are. Acceptance may be difficult, but in the long run it's easier than coping with the harmful effects of chronically released stress hormones. Consider that often these issues are painful not because of the actual facts of the situation, but because the situation somehow didn't conform to your idealized notions of how it should be. If a relationship was bad for you, it almost certainly wasn't the right one, no matter what you kept telling yourself.
- Look for the upside. As the saying goes, "What doesn't kill us makes us stronger." These stressors can often provide you with an opportunity for personal growth. If your own poor choices

contributed to a stressful situation, reflect on them and learn from your mistakes.

- Share your feelings. Talk to a trusted friend, a coach, or a medical professional. In difficult times, the simple act of expressing your feelings can be very cathartic, even if there's nothing you can do to alter the stressful situation.
- Learn to forgive. Accept the fact that we live in an imperfect world and that people make mistakes. Let go of anger and resentments. Free yourself from negative energy by forgiving yourself and others and moving on.

Step 5: Determine Your Coping Style

In this next step in the discovery of your BestStress Zone, I'd like you to evaluate your current method of coping. It is likely to combine some elements of the various strategies described in the following passages. Coping styles vary. Recall that stress is the result of an appraisal process. Your brain identifies a situation as threatening, and if your response capacities are insufficient, this sets off the stress response. Once you are aware of an undesirable biological change or a thought or negative emotion that makes you uncomfortable, the coping process begins. Coping strategies generally fall into one of two categories.

Problem-focused coping is about aiming toward an effective and lasting resolution to a situation that maximizes positive gains and minimizes negative effects. It involves behaviors that help you take charge of changing the environment or develop an action plan that leads to a solution. *Emotion-focused coping* embraces your efforts to process the feelings and the emotions associated with a threat or a challenge. Remember that the actual demand of a challenge may have little to do with the anger, anxiety, or fear you attach to it. Your *perception* of the situation determines how you need to cope. Your coping is effective if you feel calm and capable when anticipating predictable stressful events. Effective coping also allows you to relax before and during stressful situations. Finally, effective coping helps to counteract irrational negative thoughts and behaviors when you find yourself in a stressful situation.

Emotion-focused coping focuses not on specific factual events or direct action but rather on processing the feelings and the reactions associated with a stressor. In general, this strategy is most effective when the trigger is unpredictable or leaves you with little or no control. Emotion-focused coping can be positive or negative. Proactive reappraisal (rethinking a situation), relaxation, or seeking a forum to express your emotions are positive emotion-focused coping strategies. Common negative emotion-focused coping strategies include rumination, self-blame, and wishful thinking. Many women find that simply talking with a friend helps a great deal, unless the friend provides a lower level of support than needed or there isn't a strong-enough bond of intimacy with that friend. In a worst-case scenario, that might only serve to worsen the negative effect of a lack of control, further increasing the risks.

Here are some women's comments about their coping, which can be considered emotion-focused coping responses.

- "Laugh, shrug it off."
- "I have recognized that there are times when you have to leave the stress behind to recharge your batteries, so after the last series of events I took a two-and-a-half-week vacation, something I had not done in some time, and I did my best to leave my work behind."
- "I cope by staying busy; probably a temporary fix. I listen to music, watch television, and initiate projects (garden, home renovation, and so on)."
- "At work I use humor. I joke about everything! At home I'm less flexible, much more demanding of my family. I often will cut my coworkers a lot more slack than I do my immediate family."
- "Exercise seems to help relieve stress. Talking to friends not associated with work helps because it gives me a better perspective about things. Getting away on a vacation out of the country where I can't have access to voice mail or e-mail also helps."
- "I tried occasional meditation but usually didn't take time, same with exercise. Tried deep breathing, taking a break, and so on."
- "I talked to family and a friend; sometimes cried. I wish I could deal with high stress with a calmer attitude and fewer strong physical feelings."
- "I take vacation time to deal with 'home front' issues."

Problem-focused coping directly addresses the stressful situation itself, by designing a clear and specific set of steps aimed at reducing the affect of the stressor. It might mean removing yourself from a stressful environment—such as changing jobs, for example—or altering the circumstances within your environment, perhaps relocating your work space, investigating transportation alternatives, hiring domestic help, or rearranging some component of your daily schedule. Problem-focused coping strategies (planning actions, personal growth, self-adaptation, engaging in positive thinking) have been found to decrease emotional distress and reduce the risk of depression. Most important, don't be intimidated by the concept of problem-focused strategies.

Here are some women's comments about dealing with stress using problem-focused coping strategies.

- "Thinking about the situation, analyzing it. Being prepared for the next time a similar situation occurs."
- "While I continue to work on being more skilled at the political aspects of the job, I resent that this is so important."
- "On the issue with my daughter, I had to drop everything at work and deal with the crisis immediately. I told my immediate boss that I would be out of the office dealing with a personal crisis for a week, and he helped me cover."
- "I recently made a discovery. If I work from my home the day after I return from a trip, I am much less stressed. It's not always enough time to reduce the stress, but it certainly helps. Working from home gives me about three extra hours to work, instead of commuting and dressing. My children are thrilled that I'm in the house and don't seem to mind if I'm working at the computer."
- "I identified the smaller steps that were needed to address the issue, reached out to others: intermediate fixes that resulted in permanent fixes."
- "I tried to focus exclusively on the issue."
- "As long as I can take some action, I feel that I have some level of control, and this serves to alleviate my stress."

● "The day I received my rating this year, I was embarrassed and discouraged. I felt this way for about a week, even though I realized I had made a conscious decision to slow down at work. I don't like being rated 'average,' and it made me feel as if the firm thinks I'm not doing enough. It still bothers me, but I am continuing to focus on the home front, because I have to. I'll accept the lower rating again this coming year, although it will continue to discourage me, knowing it's the consequence of not being able to put the focus I have in the past on my career."

In addition to emotion-focused and problem-focused coping, women have an additional coping strategy, "tend and befriend," originally theorized by UCLA psychologist Shelley Taylor and discussed earlier in chapter 3. Taylor believes that this describes the stress response in women more accurately than does the more common notion of "fight or flight."

Please don't assume that a particular style of coping reflects a specific personality style or trait. There is no solid research evidence that any coping technique is more successful or more adaptive than another. Following is a list of some common methods of coping with stressors. Choose the ones that you are likely to employ when you feel stressed out or fall out of your BestStress Zone.

1. I ignore my own needs and work harder and faster.
2. I seek out friends for conversation and support.
3. I eat more (or less) than usual.
4. I engage in some type of physical exercise.
5. I get irritable and have been known to be rude to those around me.
6. I take a little time to relax, breathe, and unwind.
7. I smoke a cigarette or drink a caffeinated beverage.
8. I give thought to the source of the stress and I think of ways to deal with it.
9. I withdraw emotionally.
10. I try to reframe or rethink my perspective.
11. I sleep more (or less) than I need to.
12. I listen to special music.

13. I go out shopping and buy something to make myself feel good.
14. I joke with my friends and try to use humor to take the edge off.
15. I drink more alcohol than usual.
16. I meditate or pray.

The even-numbered items are more closely associated with healthier responses than are the odd-numbered items. If you chose mainly odd-numbered items, make a commitment today to integrate more healthy coping practices into your life.

A clear understanding of your personal approach to problem solving is a crucial component of your BestStress Zone. Most of us already possess powerfully sharp problem-solving skills, fundamental skills that we often don't think to apply to stressful situations in our lives. There are five logical steps to problem solving around the stressors in our lives.

1. Identify and label the problem.
2. Generate alternative solutions for a clarified problem and set realistic goals/solutions.
3. List the advantages and the disadvantages of each approach.
4. Make a rational choice and consider the obstacles you can expect.
5. Evaluate the desired outcome and return to steps 2, 3, or 4 as needed.

I can't tell you how many high-performing, high-achieving, and powerful women I encounter who tell me that they feel stuck. These are emotionally stable, rational, highly functioning individuals who each have a particular "problem" that is creating havoc in their lives. Given the essential nature of problem solving in building the foundation of your personal BestStress Zone, I want you to practice with a category A or B stressor that you have identified as a "problem" in step 4. Remember Deepak Chopra's admonition that the mechanism for manifestation in your life is attention. You will need to commit to and focus on solving this problem. Each time you encounter the problem in the future, you should have to go through less and less of this process, but it's a handy thing to keep in your toolbox.

Following are two completely different but complementary approaches to problem solving. Make use of whichever one feels most appropriate for a particular situation and/or dimension of your life.

Problem-Solving Approach 1

First, let's look at the more traditional approach to problem solving, which requires you to evaluate several solutions.

Traditional Problem Solving

. . . .

The Problem

Describe your problem completely. Include the following in your description:

- A one-sentence description of the problem
- The size of the problem: is it small, medium, large, or overwhelming?
- The context in which the problem occurred (where you were, who you were with, etc.)
- What you think caused the problem
- How the problem has affected you

What Have You Tried So Far?

There is no need to reinvent the wheel. If you have tried things that work, continue them. If you have tried things that do not work, take another course. Answer the following questions:

1. What have you tried so far?
2. What do you tell yourself you should do? What was the outcome?
3. What have others suggested that you do? How helpful was that advice?

Brainstorm Possible Actions

Next, ask yourself what you could change about the situation. Give yourself permission to think of anything.

(continued)

Traditional Problem Solving (continued)

Invent More Actions and Evaluate the Consequences

Now that you have brainstormed ideas and freed up your thinking, look at the problem in a more structured exercise. In the left-hand column, answer the questions to help you think of more things you could do to change the situation. Then list the consequences that go with each action in the right-hand column.

List Possible Actions	*Predict the Consequences*
What are all of the things that I could do differently when this situation arises?	For each action you think of, write down what would probably happen if you took that action.
What could someone else do that would change this situation?	What will happen if he or she does this?
What could I do to avoid this situation?	What will happen if I do?
What actions will lessen or minimize the problem?	What will happen if I do them?
What actions will make the problem worse?	What will happen if I do them?

Evaluate the Possibilities

Look over both columns. Review all actions and the consequences of each action. What looks like the best possible action? Which consequences do you like best? Choose the best possible action; then pick two alternate actions that are also good.

Make a Plan

Now that you have figured out the best thing you could do to solve your problem, you can make a plan to do it. Some solutions will be so simple, they may not need much planning. Some will be complex enough to require careful planning. Start with the best possible action you picked, and list each small step that is necessary for you to succeed.

(continued)

Traditional Problem Solving (continued)

1. List the steps you will take to complete this action.
2. List the resources you will need to complete this action. (Try to make sure that the entire solution you choose does not depend on another person changing and is not based solely on another person's action.)
3. Explain how you will know when the problem is solved.
4. Decide when you will take each step and write it on a calendar. (For really complex or serious changes, it's a good idea to wait twenty-four hours, review your decisions, and then proceed.)

Make a Backup Plan

Take some time to think through the possible consequences of each action.

1. What could go wrong?
2. How can you prevent this from happening?
3. How will you fix it if something does go wrong?

Problem-Solving Approach 2

We have all experienced this approach to problem solving. You can recall times when you were consumed with finding a solution to a problem when suddenly the solution comes to mind. These "aha moments" usually occur when you are doing something ordinary like showering or dressing. The mechanics of what occurs in this type of problem solving was described by Dr. Herbert Benson, a cardiologist from Harvard Medical School and the guru of relaxation who first popularized the idea of the "relaxation response." Benson documented the value of restoring the mind when we are "blocked." In his book *The Breakout Principle*, he describes how we can harness the natural processes in the brain to elicit the relaxation response, so that our minds are free and clear and ready for optimal problem solving. He details a four-step process in which you first push yourself to the limit mentally, and then, just as you feel yourself flagging, you disengage entirely by turning to a completely unrelated activity. If you already make use of a formal relaxation technique (see chapter 9), you would apply it at this point. Or you can just walk your dog, take a shower, go for a run, or listen to your favorite music. Brain scans have shown that as the brain quiets down, blood flow increases to areas of the brain that are associated with attention, space-time concepts, and decision making. This phase can lead to a sudden creative insight, which Benson refers to as the *breakout*, or step 3. He describes the fourth and final step as the achievement of a *new-normal state*, in which an individual finds improved performance and clarity of thought. We will explore the relaxation response in detail in chapter 9, and you can choose to use it for the purpose of problem solving in the future.

Now let's apply all of these insights about coping styles and problem solving in the following exercise.

Coping with Specific Stressors

For each of the two stressors/triggers you identified in step 2, list the coping action that you will use to handle them: (1) emotion-focused coping actions, (2) problem-focused coping actions, or (3) tend-and-befriend coping actions.
   Complete these statements.

1. In dealing with these stressors, the strategies that work best for me are: __
2. My least effective strategies for dealing with these stressors are: __
3. I am adjusting and expanding the coping strategies in my BestStress Zone toolbox by including the following emotion-focused strategies: __
4. I am adjusting and expanding the coping strategies in my BestStress Zone toolbox by including the following problem-focused strategies: __
5. I am adjusting and expanding the coping strategies in my BestStress Zone toolbox by including the following tend-and-befriend strategies: __

Step 6: Establish Your Zone Boundaries

The final step for living in your BestStress Zone is to establish *zone boundaries*—techniques and strategies that can prevent you from crossing the threshold (represented by the vertical line on the right in the illustration on page 205) from peak performance into burnout or stressed-out states. What's most important is to identify when you are living on the edge and about to fall out of the BestStress Zone.

Understanding the signs and signals that warn you when your boundaries are about to be crossed is necessary for daily life in the BestStress Zone, enabling you to live with the stressors that are inevitable and important for your 3Ps. Hopefully, you'll be able to maintain internal tranquility, harmony, and a stable emotional tone in your life. I'm not suggesting that you establish boundaries to deal with a particular event or situation. Rather, the goal is to establish boundaries that protect the cocoonlike environment you have been creating or discovering throughout this chapter. You'll need to rely on the self-assessments you conducted in earlier chapters.

Be mindful of your physical and mental signs and symptoms that warn you when your personal stress response has been triggered. You know that the edge provided by adrenaline in an acutely stressful situation no longer benefits you. Instead, it causes you to enter the stressed-out zone as noted in the previous illustration. Are your signs and symptoms a rapid heartbeat, a headache, a belly pain, or constipation?

AN EXAMPLE OF LIVING ON THE EDGE OF THE BESTSTRESS ZONE

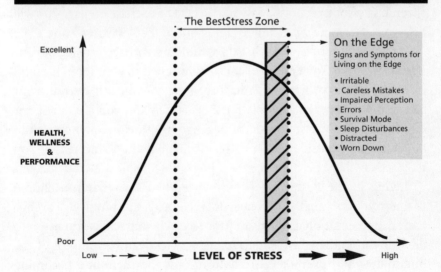

Are you suddenly making frequent trips to the smoking area on the job? Are you unexplainably irritable? Forgetful? Do you find it hard to concentrate? As you enter the stressed-out zone and begin to experience your symptoms, you may be chronically fatigued. You may live in this part of the curve for a week or two. You are still driven, but you may have a tendency to make small errors in judgment or when executing tasks. Although you feel that you have left your BestStress Zone, you still can't say no. Your sleep pattern may be just enough to get by, and even though you know you could sleep through the whole weekend, you don't. You may turn to stimulants or pure discipline to get things done. Most observers, even those in your household, may think you are okay, but that runny nose could be due to your impaired immune system. Maybe you forget where you put your keys. Or you may have a flare-up of indigestion. You are basically on autopilot.

You should know by now what your own telltale signals are and what they mean. You may still be at a stage that you can recover from without major health problems developing. If those symptoms are left unchecked, however, they could lead you down a slippery slope and land you in the emergency room! Remember that some symptoms can be extremely subtle. For instance, you might recognize a sudden mood swing associated with an obvious or acute stressor, but the low-level emotional responses and mood changes connected to a less obvious but persistent chronic stressor may not be easy to detect. The exercise on page 207 will help you determine when you're falling out of the BestStress Zone.

It's so easy to slide down that slope and find yourself outside of your BestStress Zone. You end up exhausted, resigned to your lot in life, and in denial about your stress. You lose sight of your self-esteem, your 3Ps, and your energy. Key relationships suffer, and you are at risk for developing significant long-term negative health consequences. It can be frightening outside the BestStress Zone, but there's no reason you have to stay there permanently.

Living in the BestStress Zone is a learned skill that you choose to master. Your goal is to learn to recognize the physical, psychological, and emotional signals in time to catch yourself as you begin to drift. If you know your unique responses, you can be mindful of the boundaries and prevent yourself from crossing them and becoming stressed out.

Staying in the BestStress Zone

Answer the following questions.

1. What is the first signal (feeling, thought, action) that I am leaving my place of optimal functioning or BestStress Zone?
2. What is or are the signal(s) from my loved ones, friends, and coworkers that I am leaving my BestStress Zone?
3. What is my overall emotional mood just prior to being stressed out? Look back and assess for patterns of how you really feel on a gut level for a few days before you find yourself stressed out. Anxious? Sad? Pumped? Eating more?

If you're having difficulty with this exercise, you may need to examine the last time you were out of the BestStress Zone; that is, the last time you felt that your stress was out of control. Work backward and see whether you can determine the month, the week, the day, or even the final straw, as it were, that precipitated your leaving the zone. Maybe it was an e-mail notifying you of a new department director or a parent's receiving a diagnosis of Alzheimer's disease. Perhaps you discovered your spouse in an affair or learned that your teenager was cutting school. Maybe it was a big promotion—something potentially wonderful but also equally terrifying.

Complete the following statements.

These are the best signals for me to monitor when I drift out of my BestStress Zone and into the stressed-out zone.

1. My overall feelings and emotional tone are: __
2. My thoughts tend to focus on: __
3. My work relationships become: __
4. My personal relationships become: __

Wrapup

Congratulations on getting to this point in the book. If you have made it to the end of this chapter, you have the knowledge and skills to establish your personal BestStress Zone. Putting this knowledge and skills into use every day will require practice. You must make a decision to be methodical and diligent. Here is a review of what you have achieved in this chapter.

- Reviewed the BestStress Process and understand how it provides an alternative way to think about managing stress
- Identified two stressors or triggers that are currently concerning you
- Identified the factors that influence your perception of these stressors
- Identified the triggers (the demands and challenges) in your life associated with your 3Ps
- Sorted and categorized your stressors based on their significance and controllability
- Examined your personal coping strategies
- Established boundaries/signals for your personal Best-Stress Zone

Discovery of your BestStress Zone also requires you to honestly examine some of the larger issues that may be affecting your life. If you are able to recognize that improving your technical competencies could eliminate some stress triggers, then explore continuing education options or seek other ways to sharpen your skills. If you find that time management is an ongoing challenge, as it is for so many of us, I invite you to consider alternative philosophical perspectives on time. Deepak Chopra's lessons on the nature of time, for example, are very instructive. He warns us against looking to the future or looking back at the past. He argues that the experience of time is merely a perception. If people feel that they are always running out of time, their accelerated bodily functions will manifest this, in that they prematurely stop and drop dead from a heart attack—literally running out of time.

Take a brief pause now. Think about some of these matters, both the practical concerns and the deeper, more contemplative issues. Try to get comfortable with some of these new perspectives, as well as any new insights about yourself, before moving on to the next chapter, where you will learn how you can live to your fullest potential in the BestStress Zone.

living in the beststress zone
relationships, roles, and common pitfalls

Now that you have established your personal framework and identified the stressors associated with your 3Ps, let's talk about how to live and sustain yourself in the BestStress Zone. This chapter contains practical tools, tactics, and strategies to help you manage specific situations and events, as well as deal with the triggers/stressors that you chose to work with in the last chapter. Remember that living in the zone involves accepting your stress and sometimes actually embracing it, particularly the stressors that are associated with your three Ps—purpose, passions, and priorities—and that fall into categories A (related to the 3Ps and controllable) and C (not related to the 3Ps and controllable). Living in the BestStress Zone is ultimately about achieving harmony and health in all aspects of your life, about having the capacity to receive pleasure without guilt, and about having clarity and commitment, while remaining adaptable and flexible. There will always be challenges in the BestStress Zone, but if you recognize that stressful situations are unavoidable and are necessary elements of any life, this allows you to anticipate them with calmness and clarity.

First, we will look at two strategies you can use to launch your life in the BestStress Zone: decluttering the zone and mindshifting. Then we'll consider some triggers and stressors that are common in the lives of women and clients I have worked with over the years who use the zone strategies.

Among the sources of those triggers are the following:

- Interpersonal relationships
- Wearing multiple hats
- Finances
- Unemployment
- Time management
- Caretaking responsibilities
- Midlife and aging
- Kids, adolescents, teenagers, and young adults
- Breaking up/separation/divorce
- Holidays
- Stress related to uncertainty and the unexpected

Decluttering the Zone

To begin living in the BestStress Zone, let's start decluttering so that you can feel some relief right away. What are some of your smaller daily hassles? Doing the laundry? Shopping for and preparing dinner? Keeping track of your mother's doctors' appointments? Identify the items associated with your 3Ps that if managed more effectively would markedly reduce the clutter in your life. There are probably plenty of simple things you can do: prepare menus a week in advance; lay out your work clothes for the week on Sunday night; schedule a standing appointment once a week to spend time on self-care (exercise, outings with friends, manicures, etc.); delegate chores that need to get done but not necessarily by you; and more. You will be surprised at how effective this can be in reducing some of the high-impact stressors in your life.

Mindshifting

Before we go into specific issues in detail, I want to expand on a concept that was mentioned in earlier chapters. I've explained the mind-body connection, both generally and specifically. It's a core component of the BestStress Zone, and now it's time to explore the mind-body connection on a practical level. Following are three specific cognitive-behavioral zone strategies that I call *mindshifting*, which are essential to managing stressors.

1. *Transformational coping* allows you to see relatively minor actions and accommodations in the context of a "bigger picture." Often, the ability to step back or even step outside of yourself mentally to try to understand your own place in the larger community and culture helps lessen the effect of a specific situation, person, or event.

2. *Selective ignoring* and *psychological withdrawal* are effective mental strategies for situations that exist only for a finite period of time. You will inevitably confront people and situations that are inherently toxic to your well-being. You can maintain perspective, see these situations for what they are, and not inflate them to the point where you engage in negative emotional coping practices, such as excessive eating, drinking, rumination, or unhealthy sexual behavior.

3. *Stress inoculation* means protecting yourself from potential triggers that you cannot control, in the same way that a flu vaccine prevents infection and illness. The idea is to use your imagination to mentally rehearse your exposure to a trigger and then anticipate your response. This strategy is useful for work-related stressors, particularly the overbearing and uncaring manager or supervisor or difficult direct reports. Here's how it works. Close your eyes and imagine the entire experience of this potential trigger. Try to see and hear every sound and thought and feel every feeling associated with the trigger. Picture the encounter or the situation with as much specific detail as you can, and mentally rehearse not only your feelings and responses but also your plan for coping with and managing them. The more realistic

you make the imagined experience, the more authentic your natural response will be. On the day or at the time of the actual exposure to this person, you will find that the exposure no longer elicits the same intense response.

Triggers and Stressors

Now on to specific issues and how to handle them in order to stay in the BestStress Zone.

Interpersonal Relationships

Interpersonal relationships are the number one stressor for just about everyone. Ongoing or chronic difficulties in relationships generate the most harmful stress responses. It may help to have your own personnel policies, based on your 3Ps. How are people compensated? What are your hours, confidentiality requirements, performance appraisal standards, and grievance procedures? The effort you put into understanding, fostering, and nurturing relationships will pay regular dividends.

Acknowledge that in the real world, relationships go through good patches and bad. Conflict is inevitable, and you'll almost certainly have to have some unpleasant conversations with people you care about. My goal is to help you analyze the important relationships in your life today, to see which ones are worth the effort because they bring you in line with your 3Ps, and so are worth your accepting and managing the stress. Also, I want you to have a plan in place to anticipate and reduce the stressors in your relationships more effectively in the future.

First, you will clarify the categories of relationships in the following exercise.

Your Relationship List

Think of all the people whom you feel complete the picture of your life in the following categories.

- Family
- Friends

(continued)

Your Relationship List (continued)

- Workplace (coworkers, direct reports, bosses)
- Acquaintances (neighbors, other parents, kids' coaches, etc.)
- Key contacts (hairstylist, babysitter, spiritual leader, etc.)
- Professional service contacts (broker, banker, personal trainer, etc.)
- Others

Answer the following questions.

1. Overall, on a scale of 1–5 (1 = in disarray, 5 = ideal), how would you rate your level of satisfaction with the quality of the relationships in each category?
2. What is the most obvious unifying or overlapping element that characterizes your relationships with people (i.e., giver, taker, collaborator, doer, fixer)?
3. Do you take specific steps to maintain and nurture relationships?
4. Identify some high-leverage behavior changes that could improve all of your relationships.

Dr. Marshall Goldsmith, a psychologist and the bestselling author of *What Got You Here Won't Get You There*, is one of the top executive coaches in the world and has been one of my mentors. He developed a model for self-help and coaching that he calls *feedforward*. Here is how it can work to improve your interpersonal relationships.

Following the steps below, pick one behavior that you could change to make an immediate and positive effect on an interpersonal relationship.

1. Describe this behavior to one of the people in the relationship list you just completed. It can be very simple, such as "I want to be a better listener."
2. Ask for input and suggestions (feedforward) about what you might change in your behavior in a positive way. Be absolutely certain not to reveal any judgment in your response, and do not make comments about the past. This is about having a better future.
3. Listen attentively to the feedforward and take notes. You are not allowed to comment on the suggestions in any way, nor are you

allowed to critique the suggestions, even to make positive statements, such as "That's a good idea."

4. Thank the person for his or her suggestions.

Feedforward can often be more useful than feedback. You can't change the past, but you can improve the prospects for the future. Feedforward helps you envision and focus on a positive future, not on a failed past. You will tend to listen more attentively to feedforward than to feedback because you aren't using half of your brain to prepare your response while the other person is talking. You can focus your attention on the other person, knowing that all you need to say is "Thank you."

If you are currently dealing with an interpersonal conflict that is causing you stress, make a commitment to resolve it, taking into account the ways in which you might be contributing to the conflict—perhaps through poor listening, a desire to win at all costs, a lack of empathy, or mental rigidity that may keep you from considering other alternatives. Evaluate your verbal and nonverbal communication strengths and weaknesses and make adjustments accordingly.

Consider forgiveness to be a form of self-help. Despite the phrase "forgive and forget," forgiving does not mean forgetting. It is probably not even possible to forget a deep hurt. To forgive is to let go of resentment and thoughts of revenge, the bitter ties that bind us to the one who hurt us. The first step is to want to forgive, to want to heal that wound. Start by acknowledging the hurt and allowing yourself to feel the anger fully. Recognize that you have a right to feel that way. The next step is to consciously stop all thoughts of revenge, of hurting that person in return. These first two steps may take a long time to complete. The third step is to examine the situation from the other person's point of view. What might that individual have been thinking? Was he or she perhaps dealing with other factors or circumstances that you were not aware of? Fourth, accept the hurt without passing it on to anyone else. The more it's passed around, the bigger it grows. Squash it by choosing to own it. Finally, extend compassion to the offender. This may mean reconciling with the person who hurt you directly, or it may be something that you do only mentally. Create a list of the people you need to forgive and a time frame for addressing any unresolved conflicts.

Next, I want you to consider whether you are giving and receiving unconditional love in significant relationships (romantic or important friendships or relationships with family members). Unconditional love

- means complete acceptance of every aspect of another person—both: good and bad attributes;
- allows you to take risks and to be open and vulnerable, with no preconceived limitations;
- allows you to value others for themselves, rather than for what they do or have done for you;
- allows you to feel free to be yourself, to know that you are listened to and understood, and to believe that you are okay just the way you are; and
- frees you to express yourself with no fear of rejection, confident in the knowledge that you will be cared for and nurtured.

Another factor that commonly interferes with interpersonal relationships is a lack of assertiveness. Do you lack assertiveness? You will have your needs satisfied or met only if you express them in a way that does not hurt other people in the process. Do you feel manipulated by certain individuals or think that some people are overdependent on you? If so, you may need to do the following:

- Develop and maintain a safe emotional distance from people who have a lot of power to negatively affect your emotional outlook on life.
- Take back power over your feelings from individuals on whom you have made yourself too dependent,
- Make a personal commitment to yourself and your health by recognizing that the only person you can change is yourself.
- Help the people you love and care for to accept personal responsibility for their own actions.
- Allow people in your life to be who they really are and not who you want them to be.

Think of up to three people with whom you have assertiveness issues and are committed to pursuing adjustments.

Abusive Relationships

If you believe you are in an abusive relationship (physically, emotionally, financially, or otherwise), you should seek immediate help, help that is well beyond what I can offer in this book. You need to recognize that no one deserves to be abused. Be clear that I am not asking why you would choose to stay in an abusive relationship. You are not the problem, and it is unlikely that the situation will be resolved without outside support. The dynamics of abusive relationships are very complex. Before you take any action, you must assess your situation for safety. Are there drugs involved? Are there weapons in the household? As soon as is feasible, share your situation with someone whom you know cares about you. If you have no one close whom you feel you can turn to, or you can't locate local resources and services, call the national hotline for domestic abuse at 1-800-123-4567.

Wearing Multiple Hats

Is this problem stressor related to the multiple hats you wear or the multiple roles you execute on a day-to-day basis? If the answer is yes, then ask yourself the following questions:

- Do all individuals involved have equal expectations of you? Have you established specific recognizable behaviors that are associated with your particular roles? This is not the same formal job description that may already exist in a workplace setting. In the home setting, what does it mean when you or your spouse/partner agrees to take care of the kids while the other completes work or a project for an extra three hours on Saturday at the office? It may be useful to create something like a written job description, with expected actions and outcomes, for the people with whom you share responsibility for dependents.
- Can you relinquish a role for a specified period of time, or delegate, to simplify your life? Although you may derive fulfillment from your many roles, now that you are committed to living in your BestStress Zone, you should periodically reassess the roles

you undertake and make sure they continue to be in line with your 3Ps.

- Can you think of any roles that you may want to put on hold or eliminate over the next six months? If this is tough for you to do, consider it an experiment. Revisit your list in a few weeks or even months, and if your original choices don't feel right, go ahead and make some changes.

Do you have a support team, what I call your "board of trustees"? Use the illustration and chart on page 218 to help you define your team.

Use the definition of specific roles in the illustration as you list your board of trustees. For clarification, a *mentor* is an individual who has power or position that he or she is willing to use on your behalf. A single mentor could possibly fulfill *all* of the other roles shown on the chart, but that is unlikely. Most individuals I work with require at least three of the seats that are defined on the chart to be filled in their lives. You may need different mentors for various disciplines. For example, in medicine, a physician scientist may need a technical/researcher mentor, as well as a speciality mentor for the area of infectious diseases. Note that if you use a corporate structure as a model, you are the CEO of your organization. Your mentor can fill the role of the COO, helping you operationalize your mission, as they say in the corporate world. A mentor can show you how to turn ideas into realities. As in sports, a *coach* can offer specific how-to guidance, while a *sponsor* can help you get more exposure in your organization and find opportunities to demonstrate or develop your talent. Anyone who has walked a path similar to the one you are pursuing can act as your *guide*. This valuable member of your team can help you avoid pitfalls and dead ends. A *counselor* is a confidant or a friend with whom you can share your deepest emotions or concerns. There's no telling where you'll find a counselor. It could be a close friend or a family member, but it could also be a spiritual leader.

Using the chart on page 218 as a guide, list the names of people you would like to have on your board of trustees. You can list up to two people for each position (note that not all positions need to be filled at all times).

THIS IS YOUR BOARD OF TRUSTEES—THE PEOPLE IN YOUR LIFE WHOM YOU CAN RELY ON

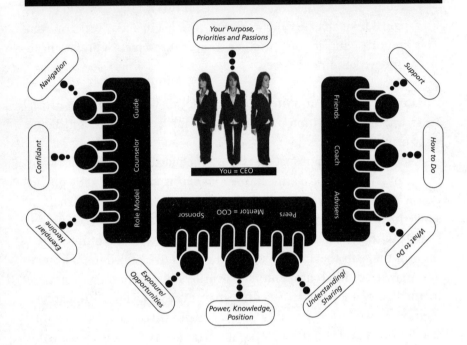

My Personal Board of Trustees

Position	Name of Board Member	Name of Board Member
Mentor		
Coach		
Adviser		
Sponsor		
Role model		
Peer		
Counselor		
Close friend(s)		
Guide		

Finally, one reason we run into trouble juggling multiple roles in life is that many of us are simply unable to say no. In her book *Civilized Assertiveness*, Judith McClure offers a number of variations on "just saying no." I've adapted them here.

1. The "No, Because" No

    "I'd like to help you on the recruiting committee, but I've spent a lot of time developing a focused marketing plan, and I promised myself that this year I would use my nonbillable time to execute it."

    (By the way, one of my clients recently used this type of no with the managing partner of her firm when he invited her to join an administrative committee at her firm. His response? "I agree. Doing business development is a much better use of your time and energy than serving on the committee.")

2. The Partial No

    "I can't chair the summer associates committee, but I would be glad to have lunch with the committee members three times during the summer."

    "I can't help you draft the proposal, but I would be glad to review it and give you my comments once you have a draft."

3. The "Not Now" No

    "No, I can't give that speech to the local bar association this year, but please keep me in mind for next year, when my schedule may have eased up a bit."

4. The Alternative No

    "No, I don't have time to write the practice group description, but I think that would be an excellent developmental project for Sue Livingston. She has indicated an interest in getting more involved in business development, and I think that this would be a great opportunity for her to get her feet wet."

5. The Just Plain No
"I'm flattered that you considered me for the position as head of the associate evaluation committee. At the moment, I just don't have time to do it justice."

Finances

Financial stress is an independent risk factor for suffering a heart attack. A recent study investigated the relationship of chronic stressors to heart attacks in a sample of twenty-five thousand people from fifty-two countries. Stress was defined as "feeling irritable, filled with anxiety, or having sleep difficulties." Financial stress was found to have a greater effect than stress at home, work, or major life events, increasing the odds of a person's suffering a heart attack by 1.3 times.

Everyone has expenses and needs to decide his or her financial priorities. Some things you have little or no control over: the prices of gasoline, food, or electricity; your income and your taxes; the performance of the stock market. Financial stress can build up insidiously over time, as larger economic forces change the overall climate. The one element you can control and that will help reduce your stress triggers over the long run is the way in which your finances align with your 3Ps.

No matter where you stand today financially, you can and should begin to rethink the role of money in your life. First, acknowledge that your finances are a likely source of stress in your life. Any number of factors may make you conscious of finances as a stressor: arguing with your spouse over money, having to use credit cards for everyday expenses, regularly making minimum payments or late payments (and incurring those hefty "default rates"), feeling overwhelmed by debts, or simply being preoccupied with worry about how you will pay your bills.

Some obvious signs that you are experiencing stress due to finances are being afraid to answer the phone or open the mailbox, stacking your bills in one pile and disregarding due dates, not paying bills and holding onto your money, or avoiding thinking about bills by indulging in poorly chosen emotional-coping strategies.

If this is a problem, let's talk about it. Recognize that dealing with the issue will be painful now, but it has no chance of getting better later if you don't get it out on the table. This may simply mean bringing the problem into your conscious mind or having a conversation with others in your household, but it could also be a good idea to consult a professional who can assist you. Decide today to address at least one single issue each day. Here are some tough questions you must answer first. What is your indebtedness? Can you refinance? What about debt consolidation? Should you declare bankruptcy? How can you manage to pay for the future education of your children? Do you have long-term-care insurance? Now let's look some simple steps you can take to eliminate financial stress triggers.

1. Know that *you* are not your debt!
2. Make using cash a habit; put your credit cards away.
3. Create an emergency fund, such as low-return but secure CDs, money market accounts, and savings accounts.
4. Become a smarter consumer.
   - What is your mortgage rate? Is it fixed or variable? If it is variable, look into refinancing at a fixed rate.
   - Are you overpaying for necessities (e.g., using the local drugstore for prescriptions vs. mail order, which allows you to order in bulk, thereby saving money)?
   - Use doctors who accept your company's health-care plan.
   - Are you paying more for brand-name products when generic ones will do?
   - Look for more competitive rates on:
     Cable plans
     Cell-phone plans (which can often be bundled with your cable and Internet service)
     Mortgage
     Homeowner's insurance
     Car insurance
   - Trim your spending for eating out, especially fast foods, by planning better or doing regular grocery shopping. If you must eat out, try to avoid appetizers, alcohol, and pricey desserts.
5. Take the time to resolve billing problems.
6. Take a second look at your kids' after-school activities (dance, sports, etc.) that require extra time and money; perhaps there are less expensive alternatives.

7. Your job is your most valuable asset. Protect it by performing your duties well. Be an essential employee. Do not give your employer a reason to fire or demote you or lay you off.

8. Set goals and plans for achieving them, such as paying off your house by the time you retire.

9. Determine the interest rate you're paying on all credit cards, and pay down higher-interest-rate cards first.

10. Subscribe to a monthly money-related magazine. It will jog your brain for new ideas, keep you updated about trends, and remind you to do some regular housekeeping on your finances.

11. Teach your kids about money literacy; it's never too early to develop a healthy relationship with money.

Finally, and perhaps most important, create a budget and stick to it. Adopt a plan for how you spend your money. You don't have to become a miser, but all of us, both as individuals and as a society, will be healthier if we learn to live within our means.

Free financial calculators are available on the Web at www.bloomberg .com and www.debtorsanonymous.org. Make use of these and other resources to get a handle on your money. You'll be amazed at how much stress you can relieve by dealing more rationally and carefully with your finances.

Unemployment

It's pretty common now for loyal, hardworking, talented people to hear the words "Your services are not needed anymore. Please pack up your personal belongings and you will be escorted out of the building." But there is also collateral damage. It may be equally troubling to be the colleague, the associate, of someone who gets the boot. What can and should you do to manage the stress that arises from the uncertainty of jobs in today's economic environment? To begin with, if you currently are employed, you must become an extraordinary employee. In a conversation with me, an internal human resources person described the following approach that her successful and profitable company uses when the numbers dictate the need for forced reductions. First, investors determine the bottom line. It is all about business. It is not personal. Often, outside management consultants assess employees, organizational structure, sales coverage models, and redundancy. You will likely be ranked based on your performance, business acumen, demonstrated skills, scores on internal tests, and attitude. There is no hiding the fact that there are objective and subjective criteria. The subjective criteria often come down to whether you are the employee who is willing to accommodate and not complain. Who is willing to do more with fewer resources? Do you add value to the team?

Many companies train managers who have to deliver the message "I'm not laying you off; the company is." If you are in the position of delivering bad news, you must distance yourself from the company because the reality is that the next round of reductions could include you! Given today's environment, take stock, literally, financially and emotionally, and research the job market immediately. Update your résumé. Decide whether you need to make a preemptive move. If you are providing health-care benefits for other people in your life, be sure to consider all of your options.

So, what do you do to live in the BestStress Zone on the day that you lose your job?

- Know that you are not defined by your job and that your skill sets and attitudes can and will lead to new opportunities. Give yourself a break. This is a natural opportunity to rethink your real needs and interests. Rediscover what you are passionate about doing on a day-to-day basis in the paid labor force.
- Despite the fact that "you knew" it was coming, you will experience a wide range of emotions, some rational and others completely irrational.
- Avoid the natural tendency to say or do anything negative in the workplace about the specifics of your situation.
- Plan and prepare to have someone to talk to who cares about you and to whom you can confide your true feelings. This may or may not be your spouse or partner.
- Be honest with your spouse or partner about the job you lost.
- Be honest with your children to the extent that they can understand.

- Now is a great time to focus on and take the time to work on your health, physical fitness, and spirituality. It is essential to get plenty of sleep, avoid mind-altering substances, and exercise regularly.
- Every day, spend some time working on your job quest. Remember that every person you know is a potential connection to a job. When you are ready, get the word out that you are an amazing employee and a great find for the right organization.

Time Management

Few things in life generate as much stress as the inability to manage time properly. We can accomplish only what we can fit into our schedules, and most of us feel as if every decision we make in life or about work is somehow dictated by time. It is possible, however, to organize our lives around a schedule that makes us happier and more productive, that accommodates our normal day-to-day routines while leaving us with the time we need for ourselves and our families.

The following quiz should help you identify trouble spots as the first step toward becoming a successful time manager.

How Do I Manage My Time?

Read each statement and choose the response that most clearly describes you. Then add up your score. The scoring key indicates your level of time-management skills.

4 = Rarely
3 = Sometimes
2 = Usually
1 = Always

1. I find that I have enough time for myself to do the things I enjoy doing. __
2. I keep track of major deadlines and schedule my work to meet them in plenty of time. __
3. I write down specific daily objectives and associated action steps. __

(continued)

How Do I Manage My Time? (continued)

4. I have a system for organizing appointments, deadlines, things to do, and general notes. __

5. I feel in control of time while at work and at home. __

6. I plan and schedule my time on a weekly and/or monthly basis. __

7. I make a daily to-do list and refer to it several times per day. __

8. I set priorities in order of importance and then schedule my time around them. __

9. I'm able to find blocks of time when I need them in case something important or extra has to be fitted in. __

10. I'm able to say no when I'm pressed for time. __

11. I try to delegate responsibility to others, in order to make more time for myself. __

12. I organize my desk and work area to prevent clutter and confusion. __

13. I find it easy to eliminate or reschedule low-priority items. __

14. I try to do things in a way that cuts down on duplicated efforts. __

15. I find that doing everything myself is very inefficient. __

16. I try to shift priorities as soon as needs emerge. __

17. I find it easy to identify sources of time problems. __

18. I find it easy to eliminate or reshuffle unnecessary paperwork. __

19. My meetings and activities are well organized and efficient. __

20. I know what I'm capable of and try not to overextend myself. __

21. I find it easy to keep up with changes that affect my schedule or workload. __

22. I know what my responsibilities and duties are. __

23. I try to schedule the most difficult work during my most productive times. __

24. I try to get only the pertinent information before making a decision, rather than trying to get as much information as possible.

25. I finish one job or task before going on to the next.

Scoring

25–40 = Excellent time manager
41–55 = Good time manager
56–100 = Poor time manager

Once you've completed the self-assessment, go back and identify the areas that are the most consistent sources of time-related stress. Look for specific behavior patterns and attitudes that interfere with your ability to organize, manage, and schedule time. The most common stress-inducing problem areas include the following:

- A schedule that doesn't connect with your 3Ps
- Lack of regularity or routine; events or activities that occur randomly throughout your schedule that make it difficult for you to plan
- Inability to delegate responsibility, causing an overcrowded schedule
- Inability to say no
- Lack of clarity regarding objectives
- No formal or carefully maintained calendar or other scheduling tool to organize commitments
- Inadequate prioritizing, which makes everything feel like an emergency
- Too much clutter and unnecessary paperwork
- Insistence on total control
- Procrastination

Most of us can improve our time-management skills, even those of you who rated yourselves as excellent. It is beyond the scope of this book to review specific time-management programs, but I assure you that many very good books and programs are available.

Caretaking Responsibilities

Caretaking can be stressful, particularly if you are in the sandwich generation and are caring for children and aging parents, relatives, or friends. If you experience stress related to caretaking, consider the following:

- Have you made a list or kept a journal of all of the tasks and responsibilities, broken down into those that *must* be done, those that *could* be done, and those that it *would be nice to* get done?

- Have you formally communicated with people you are close to, such as siblings and your spouse, partner, or significant other, who may be able to share some of the tasks identified previously?
- Have you identified and accepted the people, places, situations, and conditions that you are powerless to control regarding your children or the aging adults in your life?
- Have you examined yourself to ensure that you do not have a case of "need to be needed" syndrome? If you expend a lot of energy doing things that others could do or that will have only a minor effect over the long term, this could be your problem.
- Are you living your life vicariously through your children? Think about whether you feel stressed because you're running around providing activities and experiences that perhaps you enjoy more than they do.
- Have you set limits on the amount of time you spend on activities and tasks that are not essential for maintenance? You must develop a daily, weekly, monthly, and annual schedule for your time. This includes enough time for your self-care and all of the other dimensions of your life.
- Have you made a list of all of the individuals who potentially could share some of your emotional, physical, and task-related responsibilities?
- Can you communicate effectively with people in your support network to determine who is best capable and most willing to share certain responsibilities? For those who cannot spare time on an ongoing basis, have you determined who can provide periodic respite or scheduled help?
- Have you shared your feelings with these individuals to reach an agreement about shared accountability, if applicable?

Midlife and Aging

As young adults, we use the phrase *midlife crisis* as a kind of joke, something in the distant and hazy future. When we hit thirty, middle age starts to seem a little more real, and we take its inevitability more seriously. And by the time we turn forty, we suddenly realize that we've arrived at the midpoint of our lives and are not always sure how we got there. For many of us, this event can be a very stressful, if not traumatic, occurrence in our lives.

Men and women react very differently to the onset of middle age. Research has shown that men are likely to experience anxiety, feelings of inadequacy, and depression if they haven't accomplished everything they had envisioned for themselves as younger men. Middle age is a time for reassessment, when it's easy to think of what "might have been." Midlife is a time to return to being curious about the world around you and life itself. A man may become despondent over his career, believing he's gotten as far as he's likely to go or that he's fallen into a grinding, joyless routine. The sense of regret grows even deeper when a man starts to believe he's too old to try something new or to start over in a new career. A woman, on the other hand, is more likely to feel satisfaction in her accomplishments at midlife, focusing more on social and interpersonal success than on professional. She may be less bored and less lonely than a man is and may feel much better about herself and her future.

Even though men and women may begin midlife differently, they both usually end up discovering greater life satisfaction as they age. By the time they reach fifty or fifty-five, both men and women have usually gone through the worst periods of midlife and really start to enjoy their lives once again.

A little mindshifting can be the key to coping with potential midlife crises. I hear a lot of people these days saying things like "Fifty is the new thirty-five." I would not have believed this until my youngest son left for college, but it's invigorating to realize that this time of life isn't about endings as much as it's about new beginnings. More and more people are seeing these years as the time to experience new activities, explore unknown talents, and exploit new opportunities. The problems many of us face when we reach midlife are not connected to our physical or mental health, but to our inability or unwillingness to look at our middle years as a time of possibility.

Changes in lifestyle, along with advances in medical science, have created a generation of vigorous, physically fit men and women over the age of sixty-five. But despite all of that glowing health, people at midlife still commonly experience two kinds of stressors: those that are normal to aging, and those that are imposed by the environment. The stresses of illness, personal loss, diminished income, retirement, and inadequate housing combine with social stresses, such as age discrimination and lack of adequate services and an uncaring environment, to produce isolation, loneliness, and depression.

Often, older people feel frustrated and anxious because they know they're still fully able to learn and carry out mental tasks but are rarely given the opportunity. There is widespread bias against them in society and the workplace. Situations like this lead to depression, which is the most common mental disorder that affects aging individuals. As we age, we allow our negative perceptions of aging to shape our behavior and attitudes. Successful aging can be accomplished only if we eliminate those negative perceptions and learn to cope with the stresses of age in a positive way.

If you are over age forty-five, take the following quiz and see what level of satisfaction you experience.

Midlife Satisfaction Quiz

Read each statement and indicate whether you agree or disagree. Give yourself one point for each "agree" response.

1. As I grow older, I enjoy having a healthy curiosity. __

2. I am not angry or frustrated about hot flashes and other physical symptoms associated with menopause. __

3. Enjoyable intimate (emotional or physical) relationship(s) are an important and fulfilling part of my life. __

4. I expect pleasant, unexpected, and interesting things happen to me in the future. __

5. I feel my age, and it doesn't keep me from enjoying my life. __

6. I am satisfied with my physical appearance. __

7. Except for occasional tiffs, I am at peace with my relationships with my loved ones. __

8. Usually, I am not lonely, and I value time to myself. __

(continued)

9. Life is definitely worth living, and I am motivated to do what it takes to stay healthy. __

10. I have the energy to do what I need and want to do most days. __

Scoring

8–10: High life satisfaction. Age is not a factor in your life—attitude is. You are likely to have positive and fun experiences ahead of you.

5–7: Average life satisfaction. There is an opportunity for you to get more joy and satisfaction out of life now and in the future. Revisit your 3Ps. Make sure that negative attitudes and behaviors don't begin to affect your health and well-being.

0–4: Low life satisfaction. You may be putting yourself at risk for developing stress-related health problems. Revisit your 3Ps. Listen to your heart and your path will become clear.

Kids, Adolescents, Teenagers, and Young Adults

Is your stressor related to the care and nurturing of your children (regardless of age)? If the answer is yes, then ask yourself the following questions.

- If your child were to see you in your workplace or in a social setting, would you want the child to emulate the behavior he or she observes in you?
- Have you established ground rules for behavior in and out of home? Have you clearly defined "zero-tolerance" issues?
- Do you have policies about the use of automobiles and other devices or substances that can kill?
- Do you have policies about who can come in and out of your home and at what hours, which are in accordance with any applicable local laws?
- Have you established a budget and made it clear to your adolescents and young adult children how much money you will

spend, and have you told your children that you will not save or rescue them from fiscal irresponsibility?

- Have you discussed and established guidelines for emotional and physical intimacy, including health-related concerns in accordance with your moral codes (e.g., the use of contraceptives and so on)?

Adults don't have a monopoly on stress. Dr. Andrew Goliszek, in his book *60 Second Stress Management*, provides an excellent discussion on how stress affects kids. He notes that the reason that children seem less stressed than adults is that they're normally more resilient and less likely to have physical reactions or symptoms related to stress than they are to exhibit emotional and behavioral reactions. "Acting out" may indicate that a child is experiencing some sort of stress in his or her life. Stressful life events for children can include parental, family, or personal issues, such as the following:

- A change in family finances
- A parent or a significant adult's death
- A brother, a sister, or a close friend dying
- Divorce or separation of parents
- A parent, a relative, or another family member becoming very sick (developing cancer, for example)
- Failing one or more subjects in school
- A parent losing a job
- Breaking up with a boyfriend or a girlfriend

So, how do we recognize stress in children? They aren't likely to start drinking and smoking heavily and probably won't exhibit classic symptoms such as high blood pressure. There are, however, some telltale signs that we can watch for in our children.

Ages Six to Ten

Younger children have less-developed communication skills, making it more likely that they will reveal their stress as a behavioral response. Their inability to explain what's wrong can frustrate them, sometimes leading to violent reactions. Little things, which are insignificant to older children, may be traumatic for a six-year-old or a seven-year-old.

Changes in daily routines, such as their bedtimes, school, babysitters, or parents taking on new jobs, can trigger anxiety in young children that can lead to physical and emotional problems. Watch for the following:

- New or recurrent bedwetting
- Disrupted sleep patterns, especially getting up in the middle of the night with nightmares
- A persistent change in eating habits
- Regressive behavior, such as thumb sucking, uncontrollable crying, hair pulling, or clinging to their parents, if these behaviors have not been typical
- Sudden onset of nausea, vomiting, or stomach pains
- Marked change of interest in things the child has previously enjoyed
- Sudden fears about going to school, riding a bus, playing with friends, the weather, and so on

Ages Eleven to Fourteen

As children mature, reach early adolescence, and go through puberty, their stress response also changes. Some studies have shown that boys at this age don't cope as well as girls do, possibly because society still expects boys to act brave and not show their emotions. As a result, warning signs of stress may be less obvious in boys. These are challenging years for any kid—a time of increasingly complex social pressures. Kids may still want to please their parents at this age, but they also crave the acceptance of their peers. The most common warning signs for eleven- to fourteen-year-olds are the following:

- Depression or a sudden onset of sadness
- Bouts of aggression or violent behavior
- A marked change in school performance and/or concentration
- Withdrawal and isolation
- Regression to more childlike behaviors, such as thumb sucking and talking in a babyish manner
- Unwillingness to participate in family or school activities

- Unwillingness to talk or to ask questions, especially if the child has been normally vocal or curious

At this age, children are generally still open and willing to talk. Take advantage of that by listening to their complaints and picking up on the distress signals they may be sending. Helping them handle stress during the middle school years will prepare all of you for those difficult teenage years.

Ages Fifteen to Eighteen

Once those teenage hormones kick in and a child reaches the high school years, an entirely new set of issues comes into play. A teen's world is full of dilemmas, mood swings, confusion, anger, and frustration over everything from homework to love. Teenagers become preoccupied with their looks, peer and family relationships, and social status. It's easy for teens to lose perspective. It's either emotional feast or famine, and parents have to realize that at this most critical stage of life, their children need more understanding and help in coping with stress than at any other time.

Because a teenager's brain is not yet wired to avoid risks, some of the warning signs are related to risk taking. Kids in this age group react to stress by acting out in specific ways and can, in fact, place themselves or others in danger without even thinking about it. Keep an eye out for warning signs, such as the following:

- A breakdown in interpersonal relationships
- Isolation and withdrawal, especially when the teen was previously outgoing
- Unwillingness to accept responsibility at home, at school, or on the job
- Unusual boredom, fatigue, and/or loss of interest
- Decreased self-esteem
- Sudden depression and/or irritability
- Sudden onset of physical problems, such as loss of appetite, increased blood pressure, stomach pains, exhaustion, asthma, or skin disorders

Special-Needs Children

The lives of some families are complicated further by their having special-needs children. It goes without saying that the pressures of caring for a child with physical, mental, or emotional disabilities add a whole new dimension of stressors. A parent can be overwhelmed simply by trying to comprehend the unique stressors in his or her child's world. My own expertise does not extend into all areas of disability, but I can assure you that whatever your child's particular needs are, help is available. Moreover, I urge you to take advantage of the many doctors, authors, support networks, special schools, government services, and other resources that are devoted to your particular situation. These resources can help you fulfill your daily duties and responsibilities without stressing out, so that you can live in your BestStress Zone.

It's easy to overlook stress in teenagers, because we assume that what we see as bizarre behavior is a natural part of the physical and emotional changes they're undergoing. But we need to be keenly aware of what goes on in our children's lives, so that we can distinguish actual stress-related behavior from simple growing pains.

It doesn't take much for a teenager to get stressed out under the best of conditions. Add death, divorce, illness, or a broken relationship, and you have the ingredients for real problems. As a child moves through these tough years, parents may feel as if they're constantly walking on eggshells. Don't be afraid. Don't let outbursts or arguments deter you from staying involved. Your lives will calm down as your kids grow up, but not without your vigilance and participation. By separating normal outbursts from cries for help and by identifying stress symptoms right away, especially when your children are experiencing traumatic life events, you might prevent your kid's stress load from getting out of hand and causing more serious physical and emotional disorders.

Breaking Up: Separation and Divorce

There's no easy way to get through the breakup of a long-term relationship. Even if you were the one who wanted out, the practical changes in your daily life will create stress. Change, even positive change, always generates some stress. If nothing else, you will have to deal with more tasks and less money, particularly if you have kids. You may also have fewer friends because some friendships were mutual.

Most breakups, though, create sadness in both parties. It's important to establish some kind of grieving process to help you work through the emotional turmoil. It's easy to wallow in the pain, but a little structure, maybe even a loose timetable for getting back on track, can relieve some of your stress by making life feel less random, less out of control.

Still, give yourself enough time to heal and to get comfortable with your new situation. Here are some specific suggestions.

- Have someone determine objectively whether your kids need professional counseling, even if it is just for the short term. Your children may seem okay to you, but getting a second opinion from an objective source is best for their long-term mental well-being.
- Join a singles group or a group of recently unpartnered people for support. If you don't have time or don't want to join a group that meets regularly, join an online group.
- Reach out and ask for help from family or friends. Don't feel guilty or embarrassed for not staying in a relationship that was not right for you. It may be the first time in your life that you feel you have failed at something. You haven't, so be kind to yourself and ask for the support you need.
- If you have children with your former spouse, encourage a continuing relationship between them. Your relationship may have failed, but that is no excuse for not supporting and encouraging your children to develop meaningful relationships with both you and their father.
- Always remind yourself that this is a process and you will get through it.
- Stay busy. It will take your mind off the breakup.
- Don't spy on your ex's new life.
- Focus on self-care—you deserve it!

Holidays

Are holidays or family gatherings a frequent stressor or trigger in your life? Here's something ironic: Imagine that you've followed the approach outlined in this book and established a solid routine that allows for a comfortable existence in the BestStress Zone. Now comes the holidays, and as quick as you can say "Seasons Greetings," your routine—the result of so much hard work—gets completely disrupted because of travel, family obligations, and a whole bunch of special stresses and pressures. Research based in the United States has studied the effects of Christmas and stress. Did you know that more people die of heart disease on Christmas than on any other day of the year? The New Year's holiday is right up there, too. Doctors call this phenomenon of discrete peaks around Christmas and New Year's the *Christmas coronary syndrome* and suggest some possible reasons for it.

- Changes in food and alcohol consumed during the holidays. Just like greater amounts of fats and sweets, alcohol also has a direct toxic effect on the heart, causing what we sometimes call "holiday heart," the abnormal heart rhythm known as *atrial fibrillation.*
- Respiratory diseases make people more vulnerable during the holidays. This is due to the increased use of fireplaces and to environmental toxins (particulate pollution is higher in the winter). Also, many older people with risks for suffering heart attacks also have other risk factors, such as a history of smoking, chronic bronchitis, and frequent upper-respiratory infections.
- Patients with chest pain delay seeking care during the holidays. Instead of responding quickly to abnormal pain or unusual shortness of breath, people are likely to put off going to the hospital ER to avoid disrupting the family gatherings.
- Emotional stress can trigger an acute stress response.

Here are eight tips for reducing the emotional effect of stress in your life and for your loved ones during the holidays.

1. Give yourself the first gift by committing to self-care during the holiday season. Whatever your health routine is, stick to it.

Pack meds and relevant medical items early if you're going on a trip.

- Eat breakfast every morning—proteins are a must.
- Get enough sleep. It improves your resilience in dealing with triggers, and you'll feel better.
- Don't forget fitness. You don't have to follow your normal routine, but do not abandon fitness and exercise altogether during the holidays. Even a brisk walk with your family can be beneficial, not to mention a great way to get reacquainted.
- Integrate relaxation therapy of some type into each day. It only takes a few minutes.

2. Anticipate these common holiday stress triggers and have a plan for dealing with them, if avoiding them is impossible or impractical:
   - Time constraints
   - Financial concerns
   - Entertaining
   - Gift-giving
   - Traveling
   - Decorating
   - People and relationships
   - Food and drink (make a plan for how much you will eat and drink, and stick to it)
   - Shopping (especially with children in tow, crowds and safety can cause extra concern)
   - Emotional-memory triggers (holidays can often carry the unseen emotional weight of memories—of a departed loved one, for instance, or of difficult holiday encounters in the past)

3. Be realistic about holiday expectations; establish your priorities and maintain a balanced perspective.
   - Discuss priorities with everyone involved who is close to you. What does each person *really* want most out of the holidays—reflection on spiritual beliefs, personal tranquility, shopping, good food, time with family and friends? None of this can happen when you are stressed. You may find that the

important people in your life would happily abandon the traditional holiday festivities in favor of establishing new, and perhaps more meaningful, family traditions.

- Delegate by enlisting the help of family members to complete holiday tasks. *Everyone* can have an appropriate task:

   Help in caring for pets

   Being a special host or hostess to an older relative

   Emptying the trash

   Checking in to run last-minute errands

   Help with taking down the tree

   Wrapping the presents

   Being "in charge"—cleaning up after the gifts are opened

   Giving Mom a back rub

- Establish a budget and stick with it. Reach a consensus on the "*exchange* value" of not overspending; in other words, using the money you save to spend on spring break, summer at the beach, or a college fund.

- If providing elaborate meals is a potential stress trigger for you, have the meal catered, or ask your guests to bring potluck dishes.

4. Have a sense of humor. If something goes wrong or doesn't go according to plan, shrug it off. Focus on the excitement of being with family and friends.

5. Put aside the idea of having "perfect"
   - foods;
   - decorations;
   - peoples' responses to your actions;
   - behavior of the kids; and
   - timing of events.

6. Avoid overload.
   - Simply avoid the words *should* or *must*. Think in terms of what you prefer.
   - Stick to a schedule as much as possible, but be flexible.
   - Minimize the stress of shopping by using home delivery, online retailers, mail order, and so on.

7. Practice saying no.
   - Say yes only to what you really want to do or to what aligns best with your 3Ps (purpose, passions, and priorities).
8. Be realistic about relationships.
   - Never forget that individuals and families change and grow over time, as do traditions. You might be surprised by new attitudes. Remember that growth is always a possibility.
   - Rethink your perception of the *roles* of various people, including yourself.
   - Stop obsessing about the presence of someone you have issues with, and really try to reach out. Listen from the heart to what others have to say. You'll find that the effort (1) refreshes and improves relationships, (2) creates opportunities to articulate and refine your own thoughts and feelings, and (3) helps you feel connected.
   - Consider the gift of forgiveness.
   - Check yourself for automatic negative thoughts.
   - Don't overdose on togetherness.
   - Make a holiday safety agreement with teenagers or young adults who come home for the holidays, regarding driving, curfews, and checking in.
   - Plan for predictable situations. Practice your responses to the trigger-inducing questions about your weight that you can expect from Aunt Mary, for example.
   - Family members who have experienced a recent loss need special attention. Listen with empathy; reminisce with elders. Provide reassurance, but avoid peddling guilt. Help them out with a tangible service. Don't wait to be asked. Allow them time to participate in a social gathering on their terms.

Finally, here are simple steps you can put into place to specifically avoid cardiovascular deaths in your family during the holidays.

1. If you have high blood pressure, coronary disease, or heart failure, do the following:
   - Pack your meds in your carry-on bags. Carry a copy of your EKG in case you have to go to an emergency room.

- Follow your usual self-care routine; exercise or walk if you are in a rehab program. Ask and encourage any family members to do the same. Go with them to the mall to walk if you need to, or send the kids and make it a family outing.

2. Drink in moderation or not at all.
3. Avoid known triggers, such as the following:
   - Excess physical exertion (shoveling snow, lifting heavy boxes, etc.)
   - Overeating
   - Lack of sleep
   - Emotional stress
   - Illegal drugs
   - Anger
4. Don't delay: if you feel that you need to seek medical care, do so immediately. It's okay to go to the nearest emergency room even if you aren't in your hometown.
5. Get your flu shot if you are at risk for cardiac compromise due to respiratory infections.

Stress Related to Uncertainty and the Unexpected

Expectations are embedded in your routines, roles, and norms in life. The same expectations that create efficiency in life can undermine you when unexpected events occur. I call this the paradox of planning. You can only experience "unexpected" disruptive events if you have expectations. It pays to be aware of your expectations. Expectations may create a bias in how you interpret and perceive events so that only your hunches are confirmed. You are very aware of events and situations that you agree with and may be troubled by others that may be important signals of things to come. You can lose track of reality. One way to avoid doing the latter is by being mindful. Mindfulness is a style of mental functioning characterized by having a keen awareness of context, details, and deviations from your expectations.

1. Awareness and attention are key elements of mindfulness. Mindful people have the "big picture" of the moment. Mindfulness is also called situational awareness. Mindfulness requires a certain quality of attention, and, unlike situational awareness, there is

a capacity to analyze and continuously refine and adjust your expectations based on newer experiences. It is having the capacity to invent new expectations that make sense of unprecedented events. Being mindful makes it less likely that you misunderstand, misestimate, and misidentify what you experience.

2. Mindfulness means having a clear and detailed comprehension of emerging threats. You need to notice small failures and not simplify or normalize them. If you anticipate certain problems, you can prevent unexpected disruptive events. You do this by making sense of emerging patterns.

3. Being mindful in the BestStress Zone means being committed to anticipation. As is true for most of us today, however, sometimes things are beyond your control, such as the current recession or losing your job. When things fail, you must be resilient. Resilience gives you the ability to deal with unexpected disruptive events. If you are resilient, you can absorb the unexpected and still manage to function. Resilience requires flexibility and a willingness to learn and grow. It is about being able to bounce back . . . not reacting to the point that you are disturbed, but rather bouncing back to your original point of balance and equanimity. Today, more than ever, you need to be committed to learning and growth, sometimes without necessarily knowing what you will need to learn.

In Summary

Life in the BestStress Zone requires skills and knowledge that mitigate harmful responses to stress. The underlying strategy is pretty simple and, in a way, comparable to the way things are in my ER. When I am on duty as an ER physician, I lead the clinical care aspect of the team and am the person who is most accountable. Every team member, from the team leader to the housekeeper, has a clearly defined role. They all know what is expected of them and so understand their value to the team. We have plans in place, called *triage protocols*, for dealing with common situations, demands, and challenges. We can't predict what's going to happen on any given shift, but we are fully prepared. Our combined technical knowledge and skills allow us to achieve a "flow" state by the time the third or fourth trauma victim rolls in the door on a Saturday night, when a grandmother comes in with heart failure at 4 a.m., or when a parent carries in her four-year-old asthmatic son who can barely breathe.

For less dramatic emergencies, we use what we call in medicine a SOAP assessment. Here is how this works. The nurse and the physician obtain the patient's report of his or her "sick" experience (S = subjective). Next, we assess information that can be measured regarding the experience (O = objective information). Third, the physician uses a process called *clinical reasoning* to make an assessment (A) or a diagnosis. Finally, a plan (P) of action is negotiated between the physician and the patient.

When you, the patient, leave the doctor's office or the ER, you are armed with a plan. The plan is in some ways a mini-experiment. Sometimes physicians don't have a specific diagnosis. In the emergency department, my assessment most often leads to a specific diagnosis; however, my primary concern is resuscitation and elimination of any potential acute life-threatening situation. If there are a number of concerns when a patient presents to a physician, my approach is to be systematic and methodical. Furthermore, it is important to identify the root cause of problems, as opposed to merely treating symptoms.

How does this ER experience relate to life in the BestStress Zone? Don't sweep your stress under a rug. Embrace it. Plan for it. Use potentially stressful situations as opportunities to get into a *flow* state. We may have a quiet period in the ER, but we know what's coming. Patients will walk or roll through the door. I want you to use the information you've gained so far—knowing who you are, what is important to you, what stressors you are likely to face—to do your own SOAP assessment. What are you feeling, in your body and in your mind (S)? What are some of the specific experiences in your current life that you know to be stressors (O)? Now, make an objective assessment (A). Finally, decide which zone strategies will be the most effective for you and implement them into a plan of action (P).

In the next and final chapter, I will explain how you can stabilize and maintain the quality of life that you will experience in the Best-Stress Zone.

9

defending and nurturing your beststress zone
self-care strategies, relaxation, and the power pause

The final step in this process is to ensure that the changes you've made stay with you for the long-term future. I'll show you how to defend, nurture, and sustain yourself in the BestStress Zone, that zone of health and safety and positive potential that you've created during the course of reading this book. This chapter includes many self-care strategies, including sleep, nutrition, and physical fitness. We'll also cover relaxation: what it is, how to achieve it, and how to integrate recovery, renewal, and relaxation into every day of your life. I'll explain how true control of your life necessitates having mechanisms in place to deal with the unexpected. Remember that unpredictability is the greatest source of stress. If you can establish preset response plans for different kinds of emergencies in your life, you'll be able to ease the anxiety that commonly simmers below the surface.

Think about the way a basketball team uses a *zone defense*. A rigid or static defense can be quickly penetrated, but a properly executed zone defense remains fluid, reshaping and reforming to adjust to changing conditions on the court, and thus is potentially impregnable. The Best-Stress Zone works the same way. We all know that even the best-laid plans sometimes fall apart for reasons we can't anticipate, so together we'll create a BestStress Zone filled with strategies for maintaining balance even during life's inevitable and unexpected changes.

Self-Care Strategies

The most important element of the BestStress Zone approach requires no equipment and costs you nothing. Begin by embracing the following components of a healthy attitude. First among these is gratitude. Even as you acknowledge the inevitability of stress, you can also admit that every situation in your life offers something that you can be grateful for. Learn to look for these positive and future-oriented elements in stressful situations and see how quickly your burden becomes lighter. You might even be able to find humor in these situations, which is the next crucial step in attitude adjustment. Research has proved the therapeutic value of humor: it's adaptive, a cathartic release of tension, an outlet for hostility and anger, and a defense against depression. Humor indicates emotional maturity but also triggers healthful biological changes. Laughter increases muscular and respiratory activity, and it elevates the heart rate and the production of antistress hormones.

In chapter 3, I introduced the concept of *flow*, a state of being in which you are fully engaged and challenged and able to apply your skills in a positive, productive way. In the flow state, your perception of time changes. You feel as if time is flowing smoothly forward; you are centered and directed. Part of living in the BestStress Zone is being able to get into that flow state more often or more regularly, which sometimes requires focused attention and clear strategies.

A key self-care strategy is to change or reduce any tendency toward type A behavior. You want to do away with the irritability, impatience, and sense of urgency about time that is a trait of so many driven and high-achieving women. Most people aren't born with type A behavior, but rather, it is learned, like almost all other types of behavior. We learn it early on, from parents who rush us to get up, do our chores, or finish our meals, and from teachers who demand carefully completed school-work in a limited amount of time. Later, the behavior is reinforced by bosses and managers who have similar expectations about your work-load, even when that workload has become unreasonable. For better or for worse, most of these behaviors are rewarded throughout life. Good things come to those who toe the line, or actually to those who are first in line. Perform well, and get the brass ring.

Try to observe your own behavior objectively, and look for signs of type A tendencies. Do you rush to beat traffic lights as they are turning red? Do you find yourself telling your children to hurry with a raised voice when you could just as easily stop, take a breath, and find ways to enjoy your moments with them? I don't want to discourage you from maintaining a high level of competence and productivity or to take your commitments and responsibilities less seriously. I do, however, urge you to consider the following twelve strategies.

1. Recognize that life is always unfinished. It's not realistic to believe that you'll have a chance to finish everything you need to or want to before some other task presents itself. You will always have a to-do list.
2. During a conversation, listen quietly to what other people are saying. Refrain from interrupting them or trying to speed them along in any other way. Also, ask yourself:
   - Do I really have anything important to say or to add?
   - Does anyone want to hear what I have to say?
   - Is this the time to say what I want to say?

If the answer to any of these questions is no, try to remain quiet.
3. Concentrate on one task, person, or interaction at a time. Try to refrain from multitasking.
4. Don't interfere with others doing their work, particularly if it's work you've delegated, and even if you think you can get it done faster or better.

5. When confronted with making a choice about a task or a chore, ask yourself these questions:
    - Will this task have importance five years from now?
    - Must this task be done right away?
    - What would happen if the task weren't done at all?

6. Refrain from making appointments or scheduling activities that are unnecessary. This will allow you to keep your schedule more flexible.

7. Remember that your time is precious and must be protected. Whenever possible, ask whether you can engage someone else to handle a task, possibly for pay, and free up your valuable time to focus on and execute tasks directly related to your 3Ps.

8. Make a point of going to restaurants, theaters, or other venues where you know you'll have to spend some amount of time waiting. Think about using that time to engage more fully and directly with your spouse or companion, or, if you are alone, treasure the enforced downtime. Get to know yourself.

9. Smile whenever you can, at whomever you can. You'll be amazed at how this can reduce free-floating anxiety.

10. Thank people for the nice things they've done.

11. Remind yourself daily that no matter how many things you've acquired, they are essentially worthless if they don't improve your mind or your spirit.

12. Engage regularly—daily, if possible—in a relaxation technique. There are many relaxation practices, and I'll discuss one, the *Power Pause*, later in this chapter.

Next, let's set up a self-care strategy to help control your anxiety. Earlier, I defined anxiety as a subjective feeling of tension, apprehension, nervousness, or worry that usually has its roots in irrational fears and thoughts. It often manifests as chronic worrying, fears or phobias, panic attacks, obsessions and compulsions, hypochondria, shyness, or a specific performance anxiety. Keep in mind that anxiety can act as a trigger of the stress response, or it can itself be a part of the response. When you are anxious, your body will respond as it does when you feel fear: your heart rate will become rapid, your respiratory rate and your blood pressure will increase. In other words, your biological response is turned on, sometimes in an exaggerated form. You might feel weak, faint, or numb. My approach to coaching clients with anxiety is based on the extensive work of the preeminent researcher and clinician in the area of anxiety disorders, Dr. David Burns.

Here are some quick action steps for managing anxiety in the Best-Stress Zone.

1. *Change the way you think.* Anxiety results from distorted and illogical thoughts. As simplistic as it sounds, if you can change the way you think, you will change the way you feel. When you feel anxious, worried, or panicky, you are likely thinking and telling yourself that something terrible is about to happen. Your negative thoughts will reinforce a vicious cycle.

2. *Confront and deal with or make a conscious decision to delay and avoid specifically anxiety-provoking situations for a discrete period of time.* This probably sounds overly simplistic, but I'm continually surprised at the number of my clients who repeatedly put themselves into situations in which they know they will experience unrealistic fears that trigger anxiety. If you simply can't at this time confront a trigger, then for now avoid the situation. If engaging in a task or a situation is necessary to get you closer to your 3Ps, develop a strategy for confronting and overcoming the specific underlying fear. For instance, if the thought of public speaking automatically triggers your stress response, but your professional success, which you've determined to be an important life priority, requires you to make such presentations, try to find a book, a course, or even a private coach to help you break through that fear.

3. *Make use of relaxation techniques in conjunction with imaging.* You can systematically desensitize yourself by imagining yourself in the anxiety-provoking situation *while* practicing a specific relaxation response. It helps to develop a "fear hierarchy," which essentially means breaking down the feared task or situation into smaller, more manageable, discrete elements, and then addressing each of these individually. Again, using the fear of public speaking as an example, you can imagine getting the request to make the presentation, preparing your speech or materials, the first moment when you step up to the podium before that terrifying sea of unfamiliar faces, or feeling frozen by a question that you didn't prepare for. You can even visualize the positive conclusion—the

sound of warm applause or laughter or the sight of audience members smiling and nodding their approval. Work through the steps, starting at the beginning, and practice your relaxation response for each individual step. You will be able to desensitize yourself more easily in this way, ultimately eliminating the fear from the discrete elements and thus doing away with the anxiety caused by the larger experience.

4. *Try self-talk strategies.* Ask yourself questions that keep a feared task or situation in perspective, such as "What is the real worst-case outcome?" Or "How badly could it really go?" If you prepare well and rehearse, and if you know your audience, what are the odds that you could truly fail to effectively communicate or persuade them in your presentation? Going even deeper, ask yourself how bad the ramifications would really be if you completely botched the presentation? Would you lose your job? Would the company go under? Most likely not, and if you accept that, you can free yourself to ask questions about what your real underlying fears might be. Is it about losing respect? Is it about rejection? Even at this level, asking yourself similar questions can be very helpful. Will your coworkers never respect you again because of one bad presentation? Will your friends abandon you? Would you abandon them? Talking yourself through an anxiety-provoking situation in this way can be like diffusing a ticking time bomb. Better yet, you might convince yourself that the bomb never really existed in the first place.

5. *Practice forgiveness.* Forgiveness is another powerful tool for defending your BestStress Zone. A psychologist might define forgiveness as the juxtaposition of positive emotions (such as sympathy, empathy, compassion, or love) with negative emotions of unforgiveness (anger, resentment, jealousy, and so on). Thus, you can think of forgiveness as an emotion-focused coping strategy to reduce the stressful reaction to a transgression or another negative event. This idea is supported by research that shows that forgiveness can actually lessen the physiological effects of the stress response, leading to better health. Forgiveness also offers more indirect benefits, such as increasing your openness to social support, improving your interpersonal relationships, and actively engaging your spiritual tendencies.

Following is an exercise that will determine the role anxiety plays in your life.

Anxiety Self-Care Exercise

. . . .

If you believe that anxiety is a significant problem for you, write down your thoughts in response to the following:

1. I am mostly likely to experience anxiety when: __
2. My underlying fear is related to: __
3. The advance planning that would help me avoid exposure to an anxiety-provoking situation includes: __
4. Self-talk that I can use to manage this anxiety includes: __

Physical Self-Care

"I just don't have time" is the comment so many of my clients make when it comes to self-care. You have so many responsibilities that it's easy to forget to take care of yourself. And while it can be hard to place self-care at the top of your to-do list, it is an important aspect of living in the BestStress Zone.

Nutrition

Experts don't agree on the specific relationship between stress and nutrition. We do know that stress increases the body's basic need for calories by as much as 200 percent. Stress hormones increase the body's production of heat. Ultimately, stress induces *caloric inefficiency*, meaning that the amount of energy created by the body is out of balance with the amount of fuel (food) taken in. This is one reason that we feel the need to eat more when we are stressed and why many people experience significant changes in their weight.

Many theories have been explored, with researchers hoping to demonstrate a danger or a benefit associated with various food items or nutritional patterns. According to researcher Carlos Montesinos of Amerisciences, one of the few nutritional-support companies that adheres to FDA standards for its products, nutrition can play a key role in either helping or hurting your physiological ability to respond and adapt to stress. Being mindful about what you put into your body can have a tremendous impact on your health. Maintaining a balanced diet means taking in the right proportions of the core macronutrients: proteins, carbohydrates, fats, and micronutrients. It is the micronutrients—vitamins, minerals, and other phytochemicals—that are often lacking in our 24/7 lifestyles.

Chronic stress has been shown to decrease the body's stores of key micronutrients and vitamins, with the following possible ramifications.

- Vitamin C has been proved to enhance the action of certain immune cells.
- Deficiencies in vitamins A and B12 and folate will cause impaired production of infection-fighting antibodies.

Stress also seems to increase the body's requirements for vitamins such as thiamine, riboflavin, and niacin. These and other B-complex vitamins, along with vitamin C, are the ones most negatively affected by chronic stress, and a deficiency in these vitamins can result in anxiety, depression, insomnia, and muscle weakness, independent of other personal or social circumstances. Supplementation may not only remedy clinical nutrient deficiencies, but can also provide micronutrients (cofactors, coenzymes, phytochemicals, vitamins, and others) in optimal amounts that would otherwise prove difficult to obtain from the diet alone. Micronutrients help the endocrine, cardiovascular, neurological, and other systems that are associated with the stress response. Many of these biological systems rely on specific micronutrients to effectively organize an appropriate response to such stress. The immune system, for example, depends on a readily available pool of omega-3 fatty acids to produce anti-inflammatory compounds called prostaglandins and leukotrienes. Should these micronutrients be unavailable, the body uses whatever alternative fats are available, which often promote inflammation. Proper supplementation can mean the difference between a healthy stress response and an unhealthy one. Following are lists of specific stress-related problems that you can address with proper nutritional supplementation. These supplements are available through www.stressreliefsupplements.com.

- *Sleep.* Valerian, thanks in part to its many components (valerinic acid, monoterpenes, sesquiterpenes, and so on), reduces the amount of time that it takes you to fall asleep and is generally regarded as a mild tranquilizer that you can use when you feel restless and stressed. Valerinic acid is believed to inhibit the catabolism of gamma-aminobutyric acid (GABA), increasing GABA concentrations and decreasing central nervous system activity. Unlike unnatural supplements, valerian produces no amnesia and has no addictive properties.

- *Energy:*
  - The B vitamins play an important role as cofactors in cellular energy metabolism, including glycolysis and the Krebs cycle. B-vitamin deficiency can cause fatigue and lethargy.
  - Thiamin is involved in the release of acetylcholine, and the need for both thiamin and riboflavin has been documented to increase during prolonged periods of stress (both physical and mental).
  - Pyridoxine performs functions as a cofactor for about seventy different enzyme systems, many related to stress exposure.
  - Pyridoxine, folate, and cyanocobalamin are all involved in the metabolism of homocysteine, a by-product of metabolic stress.
  - Ginseng and its triterpenoid saponins, also known as ginsenosides, have been shown to improve mental performance during extended periods of physical and mental stress. Ginseng also reduces normal insulin requirements, potentially benefiting people who have increased insulin secretion due to prolonged stress (that is not diabetes or disease related).
- *Cardiovascular disease prevention.* Omega-3 fatty acids EPA and DHA competitively inhibit the pro-inflammatory series-2 prostaglandin and series-4 leukotriene synthesis. DHA appears to have mood-stabilizing properties, as it is incorporated into the phospholipid bilayer membranes of neurons involved in neurotransmitter signaling. Though the mechanism remains unknown, EPA appears to have cardio-protective effects and may play a role in maintaining the normal electric activity of the heart.
- *Immunity.* Taking eleuthero, also known as Siberian ginseng, has been associated with increased physical stamina, cognitive abil-

ity, and immune-stimulating and -modulating effects under various stress models. Hypoglycemic and reduced insulin effects have also been demonstrated (that are not diabetes or disease related).

- *Focus and concentration.* Ginkgo biloba has antioxidant activity, as well as a peripheral circulation-enhancing activity. It has been shown to be effective at improving the cognitive ability of normal-cognitive individuals under stressful conditions (e.g., students during exam season).

Here are some suggestions and guidelines for nurturing yourself nutritionally in the BestStress Zone. It probably won't surprise you that these principles for antistress eating practices match the programs suggested by weight-loss experts, peak-performance coaches, and lately even some psychologists, as part of their memory-improvement or cognitive fitness programs. Really, there's no secret about what makes for a healthy diet.

- *A balanced diet.* Diets high in saturated fats increase the amount of cholesterol in the blood, adding to the risk of cardiovascular disease. Conversely, it's believed that low-fat diets help prevent certain cancers, such as breast and prostate cancer. A diet high in fiber is thought to lower the risk of colon cancer. Dietary fats also influence the syntheses of a group of fatty acids called prostaglandins, which mediate the immune system in relation to stress.
- *Calcium.* Stress can interfere with the absorption of calcium in the intestine, so the calcium is expelled, instead of finding its way through the bloodstream to the bones. Women, especially postmenopausal women, need calcium to prevent osteoporosis. Some may need to add calcium supplements to their dietary regimen, in addition to doing regular weight-bearing exercises.
- *Salt.* We already know that chronic stress can lead to elevated blood pressure, but a high level of salt in your diet can compound the problem. Salt can also cause your body to retain fluids, resulting in weight gain.
- *Pseudo-stressors.* These are foods that can actually produce a physical response that is similar to the stress response, by

triggering reactions in the sympathetic nervous system. Examples of pseudo-stressors include colas, coffee, tea, chocolate, and other foods that might contain caffeine or other stimulants. Most of us turn to these foods precisely because they increase the metabolism, which makes us feel more alert, but, of course, that results in the increased production of stress hormones, which elevates our heart rate and blood pressure, putting us at greater risk for developing health problems.

Here are twelve steps to healthy eating that you can start today.

1. Eat a balanced diet that includes core macronutrients—carbohydrates, proteins, and fats. Current recommendations for a balanced dietary ratio are 50–60 percent complex carbohydrates, 25–35 percent protein, and 20–30 percent fat. More important, eat four to five small meals a day, and when you eat, take the time to enjoy your food. You will decrease the amount of food you consume if you eat purposely for enjoyment, slowly savoring each bite.
2. Eat a low-fat, high-fiber diet, substituting skim milk for whole milk, for example, or staying away from fried foods and opting for whole-grain products and lots of salads, fruit, and fresh vegetables.
3. Eat cruciferous vegetables, such as broccoli, cauliflower, and brussels sprouts.
4. Limit your intake of alcohol.
5. Limit your intake of caffeine.
6. Increase your intake of vitamin D by eating cereals, leafy green vegetables, liver, and fish.
7. Get more vitamin C from citrus fruits, tomatoes, cabbages, and potatoes.
8. Add more zinc to your diet. Zinc is another necessary mineral for immune cell responsiveness Oysters contain more zinc per serving than any other food, but red meat and poultry can also supply zinc.
9. Focus more on your waist-to-hip ratio, rather than on your body mass index. This is a better measure of your risk

for developing cardiovascular disease, diabetes, and abnormal blood lipids than your simple weight or body mass index. Be realistic about your weight. Lose pounds if you need to, but don't increase your personal stress by trying to fight biology. Obsessing about your weight and body shape can lead to anorexia nervosa and bulimia, and not only in teenagers.

10. You may want to consider taking nutritional supplements. Even if you don't take supplements regularly, it might be appropriate to do so during times of high stress. Of particular importance are vitamin C, B-complex vitamins, and calcium.

11. Limit foods that contain sugar and salt.

12. Get regular exercise. Keep your bones and muscles strong—especially your most important muscle, the heart—and keep blood flowing to your brain.

Sleep

Most of us get less sleep than we need. Sleep gives your body a chance to restore its basic functions. In stress terms, it allows all of your physical processes, which are elevated when you are stressed, to return to their baseline levels. Most medical experts recommend that adults get from seven to nine hours every night.

There are four sleep stages: light sleep, intermediate sleep, deep sleep, and REM sleep.

Sleep disturbance is one of the most common symptoms of stress, and the specific pattern of insomnia changes according to the underlying cause. When you are stressed, sleep disturbances tend to occur at the beginning of the sleep cycle or in the early morning hours.

- Onset insomnia: difficulty falling asleep at the beginning of the night, often associated with anxiety disorders.
- Middle insomnia: waking during the middle of the night, difficulty maintaining sleep. This is often associated with pain syndromes or medical illness.
- Terminal (or late) insomnia: early morning waking. This is characteristic of clinical depression.

There is also a clear relationship between sleep and performance. According to Dr. Charles A. Czeisler, a sleep researcher at Harvard, four major sleep-related factors affect our ability to think and perform at peak levels.

1. The natural homeostatic drive for sleep. The body's natural need for sleep is determined largely by the number of consecutive hours that you have been awake. When you've been awake for an extended period, the brain takes over, sending signals to the body that it wants to sleep, in fact, *needs* to sleep. Sometimes you feel drowsy, but other times you feel as if you must sit down right where you are and get some sleep. With every hour that you remain awake, the sleep drive grows stronger. I can attest to this one firsthand, having tried to drive home too many times after a long and chaotic night shift in the ER.

2. The total amount of sleep gotten over several days. If you get at least eight hours of sleep a night, your level of alertness and ability to think clearly should remain stable throughout the day. But if the average person gets less than five hours of sleep a day for several days, a sleep deficit builds up. The brain finds it more difficult to function. In fact, Dr. Cliff Saper, also at Harvard Medical School, states that if you get four or less hours of sleep for four consecutive nights, you will have the same level of problems with thinking and analyzing things properly as if you had been awake for twenty-four hours—which is the equivalent to being legally drunk.

3. Circadian rhythms—the human body's internal clock and pacemaker. Paradoxically, circadian rhythms work alongside of, but in opposition to, the homeostatic sleep drive. Your internal clock sends out its strongest demand for sleep just before you habitually wake up, and its strongest demand for waking is one to three hours before you usually go to bed. It is thought that humans, unlike animals, do not take catnaps throughout the day. In fact, this circadian system serves to keep you awake at precisely the time that you are tempted to take a nap or grab a coffee.

4. Sleep inertia. This is the grogginess most of us experience when we first get up. It takes about five to twenty minutes for the brain to really wake up. Based on our understanding of sleep cycles,

this is why a "power nap" should not be longer than forty minutes—the time it takes to get into the phase of sleep that generates inertia.

Sleep problems are much more common that most people imagine, but it's such a complex issue, with roots and causes and symptoms that differ for each individual, that I can't really do it justice in this book. Don't take sleep problems lightly, however, as the long-term effects on your health can be devastating. There are sleep clinics at many major hospitals and a host of books and programs from reputable authorities available to you. Here are some quick tips for sleep hygiene.

- Establish a routine, taking into consideration your circadian rhythm and your work schedule. (Are you, for example, a night-shift worker or a traveler?)
- Establish a presleep ritual. If you are a worrier, your routine should include keeping a bedside pad to jot down things you don't want to forget to worry about tomorrow. All kidding aside, this really can help. Write the items down and let them go.
- If you are in bed for more than an hour and have not fallen asleep, get up and perform some strenuous task that does not challenge you mentally or do a bit of leisure reading.
- Use rooms other than the bedroom for activities related to your job.
- Don't consume alcohol or stimulants within two to three hours of your anticipated bedtime.
- Milk or other substances containing tryptophan or valerian are natural remedies to assist you in falling asleep.
- Take a moment to consciously express gratitude, either silently or aloud, for at least one positive thing that occurred during the day.
- If you travel across time zones and jet lag is a problem for you, consider getting *anchor* sleep—a regular period of sleep taken at the same time each day—which is believed to help train and stabilize your internal clock, or circadian rhythm.

Relaxation

The essence of the BestStress Zone is control—control of your inevitable stress triggers, control of your physical well-being, control of your whole life—and the core element of control is relaxation. So, what exactly is relaxation? You might enjoy sitting back with a good book or your favorite television show, or you might find soothing relief in activities like golf, gardening, surfing the Internet, shopping for shoes, or taking your kids out for ice cream. These are certainly stress-reducing pastimes that slow you down and distract you, but they are not relaxation. Neither is meditation the same as relaxation, although meditative states can lead to relaxation. Meditation commonly describes a state of concentrated mental attention, focused on an isolated thought or object of awareness. Usually, it involves turning your attention inward onto a single point of reference, often in a religious or spiritual context. Relaxation is a state of mind and body that is opposite to the stress state. Remember that the stress response is primarily a set of specific biological processes, and so, too, is the relaxation response, originally described in the late 1960s by Dr. Herbert Benson at the Harvard Medical School. Ideally, you want to be able to trigger the release of antistress hormones and decrease your heart rate, metabolic rate, and breathing rate. In this section, I'll introduce you to a number of different relaxation techniques and finally focus on one technique that I developed, which has been very successful for my clients. I call it the Power Pause, and I designed it to trigger your relaxation response.

The relaxation response and the stress response describe opposite processes. You experience the stress response, which is sometimes called the "flight-or-fight" response, when faced with an acute demand, challenge, or situation, whether it's a deer darting out in front of your car, a company reorganization, or the death of a loved one. The body releases stress hormones—cortisol and adrenaline—that strengthen your natural defenses and heighten your preparedness and alertness. The stress response is automatic and virtually instantaneous. It is the body's instinctive, unconscious means of protecting itself. The relaxation response works in the opposite way: it is triggered only with conscious intent. Although the stress response naturally turns itself off, containing the flood of stress hormones once the crisis has passed, that process merely brings your body back to its natural baseline levels. True relaxation is a learned skill, enabling you to actually alter your mood in a different direction. You can trigger the release of endorphins, nitrous oxide, and other antistress hormones and chemicals that will actually create a sense of heightened euphoria, a kind of "natural high." The relaxation is really a form of self-medication, without medicine.

Your body and mind need that natural healing and the restorative effects of true relaxation throughout the day every day. Relaxation is as important a cornerstone of life in the BestStress Zone as good nutrition, fitness, and regular sleep are. Imagine the liberation and joy of knowing that you can use your own internal resources to heal yourself in real time—ten minutes at your desk, on the road, or in a private space at home—with no trainers or gurus, no special equipment, and no cost.

I'll now describe some commonly used relaxation techniques. Please understand that I only want to give you a general sense of these techniques here. If any of them sound right for you or for your lifestyle, I urge you to follow up by seeking out resources to learn as much as you can.

- *Deep breathing.* This may be the most basic relaxation technique. It is the foundation of, or at least incorporated into, many other techniques. You can do it anywhere and at any time. It's simple. Inhale deeply, filling your lungs in a way that expands your abdomen outward. You can place your hand on your abdomen to make sure that it is fully expanded after you've taken the breath. If your stomach doesn't rise, either you haven't taken a deep-enough breath or you're unconsciously tightening your abdominal muscles. Once you're satisfied that the inhalation was as deep and full as possible, start exhaling, slowly, through your mouth. Repeat this cycle several times, and then rest quietly. Some people suggest counting as you breathe: inhale for four slow beats, then exhale for four slow beats. You can even pause and hold your breath calmly in between, for another four slow beats.

- *Progressive muscle relaxation.* Begin this simple three-step exercise by selecting a muscle group to focus on (neck, shoulders, lower back, legs, and so on). First, tense those muscles and try to concentrate your mind on the feeling of tension. Next, consciously relax that muscle group, again focusing your attention on the feeling of relaxation. The third and final step is mental: focus your mind on the difference between the tensed state and the relaxed state. You can begin at the head and work your way down to your feet, or you can start at your feet and work up. Ultimately, you've spent some amount of time consciously relaxing each set of muscles in your body, and you've worked to create a memory of that feeling.

- *Visualization.* Here is another relaxation method that makes use of the mind and the imagination. Assume a comfortable position and close your eyes. If you like, you can practice deep breathing as you do this. You are ready to experiment with visualization now and can choose from several options. You can imagine a tranquil scene, such as a park, a beach, or floating in water, and then place yourself in that imagined scene. Some people heighten the intensity or believability of the image they've created by adding sounds or aromas. Another technique is to visualize the desired outcome related to some specific stressor in your life. If you're worried about work, you might picture yourself finally getting your in-box cleared or your desk organized or getting praise from coworkers, customers, or your boss.

- *Biofeedback.* Biofeedback is just what it sounds like: it allows you to measure biological functions and then feed that information in a system of learning to control your body processes. Measurements include changes in skin temperature, muscle contractions, and brain-wave variations, all of which connect you more directly to the physical responses of your body. When you're stressed, you can use what you've learned to control things such as tension and can initiate other forms of relaxation.

- *Tai chi.* This ancient discipline differs from other forms of martial-arts training in that it de-emphasizes combat to focus instead on tranquility. It teaches you to remain still when faced with stress and to harmonize with aggression or fear, rather than fight against them. Through its emphasis on quiet body control, tai chi develops your strength, flexibility, and agility. There are four philosophical concepts underpinning tai chi.
  1. Silence and solitude
  2. Embracing innocence (returning to the joy of childhood) and laughter

3. Moving in accordance with the flow of nature
4. Acknowledging failure as a first step to success

- *Autogenics.* This relaxation technique is a form of self-talk. Autogenics uses self-suggestion to produce a relaxation response. You begin with deep breathing and a conscious effort to relax yourself, then follow a progression either from the head to the feet or from the feet to the head. The suggestive phrases you use might include "My arm feels heavy and warm," or "I am completely calm and relaxed." It sounds very simple but in fact requires considerable time and commitment to master. If autogenics appeals to you, you should plan to practice it on a daily basis.

The Power Pause

The Power Pause can elevate and clarify your mental state by decisively disrupting negative thoughts and emotions, which often become the stressors that plague you. It is based on Herbert Benson's relaxation response. I have linked the relaxation response with mindshifting, which I talked about in chapter 8. To begin with, keep the acronym FACTS in mind.

Focus. Focused repetition of a word or a phrase. This begins the process of disrupting your racing or negative thoughts.

Attitude. It is crucial to remain nonjudgmental of yourself and of others. Give everyone a break.

Comfortable position. Sit or lie down in a way that feels good. No torturous yoga positions are required.

Thoughts. Your goal is to focus on higher, more positive thoughts, eventually eliminating automatic negative thoughts, irrational thoughts, or wasteful thoughts.

Stay the course. This is a learned skill that requires some practice and commitment.

The Power Pause encourages you to be aware that certain thoughts and emotions can sometimes take on a life of their own, and it reminds you that they aren't the sum total of who you are. They are events in your mental life. The important thing to learn is that negative thoughts and emotions have only as much power as you give them. The level of attachment or inversion that you invest in negative thinking determines the strength of the hold that these thoughts will have over you. Who you are—your true identity—lies beyond such passing experiences. Let's break all of your thoughts down into four basic levels.

1. Negative thoughts and emotions, such as hostility, anger, fear, regret, or guilt.
2. Wasteful thoughts, such as guilt or worrying about things that might happen or should happen, when such occurrences are most likely beyond your control.
3. Necessary thoughts, such as all the things you need to remember or remain aware of every day but can clutter your mind. During the Power Pause, you'll need to let go of thoughts like "I need to fill up the car with gas," or "I have to make sure the kids get their schoolwork finished."
4. Positive thoughts, such as those that encourage peace, harmony, creativity, love, and happiness. This is the primary focus of the Power Pause.

You'll want to do a realistic self-analysis before you try to reap the benefits of a Power Pause. Survey, as objectively as you can, the kinds of thoughts that have recently dominated your awareness, and determine what level you are at currently. Of course, you will want to focus on the most positive thoughts, but don't start thinking that the Power Pause or any other relaxation technique will make your negative, necessary, or wasteful thoughts magically disappear. It's natural and appropriate to have those thoughts. Yet the biochemical reactions and changes you can achieve through the Power Pause will often allow you to view and interpret the same thoughts and information in a different, more productive way.

Some of my clients report that the Power Pause also helps them achieve unexpected but welcome epiphanies, such as an unconventional solution to a pressing problem or a new insight into a troubled interpersonal relationship. Scientific evidence supports these reports. Functional magnetic resonance imaging scans of the brain after relaxation reveal

increased blood flow into the areas of the brain associated with problem solving and memory.

I need to give you one caveat about the Power Pause: timing is very
important. I recommend a Power Pause as therapy and prevention.
For example, when you are stuck emotionally or psychologically with
a challenge on the job or dealing with a family member, or you simply
feel overwhelmed, don't push yourself through. You can't afford *not* to
stop for a Power Pause in the midst of a crisis or a stressful situation.
You can and must create an opportunity to transform your thinking and behavior and possibly the tense situation as well. A caution:
remember that the stress response can be protective. The Power Pause
is most helpful as therapy when are you on the edge of the zone and
you know that the protective elements of the stress responses are no
longer helping you. The Power Pause can also be used for prevention.
Consider a Power Pause instead of a trip to the vending machine or
grabbing a cup of coffee as a part of your break. I recommend a scheduled Power Pause at least three times a day—midmorning, midafter-
noon, and in the evening, perhaps as a transition from work to home.
You will feel the release of your innate reservoir of calming and "feel-
good" hormones and will reap the biological benefits of maintaining a
lower baseline level of adrenaline and cortisol. Using the Power Pause
helps you recover and in this way increases your resilience.

You'll recall that earlier I mentioned the idea of *focused repetition.*
There is greater power in a belief system if it is linked to a word or a
phrase and used repetitously. Dr. Herbert Benson refers to this as the
faith factor. It's okay to incorporate the Power Pause into your spiritual system or traditions, distinct from, but related to, the practice of
meditation, contemplation, or prayer. So many religious practices
contain some form of repetition, whether it's the mantras of Eastern
meditation, the repeated cycle of prayers in Catholicism or Orthodox
Judaism, or the repetitive chanting in some forms of Buddhism. Only
you can know whether certain words hold significant meaning for you,
which would be appropriate in this context. (One client of mine actually found it useful to repeat the word *power* over and over.) Even if
you don't feel strongly about any religion or spiritual tradition, you can
look into your own 3Ps—your purpose, passions, and priorities—and
find a word or a phrase that holds power for you. Ideally, whatever

word or phrase you use should be one that can be expelled in a single exhalation. If you are a runner or if you know a runner, you might be familiar with the phenomenon of "runner's high," a state of mild euphoria that is sometimes experienced about five to seven minutes into a run. Although this is partly due to the release of nitrous oxide, dopamine, and endorphins during exercise, it also occurs because of the mind-body connection with the rhythmic repetition, or cadence, of the footsteps. Focused repetition during a Power Pause can replicate that effect.

Finally, here are a few other points to bear in mind about the Power Pause before we jump in.

- The Power Pause can work for anyone, but if you have any medical or psychological conditions, you should check with your personal physician before starting this or any other relaxation program.
- The Power Pause is about focusing on yourself and putting you in control.
- Relaxation is a skill that must be developed. Don't be discouraged if you don't achieve the expected results immediately. Just like tennis, golf, video games, or playing the violin, you get good at it only through practice. Don't force it. Stick with it, and when your mind and your body are ready, you'll find yourself taking off, just like when you first learned to ride a bike.
- As with comedy, timing is everything. You will learn that you can use the Power Pause to prepare for a stressful situation or to find relief immediately after one. Or you can use it simply to maintain equilibrium throughout the day. When you first get started, don't worry about when you will use relaxation techniques; just focus on mastering the technique, and the best times will reveal themselves to you.
- As you get better at the technique, you will notice a slowing of your heart and breathing rates. These are normal and should not concern you.
- Don't get overwhelmed by performance anxiety over the Power Pause itself. This will only add to your stress. There isn't necessarily a right way to feel. If it feels good and right to you, then you know you've succeeded.

You are now ready to get into the specific steps of the Power Pause. (You can also get this information and downloadable mp3s at www.optimumstress.com.) Go forward and . . . relax!

1. Find a comfortable, quiet place and be still. Whatever seat you choose or whatever else is holding you up is your *supporting environment.* If you prefer to be stretched out, the floor could be your supporting environment.

2. Survey your mind and determine your level of thoughts and emotions. First work to eliminate negative thoughts and emotions, then the wasteful ones, by focusing your attention on positive thoughts. Be nonjudgmental, especially of yourself.

3. Clench and then release your hands, feet, shoulders, and hips. Use this technique to allow your muscles to relax, and let yourself sink into your supporting environment. Let whatever negative thoughts you may have pass through you into the floor or the supporting environment.

4. Now, either silently or aloud, repeat a word or a phrase that you have chosen because of its special meaning to you. It is particularly important to be nonjudgmental and unself-conscious at this point. If you are still holding yourself outside of the moment, watching yourself do the exercise, rather than giving yourself over to it, you will probably not get what you want out of it. Let those judgments or self-observations pass out of you, along with the other negative and wasteful thoughts. Similarly, don't let yourself get caught up in worrying about whether the relaxation is working. It's not something you can achieve by working harder at it.

5. Continue this exercise, repeating your word or phrase, for ten to twelve minutes. Use a timer so that you don't have to worry about when the time is up.

6. When you are ready to end the pause, stretch, flex, inhale, and if your eyes are closed, open them. After a few more conscious breaths, you will feel a warm sense of physical and mental well-being throughout your body.

Get Ready for Your Best Future!

More than ever, our world is in a state of constant stress, chaos, and uncertainty. If nothing else, I hope you come away from this book knowing how important it is to allow yourself to be who you want to be and not feel pressured to be superhuman. Accept and embrace the reality of your personal world and that of the larger world in which you live. You can and should anticipate uncertainty and unexpected events. Living in the BestStress Zone means getting the most out of each day, even when you are frazzled, agitated, and anxious and feel that life is out of control. This book is designed to help you find and live with optimal stress. Although women may have a unique experience of stress, because we live in a gendered society with roles and responsibilities that influence the meaning, perceptions, and sources of stress, remember that we also have many unique resources at our disposal.

This book is skills based and describes what you need to do and how to do it. You are given the tools to be able to define your personal world in terms of your purpose, passions, and priorities. At the core of life in the BestStress Zone are mental skills that you can learn and use on a daily basis. First and foremost is being self-aware. In fact, it is the self that mediates between the genetic instructions that manifest in your life and the influence of your environment. I want you to be self-assured. You are okay. This is not being self-centered. You should and must maintain *emotional integrity*, a phrase promulgated by Dr. Candace Pert. The self can make choices and prioritize. This can only be done consciously through your attention and awareness. You can actually shape and reshape your brain to create memories and scripts that support a life in the BestStress Zone.

Stress is a key determinant of health, well-being, and quality of life. Stress is an independent risk factor for heart attack. It increases the risk twofold, which is similar to elevated cholesterol above 220 mg/dl!

Now that you understand stress as a process, you can appreciate the multilevel effect on a physical, emotional, psychological, and spiritual level. Much of the stress we experience consists of predictable demands and challenges that we can and should expect. Learning the skills in this book has given you added support and resilience for living in the BestStress Zone. Now, more than ever, is the time to recognize and capture your personal power. How you think can powerfully influence how you feel. Being in the BestStress Zone means knowing that you must recognize the stressors that uniquely affect you. In the BestStress Zone, you can sort out predictable demands and challenges based on your personal triage protocol according to the degree of influence or control you have over them, as well as to their relationship to your 3Ps. For example, your relationship with your daughter requires your time today, to better understand and control the future. Take the time—today. You can change the way you feel and the harmful effects of the biological response to ongoing stress by changing the way you think. You can relearn how to perceive events. Making optimistic interpretations of events is at the core of living in the BestStress Zone. In this book, you have learned how to transform potentially harmful reactions into healthy responses. This book has also provided you with specific tools and strategies that you need to be a healthier you. Date night with your partner, spouse, or significant other is as important as maintaining your friendships and girls' night out is. You learned about the biological necessity of nurturing your social networks.

Time is often the ultimate resource in today's society. Time affluence is a better predictor of well-being and health than is material affluence. I can't overstate the importance of time management in protecting your BestStress Zone. Time may be the resource that is in shortest supply, which makes it so valuable. Deepak Chopra teaches that time is merely the experience of change. It has more to do with your internal dialogue. To protect this vital resource, you are going to learn how to say no.

Finally, I want to share a learning point from a common pattern I see in the emergency room. When people think they are near death and loved ones are gathered at their bedside, the comment I hear most often is "I want you to be happy." So I leave you with this thought: Be happy now! Remember, nobody can live a life completely free of stress. Most important, nobody should want to. Every life has periods of challenge and activity mixed in with times of serenity. Too much of either is unhealthy. In your BestStress Zone, you can live your best life, your healthiest life, by channeling the stress response to guarantee your peak performance in challenging situations and by knowing when and how to turn down the volume using relaxation. As a result, you will be able to center yourself and regroup physically, mentally, and emotionally. When you do this, you'll actually be living a life experiencing optimal stress.

selected references

Aamodt, M.G. *Applied Industrial/Organizational Psychology*, 4th ed. (Belmont, CA: Wadsworth, 2004).

Astin, John A., and Kelly Forys. "Psychosocial Determinants of Health and Illness: Integrating Mind, Body, and Spirit." *Advances* 2004;20(4).

Baker, B., Szalai, J. P, Parqueet, M., and Tobe, S. (2003). "Marital Support, Spousal Contact and the Course of Mild Hypertension." *Journal of Psychosomatic Research* 2003;55:229–233.

Benson, Herbert. "Are You Working Too Hard?" *Harvard Business Review on Bringing Your Whole Self to Work* (Boston: Harvard Business Publishing, 2008).

Bergman, Ph.D., Ronald L., with Anita Weil Bell. *Emotional Fitness Conditioning*. (New York: Berkley Publishing Group, 1998).

Berman, Brian M. "Clinical Applications of Acupuncture: An Overview of the Evidence." *Journal of Alternative and Complementary Medicine* 2001;7(suppl 1):S111–S118.

Casserley, Tim, and David Megginson. *Learning from Burnout: Developing Sustainable Leaders and Avoiding Career Derailment* (Burlington, MA: Butterworth Heinemann, 2009).

Chiesa, Alberto, and Alessandro Serretti, "Mindfulness Based Stress Reduction for Stress Management in Healthy People: A Review and Meta Analysis." *Journal of Alternative and Complementary Medicine* 2009;15(5):1–8.

Cohen, Harvey Jay. *Taking Care After 50: A Self Care Guide for Seniors* (New York: Three Rivers Press, 2000).

Cotton, Dorothy H. G. *Stress Management: An Integrated Approach to Therapy* (New York: Brunner/Mazel, 1990).

Crowley, Katherine, and Kathi Elster. *Working with You Is Killing Me* (New York: Warner Business Books, 2007).

Csikszentmihalyi, Mihaly, and Isabela Selega Csikszentmihalyi. *Optimal Experience: Psychological Studies of Flow in Consciousness* (Cambridge, UK: Cambridge University Press, 1988).

Czeisler, Charles A. "Sleep Deficit: The Performance Killer." *Harvard Business Review on Bringing Your Whole Self to Work* (Boston: Harvard Business Publishing, 2008).

Davidson, Jeff. *The Complete Idiot's Guide to Managing Stress* (Indianapolis, IN: Alpha Books, 1999).

Davis, Martha, Elizabeth Robbins Eshelman, M.S.W., and Matthew McKay. *The Relaxation and Stress Reduction Workbook* (Oakland, CA: New Harbinger Publications, 2000).

Deffenbacher, Jerry L., and Matthem Mckay. *Overcoming Situational and General Anger: A Protocol for the Treatment of Anger Based on Relaxation, Cognitive Restructuring, and Coping Skills Training* (Oakland, CA: Raincoast Books, 2000).

Gergen, David, Daniel Goleman, Ronald Heifetz, et al. "Leading by Feel." *Harvard Business Review on Bringing Your Whole Self to Work* (Boston: Harvard Business Publishing, 2008).

Gill, Jit. *Stress Survival Guide* (New York: HarperTorch, 2003).

Gold, Yvonne, and Robert A Roth. *Teachers Managing Stress and Preventing Burnout: The Professional Health Solution* (New York: RoutledgeFalmer, 1993).

Greenspan, Miriam. *Healing through the Dark Emotions: The Wisdom of Grief, Fear, and Despair* (Boston: Shambhala Publications, 2004).

Hallowell, Edward M. "The Human Moment at Work." *Harvard Business Review on Bringing Your Whole Self to Work* (Boston: Harvard Business Publishing, 2008).

Hallowell, Edward M. "Overload Circuits: Why Smart People Underperform." *Harvard Business Review on Bringing Your Whole Self to Work* (Boston: Harvard Business Publishing, 2008).

Harrell, Jules P., Sadiki Hall, and James Taliaferro. "Physiological Responses to Racism and Discrimination: An Assessment of the Evidence." *American Journal of Public Health* 2003;93(2).

Hartney, Elizabeth. *Stress Management for Teachers* (New York: Continuum International Publishing Group, 2008).

Harvard Business School Press. *Essentials of Managing Change and Transition: Business Literacy for HR Professionals* (Boston: Harvard Business Publishing, 2003).

Kagan, LesLee, Bruce Kessel, and Herbert Benson. *Mind Over Menopause: The Complete Mind/Body Approach to Coping with Menopause* (New York, Free Press, 2004).

Karasek, Robert, and Tores Theorell. *Healthy Work: Stress, Productivity, and the Reconstruction of Working Life* (New York: Basic Books, 1990).

Kets de Vries, Manfred F. R. "The Dangers of Feeling Like a Fake." *Harvard Business Review on Bringing Your Whole Self to Work* (Boston: Harvard Business Publishing, 2008).

Lazarus, Judith. *Stress Relief and Relaxation Techniques* (Los Angeles: Keats Publishing, 2000).

Lecrubier, Yves. "Posttraumatic Stress Disorder in Primary Care: A Hidden Diagnosis." *Journal of Clinical Psychiatry* 2004;65(suppl 1).

Leiter, Michael P., and Christina Maslach. *Banishing Burnout: Six Strategies for Improving Your Relationship with Work* (San Francisco: John Wiley & Sons, 2005).

Linden, Wolfgang. *Stress Management: From Basic Science to Better Practice* (Thousand Oaks, CA: Sage Publications, 2005).

Loehr, James E. *Stress for Success: Jim Loehr's Program for Transforming Stress into Energy at Work* (New York: Times Books, 1997).

Loehr, Jim, and Tony Schwartz. "The Making of a Corporate Athlete." *Harvard Business Review on Bringing Your Whole Self to Work* (Boston: Harvard Business Publishing, 2008).

Lovallo, W. R. *Stress and Health: Biological and Psychological Interactions* (Thousand Oaks, CA: Sage Publications, 1997).

Maddi, Salvatore R., and Deborah M. Khoshaba. *Resilience at Work: How to Succeed No Matter What Life Throws at You* (New York: AMACOM, 2005).

McEwen, Bruce S., and Elizabeth Norton Lasley. *The End of Stress As We Know It* (Washington, DC: Joseph Henry Press, 2002).

McQuaid, John R., and Paula E. Carmona. *Peaceful Mind: Using Mindfulness and Cognitive Behavioral Psychology to Overcome Depression* (Oakland, CA: New Harbinger Publications, 2004).

Meredith, Lisa S., David P. Eisenman, Bonnie L. Green, Ricardo Basurto Dávila, Andrea Cassells, and Jonathan Tobin. "System Factors Affect the Recognition and Management of Posttraumatic Stress Disorder by Primary Care Clinicians." *Medical Care* 2009;47(6).

Morgenstern, Julie. *Making Work Work: New Strategies for Surviving and Thriving at the Office* (New York: Fireside, 2004).

Morse, Gardiner. "Decisions and Desire." *Harvard Business Review on Bringing Your Whole Self to Work* (Boston: Harvard Business Publishing, 2008).

Murphy, Lawrence R. *Occupational Stress Management: Current Status and Future Directions. Trends in Organizational Behavior*, vol. 2 (New York: John Wiley & Sons, 1995).

Noh, Samuel, and Violet Kaspar. "Perceived Discrimination and Depression: Moderating Effects of Coping, Acculturation, and Ethnic Support." *American Journal of Public Health* 2003;93(2).

O'Connor, Richard. *Undoing Perpetual Stress: The Missing Connection Between Depression, Anxiety, and 21st Century Illness* (New York: Berkley Publishing Group, 2005).

Ong, L., W. Linden, and S. B. Young. "Stress Management: What Is It?" *Journal of Psychosomatic Research* 2004;56:133–137.

Ornish, Dean. *The Spectrum: A Scientifically Proven Program to Feel Better, Live Longer, Lose Weight, and Gain Health* (New York: Ballantine Books, 2007).

Penley, J. A., J. Tomaka, and J. S. Wiebe. "The Association of Coping to Physical and Psychological Health Outcomes." *Journal of Behavioral Medicine* 2002;25:551–603.

Pert, Candace B. *Molecules of Emotion: Why You Feel the Way You Feel* (New York: Scribner, 2003).

Pert, Candace B., and Nancy Marriott. *Everything You Need to Know to Feel Good* (New York: Hay House, 2006).

Pettinato, Yolanda. *Simply Yoga* (Heatherton, Victoria, Australia: Hinkler Books, 2002).

Posen, David. *The Little Book of Stress Relief* (Buffalo, NY: Firefly Books, 2004).

Rasul, F., S. A. Stansfield, C. L. Hart, C. R. Gillis, and G. D. Smith. "Psychological Distress, Physical Illness and Mortality Risk." *Journal of Psychosomatic Research* 2004;56:1–6.

Ray, O. "How the Mind Hurts and Heals the Body." *American Psychologist* 2004;59:29–40.

Rowe, John W., and Robert L. Kahn. *Successful Aging* (New York: Dell Publishing, 1998).

Sapolsky, Robert. *Biology and Human Behavior: The Neurological Origins of Individuality*, 2nd ed., part II (Chantilly, VA: Teaching Company, 2005).

———. *Why Zebras Don't Get Ulcers* (New York: Owl Books, 2004).

Schindelheim, Franklin. *Relieving Classroom Stress: A Teacher's Survival Guide* (Bloomington, IN: AuthorHouse, 2004).

Schnall, Peter L., Karen Belkic, Paul Landsbergis, and Dean Baker. *Occupational Medicine: The Workplace and Cardiovascular Disease* (Philadelphia: Hanley & Belfus, 2000).

Seaward, Brian Luke. "Stress and Human Spirituality 2000: At the Crossroads of Physics and Metaphysics." *Applied Psychophysiology and Biofeedback* 2000;25(4).

Seligman, Martin E. P. *Learned Optimism: How to Change Your Mind and Your Life* (New York: Vintage Books, 2006).

———. *What You Can Change and What You Can't: The Complete Guide to Successful Self Improvement* (New York: Vintage Books, 2007).

Shapiro, S., D. E. Shapiro, and G. E. R. Schwartz. "Stress Management in Medical Education: A Review of the Literature." *Academic Medicine* 2004;75:748–759.

Skinner, E. A., K. Edge, J. Altman, and H. Sherwood. "Searching for the Structure of Coping: A Review and Critique of Category Systems for classifying Ways of Coping." *Psychological Bulletin* 2003;129:216–269.

Smith, C. S., and L. M. Sulsky. "Investigation of Job Related Coping Strategies Across Multiple Stressors and Samples." In L. R. Murphy, J. J. Hurrell Jr., S. L. Sauter, and G. P. Keita, eds., *Job Stress Intervention* (Washington, DC: American Psychological Association, 1995), pp. 109–123.

Smyth, Kathleen, and Hossein N. Yarandi. "Factor Analysis of the Ways of Coping Questionnaire for African American Women." *Official Journal of the Eastern Nursing Research Society and the Western Institute of Nursing* 1996;45(1):25–29.

Stack, Laura. *The Exhaustion Cure: Up Your Energy from Low to Go in 21 Days* (New York: Broadway Books, 2008).

Strike, Philip C., and Andrew Steptoe. "Behavioral and Emotional Triggers of Acute Coronary Syndromes: Systematic Review and Critique." *Psychosomatic Medicine* 2005;67:179–186.

Swanberg, Jennifer E. "Illuminating Gendered Organization Assumptions: An Important Step in Creating a Family Friendly Organization, a Case Study." *Community, Work & Family* 2004;7(1):3–28.

Todorov, Herman, Robert Nadler, and I. N. Todorov. *Public Enemy Number One—Stress: A Practical Guide to the Effects of Stress and Nutrition on the Aging Process and Life Extension* (New York: Nova Science Publishers, 2000).

Wachsman, Daniel E., and Ravin Davidoff. "Takotsubo Cardiomyopathy: A Little Known Cardiomyopathy Makes Its U.S. Debut." *Cardiology* 2004;102:119–121.

Watson, David, and James W. Pennebaker. "Health Complaints, Stress, and Distress: Exploring the Central Role of Negative Affectivity." *Psychological Review* 1989;96(2):234–254.

Weick, Karl E., and Kathleen M. Sutcliffe. *Managing the Unexpected: Resilient Performance in an Age of Uncertainty* (San Francisco: John Wiley & Sons, 2007).

Wilson, Marie C. *Closing the Leadership Gap: Add Women, Change Everything* (New York: Penguin Group, 2004).

Wilson, Paul. *Instant Calm: Over 100 Easy to Use Techniques for Relaxing Mind and Body* (New York: Penguin Group, 1995).

Worthington Jr., Everett L., and Michael Scherer. "Forgiveness Is an Emotion Focused Coping Strategy That Can Reduce Health Risks and Promote Health Resilience: Theory, Review, and Hypotheses." *Psychology and Health* 2004;19(3):385–405.

Zalaquett, Carlos P., and Richard J. Wood. *Evaluating Stress: A Book of Resources* (Lanham, MD: Scarecrow Press, 1997).

index